John Hohenberg

UNIVERSITY PRESS OF FLORIDA

Gainesville / Tallahassee / Tampa / Boca Raton / Pensacola / Orlando / Miami / Jacksonville

John Hohenberg

THE PURSUIT
OF EXCELLENCE

★

John Hohenberg

Copyright 1995 by the Board of Regents of the State of Florida
Printed in the United States of America on acid-free paper ∞
All rights reserved
Design by Louise OFarrell

00 99 98 97 96 95   6 5 4 3 2 1

Library of Congress Cataloging-in-Publication Data

Hohenberg, John.
    John Hohenberg: the pursuit of excellence / John Hohenberg.
        p. cm.
    Includes index.
    ISBN 0-8130-1339-9
    1. Hohenberg, John. 2. —Journalists—United States—Biography.
I. Title. II. Title: Pursuit of excellence.
PN4874.H59A3   1994   94-36717
070.92—dc20
[B]

Frontispiece: John Hohenberg after twenty-two years with the Pulitzer prizes.

The letter from William Faulkner cited on page xi of the preface is quoted with permission.

The University Press of Florida is the scholarly publishing agency for the State University System of Florida, comprised of Florida A & M University, Florida Atlantic University, Florida International University, Florida State University, University of Central Florida, University of Florida, University of North Florida, University of South Florida, and University of West Florida.

University Press of Florida
15 Northwest 15th Street
Gainesville, FL 32611

This book is gratefully dedicated
to JoAnn and Pam, Tracey and Eric.
It is also written in fondest memory
of my parents, Dorothy, Sue and Dick.

CONTENTS

The Pursuit of Excellence   ix

Part 1 ★ Beginnings

1. Growing Up   3
2. Starting Out in New York   14
3. The Grand Tour of Europe   23
4. Surviving the Crash   32
5. The Professional Life   40

Part 2 ★ In War and Peace

6. Service in World War II   49
7. Peace, It's Wonderful   61
8. A New World   71
9. Land of Promise   82
10. After Fifty Years   94

Part 3 ★ Back to Academe

11. New Times on Morningside   107
12. On Journalism   117
13. Conflict on Campus   130
14. "I Tread the World …"   140
15. Looking Back   150

Part 4 ★ The Pulitzers and I

16. Problems and Prizes   161

17. Fighting Words   169

18. Among My Souvenirs   177

19. The Prizes and Vietnam   186

20. The Prizes and the Law   195

21. The Presidency and the Prizes   203

22. Winding Down   210

23. Expanding the Pulitzer Prizes   216

Part 5 ★ A Different Life

24. Change and Circumstance   227

25. Comeback   235

26. Second Chance   243

27. The Making of a Southerner   253

28. The Uses of Teaching   261

29. Moving On   276

Index   289

ILLUSTRATIONS

Frontispiece, John Hohenberg after twenty-two years as Pulitzer administrator
My parents' engagement picture, 1905   6
At age three, my first travel picture   6
Me in the fifth grade in Seattle   7
A high school track star, Seattle   7
Dorothy as I first saw her   30
The picture Dorothy gave me   30
Our Columbia graduation picture   31
The bridegroom in Atlantic City   31
In shock after the Wall Street crash   54
My Chickering and I   54
My rose garden scene with Freckles   55
The unhappy warrior   55
With President Harry Truman at the UN   100
With Bernard M. Baruch at the UN   100
With Canadian General A. G. L. McNaughton   101
With Soviet Andrei Gromyko at the UN   101
Interviewing Secretary-General Dag Hammarskjold   124
Interviewing U. S. delegate Henry Cabot Lodge at the UN   124
Criticizing a student's page makeup   125
With Soviet UN delegate Yakov Malik   125
Joseph Pulitzer, Jr., Dr. William McGill, and I   196
A Pulitzer board vote   196
Dorothy and I at a Pulitzer party   196

The Pulitzer board, 1967, before the Liberty window   218
Interviewing Ambassador Samuel Berger in Seoul   219
Honored at Wilkes College with L.H.D.   219
JoAnn on her first trip to Columbia   248
JoAnn at the Long Island homestead   248
JoAnn and I   248
Wedding picture, JoAnn and I   251
JoAnn and her teen-age children, Pam and Eric   251
Eric and Tracey's wedding photo, Pam as bridesmaid   264
I play the wedding march   264
Farewell to the old homestead   264
Liv Sawyer   273
Where I worked at the University of Tennessee   273

THE PURSUIT OF EXCELLENCE

When William Faulkner won his first and long-delayed Pulitzer Prize in 1955, he sent me a letter from his home in Oxford, Mississippi, in which he wrote:

> I believe that no man's—artist's—work is to him as good as he wanted it to be; maybe it is never as good in the opinion of others as it should have been or maybe could have been. But at least it was the best he was capable of at that moment, and it makes him feel very good and worth-while when a committee of people dedicated for that moment at least to judging it, publicly affirm that they too believe it was the best he could do at that moment, and that that best was good enough for that formal affirmation.

It was in this manner that one of the most distinguished of American novelists accepted the award for one of his lesser works, *A Fable*, while at the same time affirming his own pursuit of excellence that had led him in his earlier years to publish such other highly regarded novels as *The Sound and the Fury* and *As I Lay Dying*. I cherish his letter as one of the mementos of my twenty-two years as the administrator of the Pulitzer Prizes, because it defines so precisely those limits within one's self that serious writers inevitably struggle against for all their days and sometimes wakeful nights.

Faulkner's pursuit of excellence and the rationale by which he judged his own work apply to others among the treasures of my academic experience at Columbia, Florida, Tennessee and other universities. Among them are the volume *Profiles in Courage* that John F. Kennedy signed in his copperplate script before he handed the book back to me; a sentimental affirmation of many years of friendship, written and signed by Bernard M. Baruch in *My Own Story*; an autographed copy of *Lyrics* by the finest lyricist of my time, Oscar Hammerstein II; and a book by Ralph McGill, editor of the *Atlanta Constitution*, about our adventures together during a month-long trip in the state of Israel.

This autobiographical account, in a quite different sense, also illustrates Faulkner's "pursuit of excellence under the limitations of the moment." I only wish I might have had more space to recount the enormous range of travel, around the nation and the world, that I undertook in my later years with my wife. Much of this was on a government mission across Asia; the rest was mostly across the United States. Still, to have to tried to flesh out so important and often entertaining a narrative would have made a book almost twice as long. And so I agreed reluctantly to severe limitations for what will eventually provide the basis for a new kind of travel book.

There is also a bit of history in these pages: about a career that has from time to time made me a journalist; a government servant at the Pentagon and the State Department; a university professor here and abroad; a soldier in World War II; a pianist with a lifelong love of music; and a prize-giver. I am among the last of a generation of Americans who fervently believed that their children would have a better life than they did. Today, I am sorry to concede, too many of the baby boomer generation have their doubts.

The core of my generation in my native New York City was formed from a different background. We were the descendants, for the most part, of immigrants from Europe who had streamed through the Ellis Island immigration station, long since closed, at the rate of more than a million a year in the late eighteenth and early nineteenth centuries.

To them—and I heard it often as a child from both my parent—the Statue of Liberty with her lighted torch in New York Harbor meant that this new land of their dreams was the home of a free people. Indeed, it was fitting that it was a Hungarian immigrant, Joseph Pulitzer, who raised the money to place the Lady with the Torch on her pedestal where she still stands today.

But the vast majority of these new immigrants did not have the vitality or talent that made Pulitzer the founder of an American tradition in journalism. Most of them had little more than the clothes on their backs and the few belongings they carried in paper packages and cardboard boxes. Few of them could even afford a suitcase.

The great mass of these impoverished newcomers knew little or no English. Few had American relatives they could rely on. There were no jobs waiting for them, nor would there be at a later date. The 100 percent Americans of their day taunted these immigrants because they sometimes worked for a few cents a day, becoming the targets of an outrageous slogan of the time: "A dollar a day is a white man's pay."

It was years before my father earned a dollar a day. Often he had to work two jobs, sometimes three, to support my mother and me. He went to a musty night school at the outset to learn English. Yet, out of his generation came some of the leaders of the land. And like my father they truly believed that their children would have a better life than they made for themselves, a sentiment my generation proudly inherited.

If anything I have written in these pages can change the pessimistic outlook I have detected so often among the thousands of talented hardworking young people I have known in my classes across the land, then I shall feel well rewarded for having exerted still another effort in this book, my fifteenth, to do my best work within the limits that were set for me.

Finally, I call particular attention in this volume to the section about the Pulitzer Prizes, which remained a part of my life long after I left Columbia University. I was teaching elsewhere and therefore was unable to attend the seventy-fifth anniversary celebration of the awards in 1991. However, I urged the Pulitzer Prize Board at the time to broaden the range of the awards, to encourage greater attention to meritorious public service in this country.

In a letter to Michael I. Sovern, then the president of Columbia, I proposed that the Pulitzer gold medal for public service should be offered for excellence in fields other than journalism, to which it had always been restricted.

I have expanded that theme by making public my proposal to offer annually several gold medals for excellence in public service in other major fields such as education, public health, civil rights, and social progress. It is, in effect, an adaptation of Faulkner's theme to stimulate the pursuit of excellence in public life by broadening the range of the oldest and most prestigious of American awards. The journalists of America should be the first to see that something must be done in this country to recognize and support new leadership in other important aspects of our existence as a nation.

I cannot conclude these prefatory observations without extending my thanks to the editors at the University Press of Florida for their efforts to bring this book to public attention. I am grateful as well to Ralph L. Lowenstein, former dean of the University of Florida's College of Journalism and Mass Communications, for the recent year I spent there with an endowed chair, during which I conceived the basic outlines of what I have set down her.

I owe a great deal as well to my successors in the Pulitzer Prize Office, especially the late Dean Richard Terrell Baker of Columbia's Graduate School of Journalism, as well as to my assistants for many years in the Pulitzer Prize Office, Rose Valenstein and Robin Holloway Kuzen.

To my wife and beloved traveling companion, JoAnn Fogarty Hohenberg, I owe the greatest debt of all for her wise counsel and steadiness of purpose that have sustained me throughout our long and happy marriage. In my continued pursuit of excellence, she shall have her travel book in the not too distant future and it, too, will be my best.

J.H.

PART I

Beginnings

1 ★ GROWING UP

I owe my existence to a cargo of Alaskan whalebone.
My father, Louis Hohenberg, a youthful and industrious Hungarian immigrant, had picked it up in the far north early in this century when he failed to find gold there. He sold it at a profit in New York and promptly used the proceeds to finance his marriage to my mother, Jettchen Scheuermann, a lovely and gracious German immigrant.

From that union, I arrived in due course on February 17, 1906, in a tenement on New York's lower East Side of Manhattan. However, our little family didn't stay there long. When I was eighteen months old, we rode the rails across the continent to Seattle, where my father set up the first of several small businesses he was to operate over the years.

That, too, didn't last long. When I was three, we took off again, this time to Germany and Austria-Hungary for an extended visit to my parents' native villages.

By the time we returned to Seattle, as might be expected, I'd forgotten most of the English I'd ever known and spoke instead a garbled mixture of German, Slovak, Hungarian, and even a few words of Yiddish. Scant wonder, then, that I became a journalist—an enthusiastic seeker of information about everybody else's affairs but my own—and eventually a teacher and prize-giver, by grace of the benefactions of another Hungarian, Joseph Pulitzer.

Through my early travels, I learned to be respectful of all peoples on the move, and Hungarians in particular. But all that did not help me on my first day of school in Seattle when my classmates crowded around me jeering, "Yah, can't speak English! Heinie, Heinie, Heinie."

For the benefit of a younger generation who do not know the ways of foreign peoples in a comic strip called "The Katzenjammer Kids," "Heinie" was the name given at the time to an unreconstructed German immigrant. After that noisy initiation into the niceties of American education, I needed no urging to learn English again in a hurry.

Most of my other early childhood memories are dim recollections of sights and sounds. I can never forget the sound of my father's low voice as he read aloud from his daily newspaper, wherever we were, to fill my mother and me in on the events of the day. It was a habit for him, and it impressed on me, from childhood onward, the importance of unfolding events. I am sure the habit I acquired of listening to the daily news at night nudged me ever closer toward a journalistic career.

The alternative was music, which I loved, mainly because my mother had a beautiful voice and often sang to me when I was very young. I was always quiet and wide-eyed, she told me in our later years, when she sang from her favorite operas or a Schubert *lied*. From her, I learned to appreciate music and to study the piano sufficiently to be able to perform without embarrassment.

Even in my earliest years at school, my parents saw to it that I was given a respectable background in both music and the theater. As an only child, I was treated as if I had been a prince, regardless of our family's modest means. There were always books and newspapers in both English and German around our home in Seattle. We attended concerts regularly. And my parents were devoted supporters of our local theater stock company, which staged the recent Broadway shows and others on a regular basis, a different attraction every week. Even so, I remember little except the fun of it all.

Then, when I was nine years old, a quite different sound came into my life—the brisk clacking of a typewriter. My father brought home to me a green second-hand Oliver typewriter, a squat little machine that fascinated me from the moment I inserted paper into the roller and picked out my first sentence.

Of course, my father had meant the machine to be used to improve my schoolwork, but almost at once I was creating stories to please myself. Without instruction, I learned to type rapidly with four to six fingers and thereafter was always happiest when I could dream on my Oliver.

From then on, the typewriter diverted me from the Kimball piano my father also had bought for me at my mother's insistence. Not that I gave up the piano, by any means. But the creative spirit, such as it was at that early age, could scarcely be contained once I found my classmates at school liked the stories I typed about them. I also began experimenting on the piano with childish songs I'd put together with my mother's encouragement. For awhile, I wasn't sure whether I was more interested in songs or stories, then I settled by trying to do both along with the typical American schoolboy's devotion to sports after school.

I remember hearing my father remark to my mother one night after he'd finished reading the news to us from the *Seattle Times* that I was trying to do too much too soon.

There was a rough interlude for me at school when the United States went to war with Germany in 1917–18 while I was in the seventh and eighth grades. At once, my formerly friendly classmates were no longer interested in my stories or songs because, as it pained me to discover, all people with German-sounding names now were enemies of the republic. I was shocked to hear the name Hohenberg transformed at playtime on the school grounds into Hindenburg, the leading German general on the Western front. Then, by degrees as the war went on, I became Hindy and, in the opinion of one ferocious grade-school teacher, a Hun.

All this was confusing to me, especially when my father tried to explain to me after his nightly recital of the war news that some American superpatriots were persecuting people whom they suspected of German sympathies. What it meant to me was that I had to keep to myself as much as possible and grow up in a hurry.

Then another sound came into my young life—the growling sixty-cycle signal of a home-made radio station, call letters 7 UL, which I set up in my mother's kitchen directly after the end of the war and operated nightly by punching out the Continental code on a telegraph key. My CQs (call-ins) were answered from as far away as North Dakota. Between the radio, the piano, and the typewriter, I was lucky to do well enough in high school to be able to enter the University of Washington in the fall of 1922 as an engineering student.

Why engineering? My father had so decided. And being a dutiful son, I

My parents' engagement picture in New York City in 1905. I came along a bit more than a year later.

My first travel picture, age three, Europe-bound with my parents.

I am in the fifth grade in Seattle, age nine, and next to a pretty girl, second row from the bottom, second from the left.

I am under the illusion that I am a high school track star, age fifteen, at Broadway in Seattle.

gave it a half-hearted try. However, I'm sorry to say I spent more time working for the *University of Washington Daily* in the *Daily* shack across campus than I did at my engineering studies, and predictably, at the end of my freshman year, I was barely passing.

I told my father quite honestly then that I wanted to switch to liberal arts for my sophomore year. He was disappointed. My mother cried. And the upshot was that I was told, kindly but firmly, in my father's most authoritative news-reading voice, that thenceforth, if I wanted a liberal arts education at the university, I would have to pay my own tuition. To lessen the shock, he added that he and my mother still wanted me to live at home. I was thankful that I did not hear the door slam, but I realized with a sinking feeling that I was on my own. At the time, I was seventeen.

One evening in early June in that year of 1923, my father picked up his *Seattle Times* after dinner for his usual recitation of the evening news. He glanced at me and said, "The President's going to be in Seattle day after tomorrow."

The President, Warren Gamaliel Harding, may have been one of the least distinguished occupants of the White House, but in that distant era any Presidential visit to the Pacific Northwest was an event. As my father read on, I learned that the President was due to arrive by ship from Alaska, following a visit there, and was on his way to San Francisco.

I didn't listen very carefully to the rest of my father's recital or his explanatory remarks, which were addressed mainly to my mother. Instead, I wondered hazily if in some strange way the President's visit might give me a chance at a summer newspaper job downtown, to help me finance my sophomore year at the university.

Without confiding in my parents, I set out next morning to try my luck in a professional newsroom for the first time. What I had to offer was very sketchy training in college newspaper work, but I hoped that some editor might need an extra pair of strong young legs to help out during the presidential visit.

I began at the *Seattle Star,* then the third largest of the city's four newspapers, where a beleaguered city editor with thick eyeglasses, a moth-eaten brown sweater, and ink-stained pants demanded, with a long-suffering air, "Whaddya want, kid?"

I managed to choke out a request for summer work, to which he responded loudly, "Listen, kid, the President of the United States is coming to Seattle tomorrow. You get me an exclusive interview and I'll give you a job."

There were a few guffaws from the handful of staffers in the smoky little newsroom. A more considerate man, sitting across the double desk from my tormentor, suggested I might learn something by talking to a reporter who was arriving on the President's ship.

"No, my offer stands," was the gruff response. Then, to me: "Hey, get going, will you?"

On the way out, a friendly woman at a telephone switchboard informed me with an encouraging smile that I'd been talking to Ray Felton, the city editor. She added, "Don't let him discourage you. That's the way he treats people who come in looking for work—gives them impossible assignments."

For the rest of the day, I digested all the details of the President's arrival from the local papers and began thinking of what I might ask the President if I could get close enough to him. In the blissful ignorance of youth, I assumed I'd be able to reach the President's side without credentials of any kind.

It hadn't occurred to me that the local police, National Guard, and Secret Service would make things difficult for an interloper trying to speak to the President, much less interview him.

It seemed to me as if all Seattle had turned out next day to catch a glimpse of the President. In the mild sunshine of a June morning, I watched the President's ship end its journey from Alaska by tying up at a pier on the north side of the harbor, Elliott Bay. Between the hill where I stood and that pier, two freight engines were moving freight cars to a siding. The only other way to the pier from my hilltop was across a bridge that spanned the railroad tracks, but that rickety structure already was jammed with people.

I did what I had to do—ran down the hill, crossed the tracks, dodging the freight engines, and struggled up a smaller hill, to the pier where the President's ship by that time had put out a red, white, and blue gangplank. As I reached the pier, I could hear a band pumping out "The Stars and Stripes Forever," and I caught a glimpse of a crowd of dignitaries about an open limousine at the foot of the gangplank.

But there I had to stop. A youthful National Guardsman, uniformed and helmeted, halted me with the business end of a shakily pointed rifle, his forefinger on the trigger. Ignoring my protests that I was a reporter, he marched me off to his commanding officer. There, I underwent a stiff grilling until I had the presence of mind to ask the commander to call City Editor Felton at the *Star*.

Mercifully, by grace of the kindly Jehovah that watches over babies, pretty girls, and addled young men, the city editor remembered me and was sportsman enough to clear me for passage to the pier as a *Star* reporter. Within a few minutes, wonder of wonders, I found myself beside the President's open limousine next to a fine-looking older man who, when I told him I was a reporter for the *Star*, identified himself as a member of the staff of the local United States Attorney.

Just then, the President and his party started down the gangplank. An honor guard came to attention. Two Boy Scouts moved up between the limousine and the gangplank, eager for a look at the great man. All the rest of us around the car squeezed ourselves together so closely that I wondered how the President could possibly get past us.

I saw that I was caught between the crowd, the President's security people, and the open rear door of the limousine. No matter how frantically I struggled to free myself, I was stuck. But all at once, the President was beside me, shaking hands with everybody around him. Somehow, a small man in a blue shirt, no tie, and work pants grabbed his hand and shouted a greeting from a labor union. The two Boy Scouts pushed by me, and I saw the President had his arm around one of them, saying something I couldn't hear.

By reflex action more than anything else, I pulled at the President's arm, told him I was a reporter, and was about to ask him a question when he rattled off what must have been a stock greeting for the people of any city he visited. And all this happened while the dignitaries on the pier were milling about us, pawing at him for a handshake.

Suddenly, it was all over. The President and two of his escorts entered the car. The door closed. The crowd cleared from the front of the limousine, and it rolled slowly from the pier to join a honking cavalcade bound for downtown Seattle. After that, for the first time, I tried to act like the reporter I had pretended to be, and called the *Star*'s city desk from a pay phone on the pier.

When I heard Ray Felton's rasping voice, I gave my name and reported with what I thought was professional assurance, "The President's just left the pier in a car bound for downtown."

"You're on deadline," the city editor replied. "Give what you've got to Les Rice and make it fast." A pause, then the magic words: "Come in."

I did as I was told, received a warm welcome when I made it back to the *Star*'s little newsroom and had to repeat everything that had happened to me for Felton's benefit. He was still skeptical: "Think you can write that?"

Of course I said yes, but I had an empty feeling in the pit of my stomach. When he pointed to an old Underwood typewriter I pretended it was my green Oliver, hitched my chair up close and let fly. The result—three pages of hastily typed copy—was reproduced with byline on the front page of next day's *Star*.

For better or worse, I had become a newspaperman.

Neither Harding's death in San Francisco less than a month later nor the subsequent involvement of some of his cronies in the Teapot Dome oil scandal dimmed the memory of my first encounter with an American President. There have been others since, of much more consequence, from Franklin Roosevelt and Dwight David Eisenhower to Jimmy Carter, but none quite as important to me as that first fumbling experience.

What it led to at once was a chance to cover news and sports assignments at the *Star* that summer. When there was nothing else for me to do, I ran copy for the more seasoned reporters, answered phones on the city desk, and got my first experience at editing copy, writing headlines, and helping with makeup in the composing room. The pay was small, the work was hard, but I earned enough to put me through my sophomore year at the university—a surprise for my parents as well as myself.

My work at the *Star* continued during the fall and for much of the rest of the 1923–24 academic year, although not as regularly as in the summer because I was much more interested in my liberal arts courses at the university and didn't get away quite as often as I had during the summer.

What I was introduced to at the *Star*, in sum, was a trade that was struggling to become a respected profession—a trade that was poorly paid, for the most part, and limited in opportunities for growth. Radio, as my experience as an amateur had already taught me, was scarcely a rival to print then. Movie newsreels—with their stiff, exaggerated images of people walking as if they were on stilts—gave the public relatively fuzzy images of news events. As for television, that was nothing more than a dream at the time I broke in as a newsman.

However, for all the trade's faults and its lack of status with a less than admiring public, newspapers did have more power and authority than most of them do today. The *Atlanta Constitution*, the *Boston Post*, the *Indianapolis Times*, and the *New York World*, as well as a number of smaller papers, were exposing political corruption. Another target for some of these and other papers, including the tiny *Columbus (Ga.) Enquirer Sun*, was the Ku Klux Klan. And reporters like Herbert Bayard Swope, Louis Seibold, Alva Johnston, and Al Goldstein were winning national acclaim for their work.

Swope, in particular, was a legendary figure to every youngster in an American newsroom swinging wildly at the prospect of exposing master criminals. After being a reporter for only two years, Swope had broken the murder mystery of a gambler, Herman Rosenthal, for Joseph Pulitzer's paper, the *New York World*. The reporter proved the guilt of a corrupt police lieutenant, Charles Becker, who had had an assistant hire four gunmen—with picturesque names I've never forgotten, Lefty Louie, Dago Frank, Whitey Lewis, and Gyp the Blood. All of them went to the electric chair, and Swope won the first Pulitzer Prize for reporting in 1917.

Al Goldstein and Jim Mulroy of the *Chicago Daily News* were similarly honored when they broke the 1924 "thrill murder" of a fourteen-year-old boy, Bobby Franks, by two wealthy college students, Richard Loeb and Nathan Leopold. Goldstein and Mulroy were only cub reporters, but they provided the proof that sent Loeb to prison for life and Leopold to prison for thirty years. Had it not been for the histrionics of their defense attorney, Clarence Darrow, both Loeb and Leopold would have gone to the electric chair.

Needless to say, my year at the *Star* was mild indeed compared to such feats as these in the investigation of crime and the support of good government. Nevertheless, I thoroughly enjoyed the work, and my grades at the university improved remarkably once I left the engineering school behind me. I felt I had been given the incentive to develop whatever talent I possessed, and I resolved on a journalistic career. Even my radio station no longer interested me and soon was removed from my mother's kitchen. But I still enjoyed the piano and continued to compose little songs just because I liked doing it.

My parents also made a major decision that year. Mainly because my mother wanted to be near her three sisters—two in New York City and one in Atlantic City, New Jersey—my father decided to sell his latest and most successful business and move east with her. Theirs had been a lifelong love affair, in which each had made sacrifices for the other so that they could stay together. It was a relationship I appreciated all through my growing years, and long after they were gone the way they conducted themselves in their marriage became a fitting example for my own.

It was because of this intimate link with my parents that I hesitated not at all when my father told me quietly at the end of my sophomore year at the university that he was selling out, moving East with my mother, and as he put it, "We don't want to leave you behind." I told him at once that I would go with them. Truly, I was thrilled with the idea that I might finish my education at one of the pioneering journalism schools, the one Joseph Pulitzer had endowed with his $2 million deed of gift that also created the Pulitzer Prizes, at Columbia University.

So, that summer, we traveled east together in our 1919 Dodge. And when we put up with relatives in New York City, while my parents looked for a home and a business opportunity, I decided I would have to find a job somewhere in that vast metropolis before I dared apply for admission to Columbia University.

2 ★ STARTING OUT IN NEW YORK

On my first day of job-hunting in New York City that summer, I developed an acute case of stage fright at my first stop, the offices of the *New York Times* in mid-Manhattan. I was only eighteen, fresh out of Seattle with just a year's more or less part-time work on the *Star* behind me. I was afraid nobody would even look at me—beginning with the stern-faced uniformed doorman.

When I felt so shaky I couldn't even force myself to go inside the building, I detoured instead to the general area nearby. There, I spotted the offices of Harms, Inc., then a power in that byway of songwriting, Tin Pan Alley. On impulse, I decided to try my luck, without even a sheet of music to show a professional manager.

However, the one who was gracious enough to welcome me, Dave Stamper, didn't bother with formalities. He waved me to a battered old upright outside his office, told me to start playing some of my compositions, and then went on about his business. I went through my routine—all the precious little songs I'd composed for my mother, my schoolmates, my high school, and a crew song for the University of Washington.

When I finally ran out of material, Stamper drew up a chair beside the piano and asked, in as kindly a way as possible, "What else can you do, kid?" I told him about my year at the *Star* in Seattle, and he sighed, patted me on the back, and said softly, "Kid, be a newspaperman."

At eighteen, one is better able to take disappointment in stride. Within the hour, more to bolster my courage than anything else, I was inside the *New York Times* building getting an assignment from an agreeable elderly feature editor (he was probably all of forty-five or fifty) to do an article about the attractions of Yellowstone Park for the *Times*'s Sunday travel section.

I'd been to Yellowstone several times, most recently that summer with my parents, so the job wasn't hard to do. When I returned next day with a hastily written 2,000-word account banged out on the old Oliver, the editor read it at once, bought it and paid me $50—more than I'd earned in two weeks at the *Star*.

Then he told me to hurry to City Hall Place downtown because a new newspaper, the *New York Truth,* backed by a millionaire magazine publisher, was hiring a staff for publication within a week or so. I was in luck. In two minutes flat, I was out of the *Times* building, heading for the crosstown subway shuttle and the Lexington Avenue subway line downtown. In my excitement, I lost the business card of my benefactor, on which he'd noted brief directions, and I thereafter forgot his name. No matter. He got me started.

City Hall Place turned out to be a shabby, one-block street, and the address the *Times* editor had given me was an old unoccupied building that formerly had housed a newspaper, long since forgotten, but with its press room and other mechanical facilities now under repair. Once inside, I came upon a lean young man sitting at a large bare desk, a telephone in one hand and a crumpled brown fedora on the back of his tousled blond head. He motioned to me to pull up a chair, hung up the phone, and asked, "What can I do for you?"

It was my first successful job interview in New York City. I emerged with a district reporter's job at $30 a week, and I was receiving instructions from the editor in charge, Howard Swain, when there was an outburst of handclapping just outside his door. As we discovered upon entering a large room next door, a small man wearing gym pants, his arm muscles bulging under a short-sleeved white shirt, had jumped on a desk in front of a group of men who were applauding in greeting.

The newcomer tilted back his shaggy grey head and shouted, both fists raised, "Next week we're going to show this town a great new newspaper." He raised his voice a notch higher: "I'm going to out-Hearst Hearst."

Everybody cheered including Swain and myself, for he had raised his voice above the hubbub to inform me, "That's the boss." Still, despite my youth and lack of experience, I had to wonder just a little about the appearance of the boss—he was in his white stockinged feet—as well as the extravagance of his aims. However, nobody else seemed worried so I went along with the crowd, applauding and cheering as he outlined his credo for his paper. In addition to out-Hearsting Hearst, what he apparently was after was true stories—a lot of true stories, the more stark and shocking the better. He kept coming back to that subject repeatedly. I don't suppose the man spoke more than ten minutes when he stopped in midflight, jumped off the desk, and padded out the nearest door in his stockinged feet.

Noticing my dazed expression, Swain chuckled. "Guess you folks out in Seattle never heard of Bernarr Macfadden and his Physical Culture and True Story magazines," he said. "But next week, fella, you better be sharp because we're going to have a tough job selling this new newspaper."

"The *New York Truth*?" I asked hazily, using the name the *Times* editor had given me.

Swain gave me a peculiar look. "We're calling it something else—the *Graphic*."

That was my introduction, in the summer of 1924, to New York's dizziest tabloid and its publisher.

The scene was much more conventional the next day at Columbia University when I applied for admission at its journalism school. The director, Dr. John Cunliffe, an English gentleman journalist complete with white goatee, velvet jacket, and pipe went over my credentials from the University of Washington with me. He suggested that, since I had a time-consuming job on a newspaper, I might need as much as two semesters of makeup work before I could qualify for the journalism school. It was then a two-year undergraduate institution limited to juniors and seniors, with the degree of Bachelor of Literature as the reward for successful completion of the course of study.

All this was courteously spelled out for me by Dr. Cunliffe who seemed slightly aghast at the idea that a full-time tabloid reporter would be interested in an academic degree.

However, I seemed to convince him I was serious, upon which he sent me across the street to the School of General Studies where I was able to enroll for a semester's night course in my make-up work for the fall. With a $50 *Times* check and a prospective $30 a week from my district job on the *Graphic,* it seemed to me that I'd be able to meet Columbia's tuition requirements and other expenses.

My parents thought so too that night, when I reported both my job prospects and the resumption of my efforts to qualify for a university degree. On their part, they also had good news—they had found a small but well-appointed four-room apartment in a decent part of town as our home, and a vacant store nearby in which my father planned to start a new shop for children's clothes. So, pending the arrival of our furniture from Seattle, we would shortly be reestablished.

It had been quite an experience, even for a native New Yorker, to plunge from the journalistic heights of the lordly *Times* to the lower depths of tabloidia, the as-yet-unborn *Graphic,* and then bounce back up to Columbia University all in the same week. To prepare for my double life, I rented a dark and smelly dormitory room at Columbia, bought the required texts at the bookstore, and tried to imagine a decent schedule to combine work and study and still find time for sleep.

It was tough. I still shudder when I think of what this youngster had to endure to cram some kind of education into a brain that also had to produce sex and murder stories at a tabloid twinkling. But somehow I made out, with a lot of sympathetic help from a few others who started in the lower depths with me—Walter Winchell, the prematurely grey gossip columnist of the *Graphic*; Ed Sullivan, the wooden-faced sports editor who became an electronic media star later in life; and an impatient young political writer fresh out of Georgetown University, Leo Casey. They all coddled me, encouraged me, sometimes woke me up when I fell asleep over my typewriter in the *Graphic* office. If I hadn't been young enough to stand the strain, I suppose I might have developed a split personality.

Consider, for example, the first major Macfadden contribution to the deathless annals of American journalism through his tabloid, once it hit the sidewalks of New York: the announcement of the marriage between an elderly realtor and a teenage girl barely out of grade school. The affair was illustrated on the front page of the *Graphic* with heads of the loving newlyweds pasted to shapeless bodies partly concealed under bedcovers. Under the sprawling red headlines, to one side, was a cartoon of a duck, perched on the bedstead, with a speech balloon carrying the legend: "Honk, honk, it's the bonk."

For this exercise in the public interest, the delighted executive editor, who formerly had presided over a first-rate New England newspaper, the *Hartford Courant,* posted a notice on the *Graphic*'s bulletin board: "We tore the guts out of the presses."

There was a lot more of this nonsense in the 1920s, and it was by no means confined to New York's three tabloids, the *News, Mirror,* and *Graphic*. The craze for sensation spread to supposedly respectable newspapers as well, with such hippodromes as the Snyder-Grey murders, the celebration of gangland killers, and the daily grist about the love lives of the famous and infamous. But on the first afternoon I was able to leave all that and Columbia behind me for two hours, I also heard a young pianist—George Gershwin—play his first major composition, "Rhapsody in Blue," with Paul Whiteman's band at Carnegie Hall.

That, too, was New York in the 1920s.

My assignment at the *Graphic* was West Side Magistrates' Court and the sodden riffraff of Broadway that landed there for crime and punishment. It was a far from edifying daily spectacle—the Broadway girls (to give them a polite name) and the johns who beat them up or were robbed while sleeping with them; the continual procession of alcoholics, rich and poor, who were hauled in for offenses against conventional decency; and the humble grist of the day's news of thievery, shootings and murders.

This, save the mark, was what caused the era to be known (among those who didn't have to put up with it) as the Roaring Twenties.

But at the Columbia end of my day, in the late afternoon and evening hours, I found my reward. It was then that I was able to escape, for at least a few blessed hours, the bawling uproar of the newsroom as well as the human meat grinder that passed for justice in the New York lower courts.

In the dim-lit halls of academe, I stuffed myself for two semesters that year with the necessary requirements of economics, American history, and the classics of English and American literature courses, as well as a

German language refresher. And at the end, I was welcomed into Joseph Pulitzer's journalism school by Director Cunliffe, the author, among other works, of *The Influence of Seneca on Elizabethan Tragedy*. To me at least, this was preferable to my own output in a regular day typified by the headline "GIRL RAPED ON BROADWAY."

Once I made it known at the *Graphic* in the summer of 1925 that I would be attending daytime classes in journalism that fall and wanted to be shifted to the night side, I had an anxious time of it while I awaited a decision from Swain and the other editors. Certainly, I needed the work. I didn't know where else I could turn at that time to earn enough money to keep me going. It was one thing to feel myself superior to tabloidia while I was covering the courts or police news, quite another to be set loose to do as I wished without even a modest income to support my ambitions.

Fortunately, the *Graphic* kept me on, gave me a raise to $50 a week, and put me on the night copy desk writing headlines and editing copy for the first afternoon edition. And I had another lucky break. My father's brother, Dr. Bernhard Hohenberg, a physician with an office on East 13th Street in Manhattan, offered me a bed whenever I had the chance to sleep a few hours during the daytime between night work and my Columbia classes. Better still, I was able to give up the dark and smelly dormitory room. As for my parents' apartment, that was too far from my regular routine and I had to see them whenever I had an hour or two to myself.

In preparation for the opening day of classes at Columbia's journalism school in the fall of 1925, I finished work on the *Graphic*'s first edition at 6 A.M., then napped on Ed Sullivan's desk in the sports department until Ed came in and woke me up.

As a result, I was among the first to appear that day, one of the most important in my young life, for the debut of the Class of 1927 at the Journalism Building. While sitting among a cluster of uneasy young men in the newsroom, I was attracted to the first girl to appear—a dark-haired beauty in a blue dress, flat-heeled shoes, and a well-worn raccoon coat. As soon as I decently could, I moved as close as possible to her desk, introduced myself, and received a nod, a vague smile, and the back of her head for my efforts.

This was how I met Dorothy Lannuier, my beloved classmate who became my wife for forty-nine years—the most precious of all the consequences for me of Joseph Pulitzer's gifts to Columbia. She was the daughter of a New York hardware merchant of French-Canadian ancestry and had come to Columbia after two years at Skidmore College in upstate New York. If I had ever had the slightest intention of dropping out of journalism school, the thought would have vanished at once from my bemused mind after I first saw her. That first day of classes in the Journalism Building, however, she gave me no time. And when the first assignments were handed out after an opening lecture and the newsroom rattled to the explosion of sixty typewriters operated by the Class of 1927, I feared she had completely forgotten me.

Fortunately, I was wrong. It wasn't long before Dorothy became the dominant influence in my young life. I don't believe she fully realized how serious I was about her, mainly because other young men in the class had preempted her attention. For me, important though my work at the school had become, any spare moment I had was devoted to my continual struggle for Dorothy's attention. Between that and my postmidnight copyediting job at the *Graphic,* I didn't get much sleep at my Uncle Bernhard's apartment, and I'm sure he and my aunt worried about me.

Eventually, I did manage to arrange a lunch date with Dorothy, a promising start that soon led to other dates. And by the end of the first semester of the 1925–26 academic year, she seldom was seen, in the newsroom or elsewhere on campus, without a gawky six-footer, dark rings under his blue eyes and a head of overgrown black hair, hovering anxiously around her.

Mainly because my night work prevented me from being with Dorothy as much as I wished, I decided to try for an afternoon job so I could give up the *Graphic* and have longer evening dates with her. My first chance came with an offer of four hours of afternoon rewrite at Pulitzer's *New York World* in the great redstone building under the golden dome on Park Row at the Manhattan end of the Brooklyn Bridge.

I'd taken on seemingly impossible jobs before, but this one stretched me to my nineteen-year-old limit. What I had to do was work the midnight-to-seven trick reading copy at the *Graphic;* handle my schoolwork at Columbia roughly from nine to noon, except for special reporting assignments that might take longer; do afternoon rewrite at the *World* from two to seven; and try to get in a few hours of sleep afterward at Uncle Bernhard's.

Of course it didn't work out. The city editor, who sat on a raised dais behind an enormous desk so that he could survey his newsroom domain and his staff with a flash of his eyeglasses, kept me going six afternoons a week handling the City News wire service, and reporters' rewrite. But eventually—mainly out of pity for my circumstances, I believe—he called me over and said it just wasn't possible for me to do my best work—and he was sorry.

At least, I'd had an invigorating breath of the atmosphere of a great newspaper, something I never forgot. The only memento of my experience that I bore away with me was a vivid recollection of the gigantic stained-glass window in the lobby of the *World* building—a triumph of the glaziers' art—that set off the Statue of Liberty on her pedestal in New York Harbor. It was a symbolic tribute to Pulitzer's feat, preserving Bartholdi's masterpiece as a splendid vision of the American dream.

As a member of Columbia's journalism faculty and the Administrator of the Pulitzer Prizes many years later, I was able to rescue the Liberty Window from the wrecking ball when the *World* building was razed and cause the memorial to be set in a massive frame at Pulitzer's school, in what we called the World Room. But as a student, all I could do was tell Dorothy about the window and take her downtown with me so that she, too, could see it while the *World* was still alive and functioning.

To both of us in our student days, it seemed that Pulitzer's newspaper under its golden dome and the stained glass memorial to his gift of the Statue of Liberty would last forever. Would that it had been so.

As the end of my Columbia experience approached, with Commencement Day for the Class of 1927, I couldn't help noticing how frequently my classmates, Dorothy in particular, kept speculating on my chances for one of the three Pulitzer Traveling Scholarships—prizes for excellence in journalism. In my year, they amounted to $1,800 each, sufficient at the time for at least a part of a year in Europe or elsewhere, but Paris was more often than not the goal of every young journalist in the 1920s.

To my surprise, I did win one of the three awards. In that far-off era, the *Graphic*'s editors could scarcely be blamed for celebrating the event prominently with a picture and an overblown account of a night copyeditor's honors—an implied effort by my shaky tabloid to pose briefly as superior to the two competing tabloids, the *News* and the *Mirror*.

However, I submitted my resignation, effective the week of my graduation. At the same time, I proposed marriage to Dorothy upon my return from Europe, a proposition she promptly accepted on condition that I behaved myself while I was abroad. And so, whatever my merits or demerits, I had come of age at twenty-one with the world as my field of study for the coming year.

3 ★ THE GRAND TOUR OF EUROPE

While I was in Prague, at the outset of what I had hoped would be a peaceful *wanderjahr* in Europe, I recorded in my diary: "Hell seems to be popping in Vienna and I'm going to try to get past the Austrian frontier today. . . . The whole thing was brought about by the freeing of two *Hackenkreuzler* (the wearers of the Swastika) who were on trial for the murders of two workmen."

The date: July 19, 1927. The record: My account of my Pulitzer Traveling Scholarship, and the first mention of Adolf Hitler's brawling National Socialists, the Nazis, who already had been bold enough to try to seize hapless little Austria, his native land.

The wild-eyed Czech press in Prague was having a field day with a pumped-up war scare. It reported Mussolini's Italian troops poised at the Austrian frontier, proof that the trains were running on time. Reports also had the Yugoslavs ready to fight; the Hungarians and Czechs on military alert; the Austrians trembling with fear, casualties mounting over the Nazi uprising; and the far-off Soviets mobilizing the Red Army.

I did get through to Vienna two days later when the Czech-Austrian frontier was reopened. I wrote: "The hospitals are still crowded with sick and wounded and the funerals are still continuing. . . . I was out until 1 A.M. and saw only a few people in the main (Ringstrasse) district."

For me, this record was no empty academic exercise. Instead of putting in all my time at the University of Vienna as a graduate student, as I had expected, I was working with some of the British and American foreign correspondents in Vienna at piecemeal rates, whatever they could pay me, when they needed help or a vacation replacement. The crisis broke while I was on a quick visit to Berlin and back for some feature stuff I hoped to sell—but now I had a much bigger story and the correspondents gave me plenty to do.

As a result, the University of Vienna and the learned lectures on "Die Deutsche Romantik" in the great Viennese lecture hall became a poor second to the news.

I stuck with the correspondents at one of their assembly points, the Café Louvre, and also was on call at the Haupttelegrafen Amt (the main telegraph office), ready to take off on any assignment I could get. My Uncle Bernhard, the doctor in New York, had added generously to my $1,800 Pulitzer grant so I was by no means strapped for funds. And whatever the correspondents were able to give me became so much velvet.

Upon my return from Germany that summer, I found the image of a careworn Vienna to be singularly affecting. The old grey city beside the Danube had become a poor relation of the world-famous metropolitan centers of the day. It could not match the loveliness of Paris, the businesslike air of London, the grim austerity and even the defiance of Berlin and Prague, or the riches of New York City.

As a fledgling foreign correspondent, I did my best work with such outstanding journalists of the time as M. W. Fodor, a Hungarian who represented the *Manchester Guardian* and the *New York Evening Post*; G. E. R. Gedye, a British correspondent who roved around Europe, and several lesser known Americans who were in and out of Vienna, Prague, and Budapest as the occasion warranted.

There were role models for me among other correspondents too—the ever cheerful Tommy Ybarra of the *New York Times,* who was based in Berlin but frequently came to Vienna, and stern, greying Jim Mills of the Associated Press, who had everybody's respect. It was strange that the loudest of all, and the most constant critic of Hitler, was the pudgy South Carolinian, Robert H. Best of the United Press, who was to remain in Vienna after World War II came to America, and who would die after it was all over in a Boston prison upon conviction as a traitor to his country.

All in all, however, I have always treasured my Viennese experience because it was there that I learned at first hand what it means to be a foreign correspondent. And when I left Vienna—at the end of the winter session at the university—to get on with my grand tour, it was with regret. The young people in the American community—mainly students—turned out at one of my favorite cafés for a farewell party.

Someone else, a dark-haired little Viennese girl whom I didn't know, also wandered in. My American colleagues good-naturedly made her a part of the proceedings. At the end, when I bowed out with the explanation that I would be taking off for western Europe by way of Czechoslovakia in the morning, everybody wished me well. I thought that would be the last of my good-byes that afternoon but outside the café door, the little Viennese gate-crasher was waiting for me. Almost mechanically, not knowing what was coming, I took her hand, pressed it, and murmured, "Alles gutes, grüss Gott" (All the best, God be with you). And I heard her reply in a low tense voice, "Bitte, nim mich mit" (Please, take me with you).

Like many other discouraged young people of the era, I suppose, she had already guessed at the terrible shape of things to come after Hitler's opening show of strength in Vienna. I've often wondered whether she was able to make it out before the roof fell in on Austria, the first of Hitler's victims.

The Nazi war scare, which I had experienced, evaporated as quickly as it had begun, mainly because the tough Viennese Socialist workmen on that occasion were still too strong for the Nazis and had made an issue out of freeing the *Hackenkreuzler*. The great powers of Europe, however, had nodded over that first Nazi-Fascist challenge. And in Moscow, the Soviet butcher, Stalin, had seen it all, realized what was ahead, and begun to plan to turn Hitler and his forces westward when the time came.

We young Americans in Vienna at the time, like the little Viennese girl who wanted to go west with me, could only vaguely sense that there was trouble ahead. Once, I wrote home to Dorothy that I suspected there would be another war in Europe, which didn't make me much of a prophet because Europe had floundered in wars large and small for centuries. But if I had by evil chance been clairvoyant and predicted that Hitler, the Austrian street fighter, would take over his own country, Germany, and most of western Europe within fifteen years, I'm sure I would have been considered raving mad.

However, when I started from Vienna next morning, I was troubled sufficiently to stop off at my father's native village, Holiči-pri-Morave, which then was a part of Czechoslovakia, to say good-bye to his youngest brother, Simon, whom I had visited now and then on the short trip from Vienna. He was a small man, slow-spoken and grave of manner, very much like my father. He had never married but lived with a housekeeper and ran a bottled liquor business from his big stone house on the village square.

Perhaps it was inconsiderate of me, but I couldn't help asking Uncle Simon just before I left whether he thought there would be another war. For answer, he sighed and said quietly, "Wars are a part of our heritage here. We can never tell what country we will belong to." Just before World War II began, my family in New York City managed to spirit him out of Czechoslovakia and bring him to America. But he wouldn't stay. He felt strange, he said, and wanted to go home, which is what he did. He died at Treblinka, a victim of the Holocaust.

There were other relatives I saw as well on my trip from Vienna to western Europe during my grand tour on the Pulitzer scholarship. When I stopped off at Frankfurt am Main in western Germany to see some of my mother's relatives, their reaction to my war talk was quite different. They seemed indignant for the most part that I should worry about a Nazi-inspired war that might affect the land of Goethe, Schiller, and Heinrich Heine.

Both a rabbi and a cantor among my older relatives were equally complacent. And as for visiting America one day, just a polite suggestion I made at the time, one of my aunts exclaimed,

"Ach, Amerika! Die sind blos schportsleute!" (Oh, America! These are only sports people!).

When the crunch came, our family did manage to rescue a younger rabbi and a cantor, whom we brought to the United States. But like so many others who believed such things couldn't happen in a civilized land like Germany, the rest died in the Holocaust.

It was a relief for me to settle down in Paris, the ultimate destination of most Americans in Europe, young and old alike. After the dour atmosphere of central Europe and the gloom aroused among those who feared both the Nazis and the Communists, it was a heady experience for me to be back in a land dedicated to freedom and a great city that was forever beautiful and exciting to me. It was no wonder that so many of us younger Americans fell in love with the French way of life and remembered, for all the rest of our days, every lively experience it gave us.

Mine, despite the shortness of my stay, were notable.

Among the first people I met was Louis Bromfield, who had established himself as a serious novelist after a modest beginning on rewrite for a New York City news service. Soon after my arrival, a mutual friend brought us together early one afternoon at the Café Deux Magots on the Left Bank, for a discussion of the ways of the world, and we spent several hours in conversation, suitably refreshed by the drinks he bought. Then there was Sam Dashiell, a true boulevardier if ever there was one, the correspondent in Paris of the *New York Evening Post,* and his wife, Hilda, both even more forthcoming than Bromfield. It was through the Dashiells that I met Ernest Hemingway.

Having read Hemingway's first novel, *The Sun Also Rises,* I was impressed at once, especially when he told me he was working on a new novel—mostly about war, he said. He was slimmer than Bromfield and taller—a good-looking twenty-eight-year-old, at the outset of his fame as a novelist. Later, when I saw him at home with his first wife, Hadley, he seldom showed the liking for aimless talk that was Bromfield's trademark in Paris.

There was nothing about Hemingway then of the self-proclaimed tough guy. Nor was he anything like the seedy, whiskered drinker of his later years, who attracted so much unfavorable publicity. I think it is curious that Hadley Hemingway made a more sympathetic impression on me when we first met; at least, that is what I find in my notes made at the time.

However, except for Dashiell, who helped me land my next newspaper job in New York City at the end of my *wanderjahr,* I never felt comfortable with the avant-garde in Paris. What I liked to do more than anything else was to wander around the city by myself. It never bothered me to sit alone at the familiar café near my little hotel, reading the newspapers and watching the passing scene. And if no one else was around at the time, I was happy to go by myself for the dish of the day, some crusty French bread, and a dose of the bitter chicory coffee that shocked the taste buds.

I never would have thought of watching a sunset in New York, London, or Tokyo, but I often did while I was in Paris that year of 1928. More often than not, I thought of Dorothy, whose letters had followed me everywhere I went and sometimes piled up in advance at a place where I was due, for I kept writing to her almost daily, and sometimes twice a day, all the time I was away.

I was winding up my European tour now, and I had just passed my twenty-second birthday. I wanted to go home, but I also wanted to see a little of Britain, Ireland, and the rest of western Europe before I boarded the Italian liner *Conte Biancamano* at Gibraltar.

When I took off from Paris, therefore, London was my destination. Although I dutifully ploughed through my sight-seeing guidebook and walked the streets from Soho to South Kensington and from the Victoria Embankment to the British Museum, what gave me the most pleasure was to gorge myself on the London theater. At the time, there was a Tallulah Bankhead play, *Blackmail,* a Noel Coward revue, *This Year of Grace,* and a musical called *Clowns in Clover* with Cicely Courtneidge and Jack Hulbert, along with a lot of other amiable claptrap. I thoroughly enjoyed everything and wished for more, but time was running short and there was much yet that I wanted to see.

I had the lamentable American habit of passing through points of interest merely to say I'd been there. Perhaps my youth was an excuse for the way I skittered around, but even my notes, scattered and incoherent as they are, constitute evidence that I simply touched base here and there and hoped for the best. So it came about that I saw a little of the English countryside, of Wales, and of Ireland (then the Irish Free State).

Luckily for me, I decided to return to London before going on to the continent for a final swing through France, Italy, and Spain before boarding the ship for home. For after I returned to my hotel in London's Russell Square (by way of the Shakespeare country, Oxford University, and Windsor Castle), a letter from Dorothy was waiting for me—with her acceptance of my proposal, by mail, for us to be married as soon as possible upon my return from my travels.

Now I had a powerful incentive to wind up my trip and get on with my life. I did stop off in Paris briefly to say goodbye to the Dashiells, Hemingway, Bromfield, and others who had been kind to me. And Bromfield, incidentally, made me promise to write a novel I had discussed with him. He gave me four handwritten letters to various New York publishers he knew, as path-breaking introductions for further discussions, or perhaps even a book contract if any editor was suitably impressed.

After that, it was only to be expected that I would leave Paris with regret. In all truth, I wondered if I'd ever see the city again, if there was to be another great war, if the French would stand and fight the advancing Germans once again as they had in 1914, if we Americans once again would come to the rescue of a democratic Europe.

Such dismal thoughts as these vanished soon enough when I saw the blue waters of the Mediterranean sparkling in the sunlight off the French Riviera. I had no sooner hit the nearest beach along the road past Cannes than I shed my clothes as quickly as I could find a place to undress and went for a long swim beyond the curling waves. Even then, I enjoyed the sea and often would pass up a meal rather than miss a good swim.

I'm afraid that I thereby shortened my already brief tour of Mussolini's Italy. I had made the typical American mistake of judging the land of the Caesars by the clown Mussolini and his iron-fisted Fascisti. As a result, I'm ashamed to say, I raced through Genoa, Milan and Venice, Florence, Rome, and Naples, before boarding a coastal vessel off Naples for Barcelona. And once in Spain, all I had time for was a mad dash that took me through Barcelona, Madrid, Seville, and Cordoba before I boarded the *Conte Biancamano* at Gibraltar.

I was one of few Americans in third class, and my mostly Italian fellow passengers regarded me more as a curiosity than anything else and left me strictly alone. It was just as well. I was exhausted by the rigors of my race through southwestern Europe, and I needed the rest. As the *Conte* cruised into New York harbor after an uneventful voyage and I saw the Statue of Liberty at a distance, I felt an inner sense of peace with the world. I was home again, safely and gratefully, and my whole life with Dorothy was ahead of me.

We were married on October 16, 1928, at her parents' home in Ridgewood, New Jersey. We moved into a tiny flat at 21 Butler Place in Brooklyn and hoped for the best.

Dorothy as I first saw her at Columbia. I took the picture in Riverside Drive Park overlooking the Hudson River.

The picture that Dorothy gave me at the time.

Our graduation picture in 1927 on the steps of the Columbia Journalism building. We were engaged to be married.

The bridegroom on a four-day Atlantic City honeymoon in 1928. Notice the moustache.

4 ★ SURVIVING THE CRASH

About a year after Dorothy and I were married, I was put in charge of makeup for the financial section of the *New York Evening Post*. I'd been working there from the day after my return from my Pulitzer year abroad, and I found the place congenial—a relief from the rock 'em sock 'em routine in tabloidia.

The *Post* then was a full-sized financial daily with a modest circulation, no threat to the *Wall Street Journal* by any means, but reasonably prosperous nevertheless because of the great stock market boom of the 1920s. The excitement about the market was still at its height then, so it was vital for us to get the Wall Street closing edition, with final stock prices for the day, on the newsstands as quickly as possible.

There had been no warning signals to date that the bull market was running out of steam, so an enthusiastic public had long since joined professional investors gambling on cheap stocks. And among the afternoon papers in the city that ran complete stock market tables, the *Post* was far more dependent than others on selling its Wall Street closing edition. Therefore, it was my job to make sure the *Post* was on downtown newsstands thirty minutes after the stock market's usual closing hour at 3 P.M. The paper's appeal to advertisers depended on it.

I'd been doing reasonably well at my new job until the last ten days of October 1929 when the stock market, caught in a flurry of sell orders, closed late for several days, beginning October 21. It was then that our managing editor, Vincent Byers, came to me in the composing room and muttered, "Stock market's gone to hell. Bankers are meeting. We'll hold the Wall Street closing edition."

That was on October 24. It was the first I'd heard that something dangerous was happening in Wall Street. As the history of the period has long since shown, the giant sell-off in the stock market beginning October 21 forced the bankers to pool resources to try to stabilize prices. They were lucky enough to do so on Friday and Saturday, October 25 and 26. But on Monday, October 28, I watched the stock ticker slipping farther and farther behind, with nearly all major stocks losing ground. Our closing edition got out later and later.

Now President Hoover came to life in the White House with a solemn announcement that the nation's business, despite what was happening in Wall Street, was "fundamentally sound." Nobody believed him. There was a full-page ad next day in the *Wall Street Journal* headed, "STEADY, Everybody." And in the *New York Times* there was an authoritative account of how the banks were prepared to withstand another major sell-off.

But, alas, on October 29, the day of reckoning, the market went into a tailspin with the opening bell, and it didn't recover for years. This was when a British paper carried mythical accounts of people jumping out of windows in Wall Street. In the midst of the panic, John D. Rockefeller, Sr., made his historic pronouncement that the public was missing a lot of good bets and he himself was picking up bargains in the stock market. But in the White House, a President who had lost his nerve was wringing his hands, not knowing what to do.

I was busy at the time in the composing room getting out extra editions of the paper with the latest stock prices. It wasn't my idea. The front office had thought, I suppose, of making a killing on the theory that people would be rushing to buy papers to find out how much money they were losing.

Editors, ours and others, did have strange ideas at the time, even more so than writers. In this particular case, most of the extra copies of the *Post* that were tossed on downtown newsstands remained there unsold. The printed prices were hours behind the market and no one could say how the disaster would end and what would happen after that. When I put out the final for the day, with the closing prices for "Black Tuesday," as it became known, it was after 6 P.M.

At City Hall, Mayor "Dancing Jimmy" Walker appealed to motion picture exhibitors to show films that would "put hope and courage back in the American people." But in Albany, Governor Franklin D. Roosevelt denounced the Wall Street plungers who had sold off the market. As for the market itself, it opened Wednesday for an abbreviated session, then shut down for the rest of the week. It was just as well. For after the stock market blowout came the onset of the Great Depression.

All I hoped to do at the time was to hang on for as long as the *Post* was likely to last under such horrendous conditions and to prepare for the worst. Dorothy, being the more practical member of our marriage, suggested that just for luck we might put in a vegetable garden the following spring at her grandmother's place on Long Island. It sounded like a good idea to me. If the worst came to the worst, we could always eat spinach. Now that the merry-go-round had stopped, almost anything could happen.

Fortunately for my parents and me, their children's clothing store in New York City seemed little affected at first by the onset of the Great Depression after the stock market collapse. And as for my Uncle Bernhard and Aunt Lily, the doctor and his wife, they'd had the good sense to get out of the market by dumping all their stocks the summer before the crash.

Dorothy's parents, my in-laws, weren't as lucky. My father-in-law's wholesale hardware business operation in downtown Manhattan was one of the first casualties of hard times. And with it went his impressive home in Ridgewood, New Jersey, little more than a year after Dorothy and I were married. What her parents had to do was to move in with her grandmother, Mary Adelaide Shirley, far out on eastern Long Island as the depression deepened across the land.

Grandma Shirley, then in her one hundredth year, lived with an unmarried daughter, Aunt Jo, in a white clapboard cottage in Aquebogue that had been built in 1827. I had come to know Grandma Shirley and Aunt Jo long before my marriage during brief summer vacations when I took the Long Island Rail Road to Aquebogue. There, I stayed in a comfortable room in an old red barn that had been plainly furnished with a bed, a rocking chair, a table, chairs, and an oil cook stove. That was when Dorothy stayed with her parents in Grandma's cottage.

I soon learned that the hard-working folk on the north fork of eastern Long Island were self-reliant and sturdy, not at all like the society people in the wealthy south fork community of Southampton. And during the early years of the depression, in which the more pretentious people were among the first to be leveled off, that always made life on the north fork more interesting to me. It was 90 miles from Manhattan.

Once we were able to settle Dorothy's badly shaken parents with Grandma Shirley and Aunt Jo (the mother and sister of Dorothy's mother), what I felt I had to do was to contribute whatever small sums we could afford to help maintain the family. And the following spring, I put in the vegetable garden Dorothy had suggested. With a hand plow and other seldom-used farm implements at Grandma's place, I had all-day Sunday workouts every week when Dorothy and I came to Aquebogue on the Long Island Rail Road.

By that time, the old Hudson automobile Dorothy's mother had driven was no longer in running order, and we had to make do by train. And now, as the youngest people in the family, both of us lived in the barn. During the week, Dan Corwin—a hired man who worked on a duck farm and lived nearby in a little one-room shack—took care of the garden for us. He often said it was about time he gave something back to Grandma Shirley for letting him live in his "office" rent-free for so many years.

This is how we got along as the Great Depression spread until the whole country was affected. Frankly, I considered myself lucky that I still had a job, no matter how inadequate the salary was in view of my needs. Considering the far from settled state of the nation, I did the best I could at the *Post* to hang on while people were being let go there, as they were everywhere else.

There came a time in 1930, while I was at work in the city and Dorothy was staying with her parents in Aquebogue, that Grandma Shirley asked to have her best black silk dress laid out in her upstairs bedroom.

"Are you going somewhere, Grandmother?" Dorothy asked.

The old lady said calmly, "I shall be dying tonight."

Dorothy was immediately concerned, as were her parents. They wanted to call a doctor, to have Grandma taken to a hospital, to have her treated for all manner of ailments. But the old lady remained firm. She had asked only to be helped into her best black silk dress once it was laid out on her bed.

And that, finally, was what Dorothy had to do for her, all assurances and protests to the contrary. Eventually, Aunt Jo cautioned Dorothy's mother, "Mama knows, she's always told me this was the way she wanted everything to end, nice and quiet, like, and no fussin'."

So Mary Adelaide Shirley, in her best black silk dress, sat by the window of her bedroom in the old white cottage beside the road in Aquebogue that afternoon, watching the sun go down for the last time. And when her people came to put her to bed later in the evening after she hadn't come downstairs for supper as usual, they found that she had died.

She was 101½ years old.

There was a service for her in the steepled white Congregational Church across the road in Aquebogue from the church's burying ground next day, but I couldn't get away from the *Post* to attend. The five-day week and time-and-a-half cash for overtime were in the distant future. But come Sunday, I was at last able to pay tribute to Grandma, standing with Dorothy beside the old lady's newly turned grave and muttering a half-remembered prayer I'd learned in Hebrew as a child. I didn't think Grandma would mind.

More than anything else, she had taught me the virtue of kindness and forbearance in her long and useful life.

For young people like myself who still had a job or a business of their own during the opening years of the Great Depression, the responsibility sometimes caused an intensely nervous strain. Day after day, I wondered what would become of us all if I, too, was put out of work and had to scramble with millions of others for the pitifully small sums of unemployment relief that then were the only cushion there was for distressed people and their families. Without doubt, if my own parents had been in difficulty, I knew that my Uncle Bernhard would see to it that they were cared for as long as he was alive. He was old now, too, and suffering from diabetes, but he still insisted on treating anybody who asked for his services, $1 to the office and $2 to the home if they could pay, nothing at all if they were broke.

This was a crisis far more devastating than any other I'd ever read about in our history as a nation. And there was no sign, even far down the road, that we'd be coming out of it very soon. At the outset of the 1930s, there seemed to be worse news every day without a break in sight and the stock market lay rolling near or actually at an all-time low.

Wherever I turned to look for help to see my dependents and myself through the crisis, there was only despair and, inevitably, blame for the unlucky President Hoover who was still proclaiming, as if it were a magic formula, "Prosperity is just around the corner."

The opposition, quite naturally, was making capital out of Hoover's irresponsibility, his inaction, his virtual paralysis. But I still wondered how any one person, President or not, could have averted this disaster to which so many different forces here and abroad had contributed. In Joseph Pulitzer's *New York World,* his chief editorial writer, Walter Lippmann, was still blaming Hoover for almost everything, including a surrender to special interests. But then, even Lippmann was under the same kind of pressure that was affecting most of the rest of us in the news business. His paper, under its magnificent golden dome on Park Row, was also dying. Its financial losses were enormous.

Some nights, when I left the *Post,* I used to walk the few blocks across town merely to stand there on Park Row and wonder what was happening to the *World.* I had a nagging memory of Don Seitz's opposition to the first of Joseph Pulitzer's proposals to build a journalism school at Columbia University and create his cherished Pulitzer Prizes with a $2 million bequest. Seitz, who became one of Pulitzer's biographers, had pleaded with his fiercely determined patron toward the beginning of the century:

"Endow the *World.* Make it foolproof."

But at the time, Pulitzer seemed to have decided he had done enough for the *World.* Instead, he wrote that he was "much attached" to the idea of prizes for journalism and literature—and that became his first priority. After his death in 1911, his journalism school was created at Columbia in 1913; it moved into its own building two years later, and his prizes followed with the first awards in 1917.

But now, as all of us knew, the *World* couldn't last much longer. Nor would its sister papers in the evening and on Sunday survive. The end came when Roy Howard, of the Scripps-Howard Newspapers, offered $5 million for all three properties, and the Pulitzer management—still having a going newspaper, the *St. Louis Post-Dispatch* and other properties—quickly accepted.

I remember how downhearted I felt on February 27, 1931, when I walked across town for the last time and watched the lights go out under the golden dome. The successor paper, the merger with Scripps-Howard's *Telegram,* became a larger afternoon newspaper, the *New York World-Telegram.* The evening and Sunday *World* editions died. And hundreds of people were let go when the once mighty *World* and its sister papers suspended publication.

I was out of a job at the *Evening Post* a year later, together with my managing editor and others of high and low degree, as the paper approached a break in its existence of more than a century and a quarter. Its losses in the depression, too, could not be sustained by its proprietors, the Curtis magazine interests that owned the then prosperous *Saturday Evening Post.* Any prospective new owner was bound to change the *Post* newspaper in format, style, and purpose. In its latter-day history, it was to become a tabloid, and old friends would be urging me to return to it.

But that kind of thing was out of the question in the Great Depression. Somehow, between temporary jobs and unexpected offers of others plus promotions, I managed not to miss a day's work or a paycheck during that altogether difficult era. And in good time, I wound up as a political writer on Hearst's *Evening Journal* at more than double the pay I had received from the *Evening Post.* I needed it!

Although I had a number of interesting assignments at the *Journal* other than politics, the trial of Bruno Richard Hauptmann and several legislative investigations among them, there was a time when we had depression tremors on that paper, too. *The American,* the elder Hearst's favorite newspaper, also was incurring heavy losses at the time, and it was published in the same building as the *Journal,* so there were continual rumors of a merger of the two papers. At one point, a *Journal* city editor suddenly was discharged for no apparent reason. And other staff changes, too, occurred from time to time.

But after a while, the rumors died down. I became more confident that the worst was over, and Dorothy and I thereafter allowed ourselves a few liberties we'd never dared even think about before—dining out now and then, a Broadway show or a concert when one particularly interested us, and even modernization of the old cottage in Aquebogue.

If we wanted to celebrate in style, we could have an elaborate French-style dinner at the Lafayette Hotel on University Place in Manhattan for only $2.50 each. Otherwise, we still had our meals at home, except when my Uncle Bernhard took us to one of his favorite Hungarian restaurants, the Café Royale on Second Avenue or the Café Abbazzia uptown.

As for Broadway shows or concerts at Carnegie Hall, these were state occasions. Usually, we attended theatrical openings or recitals when the *Journal* would ask me to do a second-string review. What we did do, if we wanted to go to a theater on our own, was buy cut-rate tickets at a place in Times Square or balcony seats at the Palace Theatre, the Valhalla of vaudeville.

Between my increased pay at the *Journal* and whatever I managed to sell to magazines, we were able to meet our family obligations and still have enough left over for Dorothy to save and make monthly payments on our first car, a 1934 Ford. That car made it possible at last for us to drive to see my parents on a weekday evening and, once the five-day, forty-hour week became a way of life, to spend weekends at Aquebogue with Dorothy's parents and Aunt Jo.

The apartment in the barn was still ours, and with Dan Corwin's help, I still managed to keep up my vegetable garden. We also moved from our tiny Butler Place apartment, first to a larger one at 226 Lincoln Place in Brooklyn, then across the street to a more glamorous one at 235 Lincoln Place. Regardless of the difficulty, we were coping with the Great Depression and doing what we could to keep our respective families going.

I never expected the lovely surprise that awaited me when I came home on a cold winter's night from the *Journal* to celebrate my twenty-ninth birthday in 1935 and found a glossy black medium-sized Chickering grand piano, its top up, reposing in the space between the triple front window of our living room. I'm afraid I disgraced myself before the assembled company for my surprise party by going emotional when Dorothy played "Happy Birthday" for me on that big, beautiful grand. I'd never dreamed I'd be able to own one, but with the first $900 Dorothy had saved, she bought it for me. And that, to me at least, meant that we had survived the worst time of our young lives.

5 ★ THE PROFESSIONAL LIFE

Most professionals in the news business who communicate directly with the public, especially during presidential campaigns, become conscious sooner or later of pressures to spin the news in one direction or another. We even have a name for those whose job it is to influence us from the White House, the opposition, or wherever: "Spin Doctors."

For all our virtuous insistence that we are well able to disregard such insidious influences in favor of certified truth, I know a considerable amount of this kind of propaganda has always got through to the public. And still does. It seems to me that this has been particularly true since television, with its marvelous mixture of images and words, has assumed much of the first reporting of the news. And yet, even if this violates the textbook image we propagate of the news columns and news broadcasts as pure and unsullied verities, I cannot think of it as a crisis for the republic because the public is now and nearly always has been aware of what is going on.

If you don't believe it, consider the historic public mistrust of the news business in America, going back to Thomas Jefferson's time. So I see no reason not to level with the public about my own concerns for our struggling profession.

I would argue first of all that the more blatant attempts at influence, whether they come from Presidential campaign sources or the front offices of concerned areas of the news media, cannot do a great deal of harm because they are so obvious. While I was preparing for coverage of the far-off 1936 campaign in which Franklin D. Roosevelt sought reelection, for example, I was instructed never to use the fatal words "New Deal" in the news columns no matter what the circumstances.

What to do? I simply used the phrase "Roosevelt administration" rather than "New Deal." The alternative, supplied by William Randolph Hearst, Sr. (the owner of the *New York Evening Journal,* for which I was writing), was "RAW DEAL." It wasn't difficult to fathom the old man's motives. He had assured FDR's nomination in 1932 in a deal in which John Nance Garner became the Vice-Presidential nominee in return for Hearst's proposal to switch Garner's delegates to FDR. But after the election, Hearst Sr. was furious because FDR's policies displeased him.

It didn't seem to matter at first to my own work, however, that the old man backed Governor Alf M. Landon of Kansas against FDR in 1936. I was by no means the only correspondent whose paper was opposing FDR. A lot of other conservative papers also were in Landon's corner. And yet, when the President came to Hyde Park to rest at his ancestral home, he paid all of us, whether we represented his friends or foes, the compliment of treating us as professionals.

To be sure, FDR could be uppity if somebody asked him a question he didn't want to answer; witness the way he told a *New York Times* reporter to put on a dunce cap and sit in a corner (a penalty for an inconvenient query). But mostly, within my experience at least, the President did try to be friendly when he communicated with us there or elsewhere at his regular twice-a-week news conferences.

These, FDR and his people fully appreciated, were our bread and butter, and they saw to it that we had more than enough to write and talk about. Nobody who covered FDR could hate him for that, including some of the opposition editorialists and columnists who also, on occasion, turned up at his news conferences. However, it became increasingly difficult for me to tell the story straight, when my publisher was cutting loose with ferocious blasts at FDR in editorial comment carried on the front page of all his newspapers. How could I contend after that, with a straight face, that I—as a reporter—was forwarding an unprejudiced view of the news even if my publisher's position was anything but unprejudiced right on page one?

Governor Landon, meanwhile, was charging FDR with leading the nation down a disastrous road to dictatorship. In Los Angeles, he elaborated on this theme, warning that New Dealers believed they had a mandate to "direct and control" business, and pleading on that basis for FDR's defeat. That was the Republican position, and it was fully reported and broadcast as it was given. There was no argument here that reporting was slanted in the news columns. The editorial attacks were something else again.

Now came a news break that couldn't possibly have been issued as propaganda because it turned out to be a colossal, in fact a fatal, error. This was the famous *Literary Digest* poll of 10 million voters, on which the magazine based its prediction of August 22, 1936, that Landon would wallop FDR. The primitive attempt of the *Digest* to poll the masses came up against a completely unscientific estimate made by James Aloysius Farley, the President's chief campaigner, who forecast that FDR would be reelected, forty-six states to two (he even named the two, Maine and Vermont). (I have never been an unreserved admirer of polls, before or since, even if the pollsters have claimed to use the most precise scientific methods. These methods were most recently found to be at fault when the British Conservative party defeated the opposition Labour party in a 1992 election, in which Labour had been the pollsters' favorite.)

Hearst Sr. may have had an intimation of what was coming, because from abroad he cabled all his papers, including the *Evening Journal*, with instructions to give equal play to the rival FDR and Landon campaigns from then on. That was on October 26, 1936, a week before election day.

For my part, I had good reason not to believe the *Digest*. One of the indicators I always watch toward the end of any campaign for the presidency is the turnout and behavior of the crowds. In the last days before that particular election, I never saw anything like the enthusiastic mobs that stormed every Roosevelt appearance I covered. It looked to me like a big Democratic victory, which is what I told my office, but of course nothing like that could be used in the *Journal* before the votes were cast.

As history has long since recorded, this was the greatest victory of FDR's political career and a record for all Presidents up to that time. In the popular vote, FDR had 27.7 million to Landon's 16.8 million. In the Electoral College, it was FDR 523 and Landon 8. Farley had hit it right: Only Maine and Vermont went against FDR. That was how I wrote the story and how the *Journal* bannered the results next day. It could hardly have been kept a secret. After Landon conceded, Hearst followed suit. In a telegram to striking workers of his *Seattle Post-Intelligencer,* he called FDR's victory "absolutely stunning," adding, "When I was a great admirer and supporter of Mr. Roosevelt, I gave him a picture of Andrew Jackson and a letter of that great Democrat. I thought then that Mr. Roosevelt resembled Jackson. Perhaps I was more nearly right then than later. . . . Perhaps Roosevelt like Jackson has given essential democracy a new lease on life and will establish it in power for a generation."

Thereupon, Hearst Sr. directed an immediate settlement of the Seattle strike and, in the following year, finally made a lot of us at the *Journal* nervous when he folded his favorite paper, the morning *American,* our fifth-floor neighbor. However, my concerns were groundless for it was the *American's* employees who were let go (except for a few who were shifted to the *Journal*). The new *Journal-American* continued to lead the evening field and remained one of the few papers in the Hearst service that did better than break even.

As for the *Literary Digest,* it went out of business unmourned and unsung—also unnoticed, except just before all future Presidential election days when its 1936 forecast is solemnly discussed on editorial pages and in television commentaries, especially by hopeful short-enders in current polls.

Once again on the *Journal-American,* we had our troubles in sustaining impartial news coverage after the Hitler-Stalin pact touched off World War II in Europe and the Nazis partitioned Poland with the Red Army that advanced from the east. The far right American conservatives became isolationists, the pro-Roosevelt liberals took the anti-Nazi line and became interventionists with the Nazis' invasion of the West in 1940. But in the waiting period before the Nazi lunge into France and the tremendous air battle of Britain, the isolationists' line was that it was, as they called it, a "Phony War."

During that 1939–40 period, therefore, the *Journal-American* gave all-out support to the isolationist America First Committee. Although "Young Bill"—William Randolph Hearst, Jr.—was now running the New York paper, his father was still very much in the news with Cissy Patterson, the owner of the *Washington Times-Herald,* and Colonel Robert R. McCormick, who owned the *Chicago Tribune*. All three, and smaller organizations that followed them, once again turned on FDR. With Hearst Sr., they opposed the later formation of the Committee to Defend America by Aiding the Allies, which FDR backed, particularly after Hitler's armies were battering west toward Paris.

Still, despite the renewed argument with the White House over World War II, the *Journal-American*'s circulation soared on the play of the war news, if not its coverage. Whether the older Hearst liked it or not, most of the professionals in the newsroom—myself included—admired the inspired and courageous radio news people, especially CBS's Edward R. Murrow, whose nightly descriptions of the Battle of Britain gripped an enormous section of the American public.

It was only when President Roosevelt plumped for a third term in 1940 and the Republicans put up Wendell Willkie, who was far from an isolationist, that domestic politics once again overshadowed the war news. For all Willkie's nonsense about FDR's supposed dictatorial leanings, I found the Republican nominee to have a warm personality and to be a realistic opponent and a gut fighter that the New Dealers would have disregarded at their peril. It was a sign of maturity that they did not.

There was, however, an agreement between the President and Willkie, in view of the way the war was going in Europe, to soft-pedal differences on foreign affairs as much as possible—a feature of the 1940 presidential campaign that was disturbing mainly to the America Firsters. I found the position fascinating, and I am sure my contributions to the coverage of the campaign must have reflected my feelings. As for the public, with the exceptions of the German-American Bund and the Communist Party of the USA, people seemed to take the Roosevelt-Willkie agreement in stride considering the wartime circumstances. Covering the Bund then was no task.

Even so, despite the passage of a Neutrality Act by a somewhat frightened Congress on FDR's initiative, there wasn't much that was neutral in his administration. The introduction of the draft, which was billed as a necessary American defense precaution, created so much anxiety that FDR had to pledge just before election day in 1940 that he would not send American boys into a foreign war.

Our coverage of this and other features of the American position on the *Journal-American* had been reasonably straight up to that point in the

Presidential campaign, but I had no illusions about what was going to happen when I registered for the draft at the age of thirty-four. Like so many others of my generation, I had already made up my mind that we would get into the war in one way or another. Not that I disbelieved FDR—that was not the point. It was my conviction that the war would be fought in such a way that we would eventually be given no choice except to fight in our own interests.

There were no surprises that election night in 1940. FDR won by 27 million to 22.3 million in the popular vote and 449 to 82 in the Electoral College. This time, however, the elder Hearst sent no congratulations; nor did he renew his comparison of FDR and Andrew Jackson as true democrats with a small "d." Our early morning election extra next day, I thought, told the story fully and fairly without any of the isolationist flourishes that had become so much a part of the reportage in the isolationist press generally.

However, I was badly mistaken when I thought that the election had settled the isolationist-interventionist debate. Just before Christmas Day, the President introduced the principle of lend-leasing American war material to the hard-pressed British who were still holding out against the punishing nightly Nazi air raids. It may have been true, as Ed Murrow kept saying in his nightly radio reports, that "London can take it." But it also was true, and the news media made no secret of it, that the British were near the end of their resources.

Still, when FDR called on the American people to support the embattled British and their allies in the West by making America the "arsenal of democracy," the isolationist press boiled over in anger. Lend-Lease, coming atop FDR's deal of destroyers for some British Atlantic bases, was too much for the isolationists. The blow-off came, I believe, when Senator Burton K. Wheeler charged that Congressional approval of Lend-Lease would "plough under every fourth American boy." FDR called it the "most untruthful, dastardly, unpatriotic thing" he'd heard in his generation.

For professionals like myself, fair-minded and decent coverage of so passionate a debate amounted to an ordeal by fire. If you were morally on the side of intervention in the war, you were in high favor at the White House and much was made of your stand. But if you were on the isolationist side, regardless of your attempts to cover the story fairly, and you needed a quick White House comment on something your editors had asked for, you could wait a long time for action, if any. It followed, therefore, that once again I was far from alone among working news people in deviating from my old publisher's views on the war.

The White House after a time recognized this clear split of opinion between the professionals and some of their publishers among the press in general. As Raymond Clapper put it in a syndicated column at the time, the President "absolved the reporters and the leaky Senators but pointed the finger at his favorite whipping boys, the newspaper owners and managers and the radio."

That, however, did not stop the publishers and managers from pointing the finger at us, the reporters, if they believed we were underrepresenting or misrepresenting the point of view they favored, whether we wrote for the news columns or not. So regardless of what FDR may have tried to do for us, and I was never as sure as Clapper was about that, in the end we reporters were the ones who wound up in the middle.

And there we remained, in one way or another, all of us who handled national, state, or local politics for the isolationist press.

I had confessed to Dorothy—and to her cousin, Dick Corwin, and his wife, Sue—that I wanted to enlist when war came, but I doubt if any of them took me seriously. Dorothy, always being so positive in nature, refused to worry about what would happen when and if we went to war. And as for Dick and Sue, with whom we'd spent so many pleasant weekends on eastern Long Island and whom we now saw almost every day as our neighbors in Brooklyn, they both simply wouldn't believe that America ever would fight in what they called somebody else's war. Sue, suiting thought to purpose, sat atop our grand piano one night, commanded me to play "My Hero," and proceeded to sing it to me with elaborate and loving gestures.

It made me feel just a bit silly, being in my thirties, but it didn't alter my convictions. And then when war came to all of us suddenly and unexpectedly with the bombing of Pearl Harbor on a chill December 7, 1941, everything changed.

The Phony War had ended. The real war had begun.

PART 2

In War and Peace

6 ★ SERVICE IN WORLD WAR II

My military career in World War II didn't turn out exactly as I'd planned. I really had wanted a combat assignment. But when it finally came, it wasn't at all what I had expected.

My story began conventionally enough with the same kind of Pearl Harbor experience that befell most of us who first heard the news by radio that December 7, 1941. I was driving along Eastern Parkway in Brooklyn, around 2:30 P.M., listening to the New York Giants' football game on NBC on the car radio when a tense voice broke in: "AIR RAID PEARL HARBOR THIS IS NO DRILL." I reacted automatically. At the next crossover, I swung back to our apartment instead of calling on my parents as I'd intended. When I burst in, Dorothy looked up in surprise and asked, "What's the trouble? Had an accident?"

I don't know why I did it, but I gripped her in my arms. Then I told her about the Pearl Harbor flash and switched on the radio. All we heard, tuning from one station to another, was an excited babble and speculation but nothing definite. The best thing to do then, both of us agreed, was for me to go in to the *Journal-American* office because the wire service teletypes would be on, somebody would be at the Sunday desk, and we'd find out what was happening there faster than any place else.

A lot of others I knew must have had the same idea because almost all the inside news staff of editors, copy editors, rewrite people, and even copy boys had come in. But all they were doing was passing around wads of wire service copy about Pearl Harbor and talking together in low voices. Even if we'd wanted to, we couldn't have gotten out a paper immediately on Sunday because the mechanical staffs wouldn't show up until their regular time.

All of us hung around anyway, alternately digesting what few fragments of news the authorities released at once about the Japanese attack and calling our homes. Then, the managing editor quietly thanked us for coming in and asked us to return two hours earlier next morning to produce the war extra. It was the best our afternoon newspaper could do with the biggest story in many years.

That night, even though the horrendous toll of the Pearl Harbor disaster was far from completely reported, Dorothy and I knew the country was in for a long and difficult war. We didn't have to wait for the official declaration and all the speech-making that followed but made plans for what we would do as soon as I was called up for duty, which we expected to be immediately. I also hazarded the guess that the great debate between the pro- and anti-Roosevelt press now was over.

I couldn't have been more mistaken on all counts.

What my draft board told me when I inquired about my status was that I had been listed as a volunteer officer candidate as I had requested because of my two years' experience in the Reserve Officers' Training Corps at the University of Washington. However, I was informed also that the military services desperately needed much younger men to fill the ranks as GIs so it would be a while before I'd be called up.

I suppose I could have stirred around and wangled myself a commission, as some of my colleagues did, or applied for a job as a war correspondent in the Hearst service or somewhere else but, quite honestly, it never occurred to me. I had had the fixed notion for so long that I wanted to see combat in uniform that nothing else entered my mind at the time. In retrospect, war correspondence would have been a far more complete experience for a journalist in his thirties. But that wasn't the way it worked out for me.

As the war fever rose across the land, I became increasingly dissatisfied both with sitting at a desk rewriting wire copy for undated summary leads of war developments and with being assigned to political differences at home. After the first shock of the Japanese treachery at Pearl Harbor wore off, the former isolationist press clamored for help for General Douglas MacArthur in the Pacific war against Japan instead of for pursuing the Roosevelt-Churchill program of beating Hitler and Mussolini in Europe first.

As the White House saw the war, by far the greatest danger to the nation lay in Europe, where Hitler still held the key to power even though he had lost the Battle of Britain. On the previous June 22, he had attacked his erstwhile ally, the Soviet Union, by sending the Reichswehr deep into the Russian heartland. What the White House now counted on was the ability of the Red Army to hold out before Stalingrad, as it had been doing since September, until fresh American troops could open a second front in the West against the Axis powers.

That, however, did not suit the Hearst-Patterson-McCormick press in its mounting dissatisfaction with the progress of the war. Not even FDR's orders to fly MacArthur out of his hopeless position at Corregidor in the Philippines appeased the opposition, which denounced the imprisonment of his replacement, General Jonathan Wainwright, and his outnumbered American forces when Corregidor fell to the Japanese after prolonged and heroic resistance.

Clearly, the renewed debate in the nation's press over the Pacific versus the European war (everybody agreed we couldn't do both because we were caught unprepared) was likely to go on indefinitely. And, adding still more to my dissatisfaction was the daily roundup of news from all the fighting fronts that showed the correspondents of the FDR opposition press, regardless of what their publishers and editorialists did, perform miracles of courage everywhere to report the war truthfully and often brilliantly.

I don't know of an instance, once my professional colleagues faced the enemy anywhere, in which they did not do their duty, regardless of personal risk and the editorial policies of their publishers. It was their performance, in fact, that increased my own dissatisfaction at having miscalculated and neglected to make an effort to join them.

What also bothered me was the repeated allegation in the anti-Roosevelt press that the President had somehow provoked Japan into attacking Pearl Harbor or even had known about the plans of the Japanese military caste in advance but had failed to sound the alarm. Neither then nor now have reasonable people ever found any basis for what amounts to a charge of treason against FDR, the Commander in Chief.

It was under these circumstances, some time early in 1942, that I received an offer to return to a quite different *New York Post* than the one I'd left involuntarily more than a decade before. Dorothy and I had made preparations for my induction into military service soon after Pearl Harbor. In anticipation of what we expected to be my prolonged absence and a greatly reduced income, Dorothy had moved us from our lovely five-room apartment on Lincoln Place to a one-room-and-kitchen at another building on Plaza Street near Sue and Dick Corwin. Except for the grand piano, which took up most of the available space in our one large room beside a combination couch-daybed and a card table for meals, nearly all the rest of our things went into storage for the duration.

Dorothy never questioned what I wanted to do in the war although I'm sure she must have wondered at times about my attitude, if not my sanity. For when Ed Flynn phoned from the *Post* to ask if I'd come back to help him out after military departures had put holes in his staff, she was enthusiastic about having me accept. We did play fair with Flynn by warning him that I might be called up at almost any time, but he was willing to take that chance. Even more to our satisfaction, he suggested having Dorothy join the *Post* staff to replace me when I entered military service.

That, finally, was how I came to leave the *Journal-American* after almost a decade of ups and downs in the Hearst service. And so I returned to a paper that I had left twice before under strained circumstances with the observation that the third time would be final. This *Post,* however, was no longer the stiff-necked Republican organ that Cyrus Curtis once had owned and lost. Now, it was a serious-minded tabloid, liberal in view and unfailingly supportive of Franklin D. Roosevelt and the Democratic Party.

The latest in a series of owners, Mrs. Dorothy Schiff, the daughter of Jacob H. Schiff of the Wall Street house of Kuhn, Loeb, and Company, had retained her maiden name after her marriage to her editor, Ted Thackrey. And he in turn had given full authority for the news side of the paper to Edward Patrick Flynn as managing editor. Having known Flynn on the old *Post* as a night side rewrite man fresh out of college while I was on the night desk there, I had confidence in him and worked well with him and his curtailed staff in the few months before my draft board summoned me into service.

That happened at last in March 1943, when I had just passed my thirty-seventh birthday—not a very likely prospect for hurry-up combat duty—but I responded gladly, even hopefully. And Dorothy, for the first time since her graduation with me in the Class of 1927 at Columbia's journalism school, began work as a journalist on 6 A.M. rewrite at the *Post*. I didn't worry about her after I had kissed her good-bye for a while when I left for basic training at Fort Bragg in North Carolina. Between Flynn, Thackrey, and Mrs. Schiff at the *Post* and Dick and Sue Corwin in Brooklyn, I knew she would be well taken care of in any eventuality.

I wish I could write that I performed nobly during my three-month basic training for field artillery duty at Fort Bragg. All I can set down here truthfully is that I tried. I had no trouble at all with marksmanship training on the rifle range, qualifying as a sharpshooter. Also, the hurry-up dawn wake-up physical training exercises didn't faze me although I was often sore in body and limb when the lights switched on in our barracks and an old-time Army sergeant bawled to us to rise and shine.

What finally did for me were all of the night-time three-to-five-mile training marches. At first, I thought I did fairly well by keeping up with the youngsters all about me. But after the first month or so, I tired after about two miles and kept going through sheer willpower more than anything else. And toward the end, even though I never dropped behind, the hard necessity of building up stamina finally overcame me and I was carted off to the post hospital with a fever.

By the time I recovered and returned to duty, I (among others) was politely informed that I could not be selected for further training at an Officer Candidates' School because the army already had all the officers it could possibly use. For the rest of the war, I wound up in the Army Transportation Corps as a technician third grade, nominally addressed as sergeant, with public relations as my specialty. Between typing press releases and taking notes for a classified record at a commanding general's staff meetings, I had virtually lost hope of active duty when I was given a strange and exacting assignment.

I had known, from my attendance at the general's staff meetings, that some of the most valuable ships in the British North Atlantic fleet were being used, along with regular well-guarded convoys, to deliver tens of thousands of newly trained American troops to Britain for what everyone knew would be an eventual cross-Channel invasion of Nazi-held France.

The day after the Wall Street crash in 1929 and I am home, wondering what will happen to Dorothy and me.

We survived the depression. I am at the Chickering grand piano that I bought with the first $900 saved.

In my rose garden at the old homestead in Aquebogue, Long Island, with my cocker, Freckles.

The unhappy warrior. I had hoped to make the field artillery when I enlisted, but I wound up in the Transportation Corps, age thirty-nine at the end of the war.

But what I didn't realize, until I was put aboard one of the largest and fastest British ships with part of a division bound for D-Day in 1944, was that these super-transports ran alone, were unguarded, and might well fall prey to a swarm of German U-boats at sea.

Perhaps the British and the U.S. Army had made provision for such an eventuality, but all I could see when I first came aboard was the regular complement of lifeboats for use in emergencies. It didn't take much of a calculation, with troops occupying every nook and cranny on the great vessel, to determine that a relatively small proportion of those of us aboard could take to the lifeboats in safety if a U-boat were to hit its mark on the trans-Atlantic voyage.

If any of my shipmates ever made the same observation, and I'm sure some of them must have done so, not a one ever mentioned it within my hearing or I would have taken note of it. It was part of my job, as a representative of the Army Transportation Corps, to make the voyage to Britain as a super-cargo and report at length on conditions aboard ship for the eyes only of my most exalted superiors, whoever they might be. Even after almost fifty years the details of that trip remain fresh in my memory, although I'm sure my report has long since been buried in some obscure file.

What the British thought of this kind of poaching on their preserve during wartime, I never knew. And the ship's commander—when I reported to him, as instructed by my superiors—was stiffly and militarily courteous in the best British stiff-upper-lip tradition.

Our supertransport, during that voyage early in 1944 well ahead of D-Day, took considerably longer than normal for the crossing, because it zigzagged sharply at irregular intervals to throw the U-boat pack off its likely course. Those of us aboard had very little to do beyond eating and sleeping and moseying around on deck when the weather was fine. But even on deck, there were such crowded conditions that I could do nothing other than study the distant horizon and the vast blue expanse of ocean on every side—a lonely and sometimes even an awesome scene.

I was in a former first-class cabin for two that had been redesigned as accommodations for a dozen soldiers, one latrine to a cabin. On either side, where two beds formerly had been installed, there was a vertical row of canvas bunks, six on each side, stacked one above the other from floor to just eighteen inches under the ceiling. This is how the dozen of us slept, each under a blanket, and I never heard a gripe.

It was, of course, a tremendous undertaking even to feed so many thousands of young, strong, active soldiers in their late teens or early twenties. On that voyage, if memory serves, we ate breakfast and dinner at eight sittings of about a half-hour at each meal in the ship's dining rooms and lunched on whatever we could scrounge mornings or evenings. However, I never heard a complaint because there was plenty of food and no one stopped us from going back for seconds or thirds.

Living, dining, and sleeping among these wonderfully alert and hardened GIs, the best soldiers America could produce, made me just a bit ashamed of my own temerity in assuming I could have matched their strengths and skills in military training, much less led them into battle. For their sakes, and the tens of thousands of others who were being transported across the Atlantic for the final assault on Hitler's Europe, all I could do was to take note of such conditions aboard the supertransport that might be improved to make later voyages safer and more bearable.

There was, however, one circumstance over which neither I nor anybody else in the Army Transportation Corps could assume any control. When it happened, I was so shocked I simply froze against the outside of a cabin on deck and never even guessed at the source of the phenomenon. I was on deck at the time, along with many others in uniform, staring off into the distant horizon or passing the lazy afternoon hours in idle talk with GIs or the ever-present British sailors on duty.

It had been a pleasant afternoon, crisp and sunny with the chill of a early spring in the air. The great ship was running smoothly, making sharp zigzags at unexpected moments to fool the U-boats that were certain to be on the watch for it and others like it. Then, well past midocean, a great geyser of seawater burst aloft with a loud swishing noise only about twenty yards off the port side of the ship's bow. More than anything else, it reminded me of the hourly eruptions of Old Faithful in Yellowstone National Park, only this display was much more forceful and menacing.

I remained braced against the wall, thoroughly shaken up, in expectation of an aftershock. But nothing else happened. The ship, within a minute or two, changed course and plowed ahead smoothly on the restless, unfathomable ocean. But among all the others on deck, I noticed somewhat sheepishly, there was neither alarm nor even a mild sign of disturbance. It was as if nobody else had even noticed the eruption of the geyser.

I pulled myself together, walked to the ship's rail, saw nothing unusual either along the ship's side or the swirling waters below. I felt a little silly because I had been alarmed over what seemed to have been a midocean display of waterworks. I never guessed at the cause and put it resolutely out of mind for the time being.

The transport was only a few hours out of port after I had presented myself, as directed, before the British commander for an oral report on my findings, that I remembered the geyser out in the ocean. After we had concluded our business agreeably, I remembered and asked the captain about the incident. He nodded grimly when I brought it up, but I pushed my luck despite that.

"What caused it, captain?" I asked.

He stared at me as he replied, "That was a torpedo at the end of its run."

So there it was, the bared edge of combat in wartime, and it had well-nigh overwhelmed me. I tried to be militarily correct, saluted the captain, took his salute in return, and left his cabin with my head in a whirl. It felt good to be out on deck again, watching the ocean waves curling away from the bow of the great ship and feeling the fresh ocean wind whipping across my face.

Not long afterward, the ship put into port in Britain. The GIs, carbines slung over shoulders and heavy packs lumped across their backs, marched to the pier, ranged themselves into formation and swung off briskly toward their military rendezvous with destiny. I wished mightily I could have gone with them. Because I could not, an arrogant assumption in any case, I fancied myself an unhappy warrior who had been left behind. It had given me a good feeling to have been one of them, if only for a few days aboard ship. On the return voyage, I often thought of might-have-beens. That, too, was a part of the war.

Except for Franklin Roosevelt's fourth-term run for the Presidency, his death, and Vice-President Harry Truman's elevation to Chief Executive and Commander in Chief, I felt little emotion for the remainder of the conflict. What I had to do mainly was to operate what amounted to a treadmill of routine military paperwork, attend staff meetings as a recorder and minute-taker, and handle associated matters. I kept up as best I could with the work of people who had been my fellow correspondents on their domestic political assignments and war reporting. And I mightily envied them.

However, it was a strange experience, some two decades after stumbling into newspaper work, to be watching a Presidential campaign from outside as I did in the fourth-term race between FDR and his strongest opponent, Governor Thomas E. Dewey of New York. The President was then in his sixty-second year, Dewey some twenty years younger, and just about the only issue that commanded public attention was the wisdom of electing the same man four times in a row to what had been, up to his time, an office with an unspoken limit of two terms. But countering the fourth-term issue was the real danger of replacing a Commander in Chief in wartime without sufficient reason.

Feeling as deeply as I did about the war and its consequences, I had no trouble whatever in casting my soldier's ballot for FDR for a fourth term even though I respected Dewey for his services in New York as a prosecutor and racket-buster. The vote, once again, wasn't even close, 25.6 million to 22 million for FDR in the popular vote and 432 to 99 in the Electoral College.

Not long thereafter, people I worked with who had seen the President were worried about what they believed to be his failing health. It was no longer possible for him to conceal what his wife, Eleanor, referred to as his "invalidism"—the heavy strain of his wartime burden plus the necessity of standing in the braces he had to use on his legs for many years following his recovery from infantile paralysis. When he addressed Congress on March 1, 1945, the correspondents noted in their dispatches that he was seated instead of standing as usual. It was also reported that he was frequently resting in the middle of the day.

These things were important to all of us in uniform—even more so, perhaps, than to the public at large because FDR, with Churchill, represented the soul of the war effort. Then, all too soon, there was more somber news for us from the White House. The President had gone to Warm Springs, Georgia, for his health after fainting one day at his desk.

He died there on April 12, 1945, of a cerebral hemorrhage—"slipped away," as Eleanor Roosevelt telegraphed her sons. It was a day when I happened to be home and Dorothy, having finished her daily chores at the *Post,* was with me in our one-room apartment on Plaza Street in Brooklyn when we heard the news by radio. Almost instinctively, she cried out and then ran to me and asked, "Oh, Jack, who will protect us now?" It was a feeling that welled up in millions of other American homes, for this President had been greatly loved and respected.

The war with Germany ended less than a month later with the surrender of the last Nazi troops on the Western front and Hitler's suicide. Mussolini had gone long before him, swung by his heels from a rope by Italian partisans after the Allies knocked him out of power in 1943. At the time the reporting of Ernie Pyle, who lost his life in the Pacific, and the AP photo of Marines raising the flag on Mount Suribachi, by Joe Rosenthal, topped the World War II Pulitzer Prizes.

What remained that summer of 1945 was fierce Japanese resistance in the Pacific despite heavy casualties and mounting losses to the island-hopping American forces. Then, in August, President Truman gave the fateful order to unleash the atomic bomb after it had been secretly tested. The bombing of Hiroshima and Nagasaki followed, after which the Emperor of Japan at last sued for an end to the war. William L. Laurence of the *New York Times* fulfilled the highest aspirations of a journalist when he rode in the bomber over Nagasaki, and in 1946 he won a Pulitzer Prize for writing the history of the nuclear effort in the United States.

Shortly before my fortieth birthday, I received my honorable discharge and concluded that I had ended my association with the armed forces of the United States. Once again, I was wrong. My number would come up again one day in a way I had never anticipated.

7 ★ PEACE, IT'S WONDERFUL!

The day I returned to work at the *New York Post* after leaving the army in the fall of 1945, Dorothy resigned and retired permanently from activity as a journalist. That, she said, was my bag.

And although she had been shifted from 6 A.M. rewrite to a daily column summarizing press comment on the news, she also had concluded that other things interested her more than newspapering now that she no longer had to support the two of us. Our parents had died during the war years, and some of our other responsibilities also had been considerably reduced.

That, as she explained it to me, now gave her time to fix up the house in Aquebogue, expand her interest in refinishing antiques, and retrieve our rose garden from its wartime growth of weeds. Then, too, there were duplicate bridge tournaments she wanted to attend with her favorite partner, Virginia Long, who also had retired from wartime service at the *Post*, and Sue Corwin, as well, had some interesting ideas.

I fully understood. But beyond Dorothy's shifting of interest under our somewhat shaky peacetime conditions, her thinking as always had a stimulating effect on me. And so I, too, began wondering if daily newspaper work was what I wanted to do for the rest of my entire career in journalism. That kind of meditation, of course, has never been unusual for people approaching forty, but in my case it turned out to be much more than a philosophical meditation on life, love, and the fate of humankind.

On nothing more than impulse not long after our discussion of her postwar activities, Dorothy suggested the possibility of my using my midweek day off to handle some of the part-time instruction in writing at the Columbia journalism school. She thought it might interest me; also, she added as an afterthought, my twenty years of covering and writing news on the spot seemed to indicate that I might be qualified to teach the subject.

I had my doubts at the outset both about my qualifications and my ability to do the job. First of all, I considered myself well treated and well paid at Mrs. Schiff's version of the *Post,* although the ghost of the founder, Alexander Hamilton, might have frowned over the burst of liberalism that had enlivened the paper. Furthermore, my current assignments at the United Nations and in Washington were much to my liking, and the prospect of a return eventually to foreign correspondence was another activity that intrigued me.

But as for teaching as a life's work, I told Dorothy, I'd never given thought to it, had no academic training for the profession, and wasn't at all sure that journalism students and I would get along well together. She replied airily in the New York catchphrase of the time, seemingly to conclude the subject, "Try it, you'll like it," and phoned Sue and Dick Corwin to ask them over for dinner.

Once again, I hesitated. But some weeks later, on my midweek day off, I did return to Columbia, felt good about being back on Morningside Heights, and found the entrance to the Journalism Building unchanged since our graduation except for the addition, on the ground floor, of J. Montgomery Curtis's flourishing American Press Institute. I dropped in, introduced myself, found Monty most agreeable to the idea of having another working newsman in the building, and was given an audience at once, following Monty's preparatory phone call, with the associate dean, Richard T. Baker.

The school was different from what it had been at the time of our graduation, Dorothy's and mine. Instead of a two-year undergraduate institution with a degree of bachelor of literature, it now was a one-year graduate school with a degree of master of science in journalism. However, the day-long course of instruction in newswriting during which the class was split into small groups, each working with an experienced professional, remained unchanged.

So yes, Professor Baker told me, he would be glad to have me around as a part-time instructor one day a week. And yes, he would recommend me heartily to the dean, Carl W. Ackerman, a graduate of the school's first class in 1913 with a wide-ranging career as journalist and public relations executive. But there the matter ended. I did not hear from Professor Baker for the rest of that year or even the next and concluded that Dorothy's hunch had been just that, and nothing more.

It didn't matter. Surveying my activities at the *Post* for 1946 and 1947 alone, I realize I had more than my share of high-level assignments—beginning with coverage of the White House and the crisis-laden period following the appearance of the United Nations in New York. Certainly, I had more than enough to sustain my interest and tax my ability as a newsman working against a lot of world-class opposition. The notion of my teaching at Columbia, so I thought, had been so quickly dismissed on Morningside Heights that I'd never hear anything more about it. And so I occupied myself completely with the coverage of the Cold War, the United Nations, and the ups and downs of Harry Truman's rough passage as FDR's successor in the White House.

There was this to be said for Harry Truman: During his Presidency, he never was afraid of anybody either at home or abroad and seemed to relish his bare-knuckled display of diplomacy against the newly expanded Soviet empire as well as his wild roundhouse blows against his domestic political foes. At any time that I was covering the White House during the absences of our regular correspondent, Charles Van Devander (a friend from my earliest days at the *Graphic*), President Truman invariably produced good copy.

To be sure, he was no FDR. He never pretended to be, which was just as well. There had been only one four-term Presidency in my lifetime, and most assuredly, with the passage of the two-term Constitutional amendment limiting the Presidency, there would not be another, except in the unlikely event of its repeal.

Truman was very much his own man—a little grey fighting cock in a wrinkled double-breasted grey or blue suit who had his own strong likes and dislikes among the White House press corps and their respective bosses. With his challenging personality, his news conferences suffered from far too much belligerence on both sides, in my view, and too little allowance for the frailties and changing nature of humankind. I make the point mainly because I found the Truman news performances before reporters to be quite different from those of FDR, who could be both a charmer and "The Champ," as Willkie had called him. Charm wasn't part of Truman's political weaponry. He wanted to slug it out with almost anybody who differed with him.

I'll never forget the first time I was virtually pushed into a hurry-up news conference with the new President after having left the Army only a few weeks previously. Instead of the row upon row of reporters eagerly seeking the President's attention so they could be called on to answer a question, I found Truman simply called the few of us who happened to be available into the Oval Office and let fly.

There he was, standing stiffly behind the big Presidential desk and chair, solemn and seemingly in a truculent mood. Whatever news he had to announce, it was some current matter long since forgotten; it was not the news that made an impression on me, it was the way we were expected to work.

This was the scene: As the President spoke, we also were standing—a half-dozen or so of us reporters. What we had to do in the absence of a speech transcript or other text was take notes on wads of copy paper as the President talked. To anybody who has ever tried to take notes while some important news source is speaking with machine gun rapidity, the difficulties of stand-up reporting are obvious. It was a time when few reporters in our business knew shorthand or carried recording equipment, and I was no exception. Accordingly, while the President was talking, I turned in desperation to a colleague, propped my wad of paper against his back and scribbled scarcely readable long-hand notes on the proceedings.

In the questions we were permitted to ask once the President had finished his initial remarks—and I noticed that he spoke without notes—almost everything had to do with verifying what he had said. He didn't help us very much and confined himself to yes, no, or refusing to respond. And before we were at all ready to leave, he abruptly dismissed us.

That, I was told, was regular operating procedure for news conferences at the White House in the Truman era, except when he had a prepared text. I don't know what the White House regulars came up with, but I wouldn't have had much confidence in either the accuracy or the integrity of my news account from that first news conference, because in the main I had to depend on my memory. My hand-written notes—scrawled on copy paper resting on the backbone of one of my colleagues—weren't precisely to be recommended as an accurate source of information for the public concerning the proceedings of the highest office in the land.

That was the way Harry Truman operated normally. But, as history will testify better than journalism, he never shrank from making major decisions affecting the security of the nation, whether it meant dropping the first atomic bombs on Japan or recalling General Douglas MacArthur, the idol of the Republican right, when he threatened to make all-out war against both North Korea and its Chinese Communist allies instead of trying to end the fighting. I know that I shall always remember Truman's grinning picture after his Presidential victory over Thomas E. Dewey in the 1948 election, holding aloft a copy of the *Chicago Tribune* that had bannered his "defeat."

The total that election night, my last to write leads on the result, gave Truman 24.1 million to Dewey's 21.9 million, with an even wider result in the Electoral College, 303 to 189, with 39 for a third-party candidate, Strom Thurmond. But I'm getting ahead of my story.

There was no nonsense in Truman's time about liking "old Uncle Joe" Stalin, an effusion to which FDR had resorted in the depths of World War II to maintain the West's alliance with the Soviets once Hitler had enmeshed his forces in the fatal siege before Stalingrad. What Truman had to contend with was the reality of Stalin's hasty last-minute declaration of war against Japan in the closing days of World War II, which was mainly for the purpose of grabbing more territory in the Far East.

Even worse was Stalin's outright encouragement of North Korea and the Chinese Communists to fight the United States and South Korea to the bitter end in the Korean War, which could not recommend the Soviets either to the White House or the American people. The Cold War in itself had been bad enough; when it turned hot, Truman had to stand fast and deliver whatever he had with force against our enemies. And he did so at the risk of destroying the United Nations before it had even settled into its temporary home in New York City.

That was my baptism as a correspondent for the *Post* at the UN, my first major assignment after leaving military service at the end of World War II. We hadn't even settled down to the long-hoped-for resumption of peace before the Soviets suddenly occupied the northern part of Azerbaijan, then a province of Iran, to encourage a pro-Communist move there to separate the Azerbaijanis and put them under Soviet control.

The way the United States got into this immediate threat to the peace was roundabout, as the available evidence shows.

Winston Churchill had set the stage for a confrontation between the Soviet Union and the West early in March 1946, during his visit to America after losing an election to the resurgent Labor Party, in which he was replaced as Prime Minister by Clement Attlee. In President Truman's presence at Westminster College in Fulton, Missouri, the old lion of Britain had delivered his celebrated "Iron Curtain" speech with this slashing thesis:

"From Stettin in the Baltic to Trieste in the Adriatic, an Iron Curtain has descended across the Continent. . . . I do not believe that Soviet Russia desires war. What they desire is the fruits of war and the indefinite expansion of their power and doctrines."

Churchill's warning against Soviet intentions was taken much more seriously than his assurances that our erstwhile allies in World War II did not want war with us. Moreover, after the disaster of the Yalta summit conference, his liking for more such meetings of heads of state was not particularly reassuring.

I well remember attending a private dinner for Churchill that same month, along with other correspondents, at Bernard M. Baruch's New York apartment, at which I heard the distinguished visitor declaim on the virtues of summit meetings—the decision making among a favored few world statesmen, as he put it, in "the rarified atmosphere at the top."

That was quite the opposite of what was then happening before the United Nations in its first meeting—and first crisis—at a quickly renovated girls' gymnasium at Hunter College in the Bronx in northern New York City. The chief combatants were Secretary of State James F. Byrnes, whom Truman had dispatched to represent the United States before the UN Security Council, and Stalin's delegate, Andrei A. Gromyko, who represented the Soviet Union. They were a striking contrast, this pair of diplomatic gladiators—Byrnes, a grandfatherly type with gold-rimmed eyeglasses, and Gromyko, a muscular younger man with a glistening shock of black hair and a permanent scowl.

What they already had done was create a world crisis before the UN over what usually is a harmless procedural motion merely to discuss an issue. Once Iran complained to the UN that the Soviets were bullying its people in Azerbaijan, Gromyko threatened to quit the UN rather than discuss the demand for an immediate pullout of Soviet troops from Iranian territory. He argued that the Soviets would leave, but only at their own time and under their own terms.

That was unacceptable to the United States. Byrnes acted to put the issue before the Security Council, after which the council's majority voted with the United States. Since the Soviet veto didn't apply to a mere matter of discussing an issue, Gromyko made good on his threat to walk out. He buttoned his tight, double-breasted blue jacket and strode from the Council's chamber at the Hunter College girls' gym.

It really did look like the UN had collapsed even before it had found a permanent home.

We correspondents fairly leaped from the press benches behind the Council's circular table and rushed after Gromyko to get a quote from him on whether this was a permanent walkout. To our surprise, and I was near the front of the pursuing press contingent, Gromyko was smiling nervously and talking with Frank Begley, the UN's chief of security.

Then, all at once, the Russian turned away from Begley and began fumbling with both hands in front of him. Just what he was doing we couldn't tell, so somebody asked Begley. The good-natured Irishman replied with mock solemnity, "The honorable delegate of the Soviet Union is unzipped and I so informed him." Then he guffawed.

Such also are the uses of international reporting.

Eventually, even though the Iranian crisis was temporarily resolved without bloodshed at that stage, it set the pattern for a resumption of the Cold War over many other East-West issues within the UN. In Churchill's words, it became "a brawling cockpit" that was more likely to separate nations than draw them together in the cause of world peace.

This was the story I had undertaken to cover for the *Post* after my World War II service, and I would not have quit for as long as the UN lasted. But it did seem to me at the time that the chances were slim that a world organization dedicated to peacekeeping could long survive.

In Matthew, there is an eloquent quotation that seemed to fit the fate that had befallen the League of Nations and now threatened its successor organization as well. It refers to the "whited sepulchres, which indeed appear beautiful outward, but are within full of dead men's bones." To my mind, the UN was not yet dead but I thought it was dying before our eyes. Indeed, some of my colleagues already were preparing suitable obituaries based on U.S.-Soviet belligerence in the Iranian case.

The temporary resolution of that issue by no means gave assurance that the world organization, so eloquently described in its charter as the great hope of world peace, would be able to survive the first major test of its ability to end a threat of war. And many more were to break almost as quickly in the postwar era, Palestine and atomic control problems among them. It was understandable, in such a topsy-turvy postwar world, that so little hope existed for the maintenance of the UN.

Strangely enough, it was a gift of $8.5 million from John D. Rockefeller, Jr., to buy land in New York City for a permanent home for the UN that finally produced signs of unity among the contending forces at that turbulent time. The proposed site on the upper East side of Manhattan, an eight-block area fronting on what was known as Turtle Bay in the East River, had to be cleared of run-down buildings and the adjacent neighborhood had to be beautified. Mayor Bill O'Dwyer promised to handle at least a part of the burden with a $15 million contribution from the city. Then, the Federal government came through with a $65 million loan to the UN to start construction.

Before most of the delegates and correspondents (including myself) fully realized how sentiment in the UN had changed, the world organization had firmly established itself in the heart of a great American city celebrated for its inner disorders, clashing peoples, high crime rate, and bumptious civic personality. At the State Department, where Dean Acheson had been plugging for a European home for the UN, he was mightily displeased, writing, "The misplaced generosity of the Rockefeller family . . . placed it [the UN] in a crowded center of conflicting races and nationalities."

However, it would be six years before the UN's new home in Turtle Bay would be completed, as Secretary General Trygve Lie from the outset repeatedly warned both the delegates and their superiors among the original membership. Furthermore, everybody realized that the girls' gym at Hunter College in the Bronx could be only a temporary expedient. So all of us—delegates, UN staff, and correspondents—soon found ourselves at Lake Success, Long Island, on the outskirts of New York City, in a refurbished factory building that had been occupied in wartime by the Sperry Gyroscope Company. In short order, the place was made into a diplomatic jungle replete with meeting rooms, offices, and circular tables for meetings of the Security Council and Economic and Social Council. For the General Assembly, a similar transformation came about when it occupied the old New York City skating rink in Flushing Meadow for its annual meetings.

Despite all that, I still maintained my dim view of the future for world peace in general and the UN in particular for as long as the Soviet Union remained a great military power under a secretive dictatorship. Even at the supposed celebration of United Nations Day, October 24, 1949, the dedication of the cornerstone for the headquarters site was marred by a plainspoken view of the proceedings by President Truman in the presence of the Soviet foreign minister, Andrei A. Vishinsky, no mean hand himself at explosive diplomatic exchanges.

Still, Secretary General Lie tried valiantly to make the occasion seem a love feast. In an impressive ceremony, he deposited copies of the UN Charter and the UN Declaration of Human Rights in the cornerstone and sealed it before a crowd of 15,000 gawking New Yorkers, who applauded dutifully against a background dominated by the thirty-nine-story steel skeleton of what would become the Secretariat Building.

The centerpiece of the occasion, however, was President Truman's speech, for which those of us in the wooden press benches set up before the speakers' stand had been waiting. This was no mere local story; both the national and international press and radio were out in force, a situation the President took advantage of when he rose to challenge the Russians. Mindful that a Soviet atomic bomb had only recently been tested, he called for Moscow's acceptance of a workable system of atomic controls under the American-sponsored Baruch Plan as "men of goodwill." Then he added one more condition for a true American-Soviet rapprochement by demanding Soviet respect for human rights, saying:

"Respect for human rights, promotion of economic development and a system for control of weapons are requisites for the kind of world we seek. We cannot solve these problems overnight but we must keep everlastingly at them in order to reach our goal."

The President won respectful applause from his mixed audience of diplomats and streetwise New Yorkers, but I noticed that Vishinsky gave only a perfunctory hand clap or two, then walked out before any of us who left the press benches could catch him for a comment. The President departed in a different direction, so the two did not meet after their short but solemn handshake at the opening of the proceedings.

As someone in the press section exclaimed while the rest of us were batting out our stories for the telegraphers operating nearby, "Peace, it's wonderful!" In the less strained atmosphere between the world's two major atomic powers more than forty years later, we may see the original United Nations Day proceedings as passing strange, but this is the way we were in the depths of the Cold War when conciliatory action for peace seemed impossible.

8 ★ A NEW WORLD

I had barely recovered from the uncertainties of World War II and the peace that failed when a concentration of events in 1948 shook me up once again. In the news business, for me at least, there seemed to be no way of coasting along at ease with the world.

Instead, with little or no preparation that year, I found myself being pushed into new, often exciting, and sometimes traumatic experiences both here and abroad. And, to top it all off, I received a most peculiar phone call that winter, which projected me before a university classroom without even the slightest introduction to teaching anybody about anything.

To begin with the summons by phone: It happened early in January while I was on assignment from the *Post* at Lake Success, preparing for the opening next day of a crucial session of the General Assembly on Palestine. The caller introduced himself briefly as a Professor Clark of the School of General Studies at Columbia, the university's night school.

I had no idea who the professor was at the time (long since I came to know him well and favorably as Dr. Donald Lemen Clark, the head of the General Studies English Department). Also, I had no interest in the problem he described to me. Briefly put, a class in journalism with a registration of some two dozen students was opening that night at 8 o'clock, but the scheduled instructor by some mischance had fallen down the stairs somewhere and broken his leg. My caller explained that I had been referred to him—and even highly recommended—not ten minutes before by Dean Ackerman of the Graduate School of Journalism.

And would I help out the School of General Studies by handling this teacherless class in journalism just for that night? I begged off at first by pleading that I had no experience in teaching and, furthermore, I was fully and even urgently occupied at the moment with a lead story for the final edition of my paper about developments at the United Nations.

Professor Clark tried argument. I insisted I was in no position to finish what I was doing, skip dinner, and rush off to Columbia to teach a night class in journalism. To that, at last, he exploded in a dour moment:

"See here, Mr. Hohenberg, if I could locate a gorilla and if it could speak enough English to make itself understood, I'd hire it for this job tonight. I'm in a fix and that's all there is to it."

I've always been an easy mark for people as honest and despairing as Professor Clark. Without really thinking through what I was doing (I still hadn't finished my piece for the *Post*'s final edition and wanted to conclude the phone call), I said, "All right, Professor Clark. I'll be your gorilla but for tonight only."

My caller, grateful for small favors, gave me the pertinent details of when and where to meet my class, thanked me, and rang off.

It was only after I'd finished my story for the *Post* and sat back to catch my breath that I realized I'd landed in what amounted to an undigested mess of literary porridge—a ninety-minute journalism class of beginners who probably didn't know the difference between quoting a source on background or putting him off the record. Not knowing what else to do, I phoned Dorothy to save my dinner for later, if at all possible, and confessed to my indiscretion.

She seemed undisturbed, even sounded just a bit smug. "I didn't think you'd mind," she said. "When Professor Baker called to ask for your number for Professor Clark, I gave it to him."

That was when I recalled my trip to Columbia just after leaving the Army when Dick Baker had promised to remember me. At a rather inconvenient moment for me, he seemed to have done so and apparently had also gone the length of giving me Dean Ackerman's blessing as well. Since I did not know Dean Ackerman, had not even met him at the time, I assumed this is what had happened.

So now, there was no help for it. I had to be off at once on the long subway ride to Morningside Heights and would have to put together an overnight piece for the next day's first edition by working the telephone once I came home to a cold dinner. Of course, I felt sorry for myself. But hadn't I, in a rushed moment, agreed to serve as Professor Clark's gorilla? I had no one but myself to blame for my plight.

I had taken along a bag of copy paper and several fistfuls of black pencils from our supplies at Lake Success with the guileful notion—at least I thought it was clever—to make my one-night stand an exercise for my class of beginners in taking notes and writing an obituary. Also, on the long subway ride, I cluttered up three pages in my notebook with what I thought was a learned dissertation on the unglamorous realities of life as a journalist. That, it seemed to me, would be a suitable lecture for the young people in what I believed, quite honestly, to be my first and last class.

In that frame of mind, I entered my first classroom as a teacher—only to find that, as Dr. Clark's gorilla, I had inherited a full house, mainly of young men, with a scattering of young women, from the intended occupant of this academic pulpit who had fallen down the stairs and broken his leg. I began in what I hoped was a businesslike way by announcing the name, number, and hours of the course, spelling out my name in chalk on a green blackboard, and proceeding to my introductory notes.

It didn't bother me that I saw few signs of interest in the proceedings, evidenced by a lot of twisting and squirming in chairs, a grimace here and there, even a few agitated whispers among my audience. Bored, were they? Then it served them right because their academic master had pulled me unwillingly out of Lake Success to conduct the class. Somewhat vengefully, I also thought that I'd never see them again—so what mattered their attitude?

What *did* make me nervous was the rapidity with which I droned through my lecture notes. At the end of about twenty minutes, with seventy minutes still to go for this marathon exercise in journalism instruction, I stood before my young people with mouth open and nothing to say. My notes were completely exhausted. At that unhappy moment, a young man with a big head and wasted legs—he had crutches lying beside his chair—took pity on me and asked me a question. Fortunately, I knew the answer. Elsewhere, I noticed a few heads perking up in interest. Other questions followed; if I knew a proper answer, I let fly, if not, I promised to look it up and communicate with the regular teacher of the course.

It wasn't long, in this kind of back and forth, before I got involved in an argument about UN coverage. Then we went at it with vigor on both sides until I noticed we'd gone well past 8:45 P.M. without a break, and I decided to kill the rest of the period, forty-five minutes, with the obit I'd decided to give them. That produced real interest, particularly when I passed out copy paper and pencils and told them how I wanted the copy prepared for my editing and grading.

Reporting the details of the obit was simple enough. I took a few minutes to tell the class about the death of Mary Adelaide Shirley, Dorothy's centenarian grandmother, and asked them to do a short piece about it. That, at last, produced action. The paper rattled, the pencils fairly raced, and, praise the spirit of Dr. Clark's gorilla, I had survived my first class in journalism at Columbia. When two dozen or more penciled obits were handed in as the bell rang for the end of the class, I wasn't at all grudging about the extra job of copyediting. Whether I liked it or not, the young people in that General Studies night class had made at least the beginnings of a teacher out of me.

Covering the reopening of the Palestine case before the General Assembly was another story entirely. The UN legislative body, which then consisted of fifty-eight members, had been summoned into special session that winter to conclude the work of the regular session. On the previous November 29, the Assembly had voted 33–13 (with eleven abstentions and one absence) to create two nations out of the territory the League of Nations had placed under British rule.

The British had posed the issue—being unable to control the continual fighting between Jewish and Arab settlers in Palestine—by informing the UN that they would have to terminate their mandate. And now, in the Assembly's special session, meeting in the old New York City skating rink at Flushing Meadow, the delegates would have to decide how to set up the two nations—one Jewish and the other Arab—that were to replace the British overseers.

The gist of the problem was that the British, tired of waiting for the delegates to come to terms with the issue, now were warning that they would pull their troops out of Palestine whether an agreement was reached or not. And in the overnight piece I wrote for the next day's *Post* after leaving my first Columbia class, I could produce no credible evidence that the Assembly was prepared to act quickly and decisively.

The Jewish Agency for Palestine, with the tremendous financial backing of organized American Jewry, was ready to support the immigration of as many as a million Jews from Europe and elsewhere to the new Jewish nation, which was frightening to both the Arab settlers and their supporters. It was certain, therefore, that some means of policing the partition agreement would have to be found by the Assembly; the British, on their part, were through and served notice that their troops no longer could be counted on to separate the opposing inhabitants of Palestine.

At the outset of the special Assembly, therefore, no way of implementing the partition resolution of the previous year appeared likely, short of forming a separate UN armed force to police the area and keep the peace. The United States and the Soviet Union, which had backed partition for different reasons, were not ready to support that kind of a universal armed unit. The Cold War already was under way. And smaller countries weren't at all anxious to send their own troops to the area to serve under the blue-and-white UN banner and be shot at in the cause of peace.

Canada's Lester B. (Mike) Pearson, the author of the partition plan compromise who had brought the United States and the Soviets together, did his best to persuade both the great powers that it was in their interests to speed the enforcement of the agreement. The United States, perhaps, might have been inclined to send troops as peacekeepers out of an idealistic consideration for the fate of persecuted Jewry. But the Soviets, having worked so hard to get rid of British troops in Palestine, weren't about to permit the Americans to replace them. And nobody, including the Arabs, wanted the Red Army in the Middle East.

That was the position throughout the long and frustrating wrangle of early 1948 when the Special Assembly grappled with its partition decision but failed to implement it. And so, on May 14, 1948, the Assembly had to give up its effort to design a suitable way to create the two new nations in Palestine.

Fern Marja and Arthur Massolo, who had been working with me at the UN to cover these and other issues, were out in the Assembly hall at the time, and I was doing a roundup piece in the cubbyhole that served as our office, when the big story broke unexpectedly.

First, the British announced that they had ended their mandate and were pulling out their troops at once, leaving Palestine to the contending forces of Jews and Arabs. Within minutes, Fern and Artie were relaying information that the Jewish delegation to the UN would have a major announcement. When it came, it was to announce the immediate creation of a Jewish state in Palestine under the partition resolution. I hadn't gotten past the first paragraph of my story about that when Fern ran in, her curly blonde head bobbing in excitement, to tell me that the name of the new nation would be Israel, restored to nationhood after two thousand years. Truman recognized Israel at once.

In a very real sense, it was a tribute to the survivors of Hitler's holocaust in which 6 million Jews had died during World War II. Only, the Arabs didn't feel that way about it. As the British force withdrew, five Arab armies from surrounding states entered Palestine to try to strangle the new Jewish state at birth. However, the Haganah, the Jewish army, was ready for them.

That war effort by the Arab nations, the first of a series, failed in a relatively short time in the face of the Haganah's defense. And when it did, the victorious Israelis by themselves changed the status of Jerusalem. Instead of a city many in the UN had seen as a trusteeship, it became part of the new state.

Israel thereby established itself as the Jewish state, provided for in the partition resolution voted in the General Assembly. The Arab state, which was to have been a new homeland for 500,000 Palestinian Arabs, remained in limbo and became a major source of continued threats to peace in the region. In the end, many Palestinian Arabs emigrated to the neighboring state of Jordan, their new homeland, while Israel suggested autonomy for Arab areas remaining within its borders.

I have often wondered what would have happened in Palestine in 1948 if the United States, Britain, and France had not been so completely preoccupied with Cold War issues. The Berlin blockade, the Soviet Communist incursions in Greece and Turkey, and the introduction of the Marshall Plan to rebuild devastated western Europe had all developed at the same time as the UN debate over Palestine. These actions were far more important to the foreign policies of the United States,

Britain, and France than almost anything that was likely to happen at the time in the Middle East.

Both the Truman Doctrine to support Greece and Turkey against Communist aggression and the Marshall Plan for Europe originated in 1947 while Palestine partition was under consideration. And while the Special Assembly was debating the implementation of partition, the Soviets began their Berlin blockade on April 1, 1948. No one should wonder that all the contending powers except the Arabs decided not to intervene with armed force in Palestine.

"What was at stake in Berlin," Truman wrote, "was not a contest over legal rights, although our position was entirely sound in international law, but a struggle over Germany and, in a larger sense, over Europe. In the face of our launching of the Marshall Plan, the Kremlin tried to mislead the people of Europe into believing that our interest and support would not extend beyond economic matters and that we would back away from any military risks."

The blockade marked the beginning of the daily American airlift to Berlin, with British help. It supplied the Berliners with food, coal, and other essentials until the Soviets had to call off their blockade in 1949. The Security Council records show that as many as 8,000 tons of food and supplies were airlifted to Berlin daily with 277,000 around-the-clock flights, a total of almost 2.5 million tons.

I stress the point because it had a lot to do with another UN Palestine crisis in the fall of 1948, when both the Security Council and the General Assembly shifted their meetings to Paris at the height of the struggle over Berlin. Ordinarily, the honorable delegates, the Secretariat staff, and the reporters who tagged along would have been inordinately pleased with a three-month session in Paris. But in the fall of 1948, the pleasure was confined largely to the wives of the principals, especially those accompanying the press (Dorothy included).

The issue that dominated the UN from September 24, 1948, onward was Berlin. On the following day, before the Security Council, the United States, Britain, and France accused the Soviets of being the aggressor. Later, the Western powers accused Moscow of violating the UN Charter, but the Soviets refused to back down. By late October, the struggle had grown so intense that it had affected the final weeks of President Truman's reelection campaign against his Republican opponent, Thomas E. Dewey. No one wanted World War III, but this was the fear that had spread through Europe and that inevitably was reflected in American opinion as well.

It was under these circumstances that a British-Chinese resolution was introduced in the Security Council to punish Israel with sanctions (of an unspecified nature) for refusing an order from Ralph Bunche, the UN mediator, to refrain from military action in the Negev, the southern desert area of the new nation. What had provoked such a threat was that the Israelis had launched attacks there against frontline Egyptian positions, beginning on October 14, while the Berlin crisis was verging on a new European war.

The position of the United States on Israel became important, particularly in the closing days of Truman's reelection campaign, when polls showed his lead in New York state was paper thin. To take New York, the state with the largest electoral total, he needed every vote he could get in strongly Democratic and pro-Israel New York City.

By chance, at the time, I was told that Secretary of State George Marshall had planned to announce, in the Security Council in Paris, American support for the British-Chinese plan for sanctions against Israel. That, it seemed to me, was news for a New York City paper and I didn't hesitate to send the story from Paris.

The reaction was immediate. I learned that overnight President Truman had sent a cable to the U.S. delegation to refrain from backing the move for sanctions against Israel before the Security Council. The reason, it was explained, was that the Egyptians should have been blamed for violating the truce, not Israel, which had counterattacked to save its settlements in the Negev.

The matter eventually was settled without punishing anybody. Four days before the U.S. presidential election on October 29, 1948, I reported that the President's policy reversal had killed the plan to punish Israel. Instead, after the President's reelection, both Israel and Egypt were quietly persuaded to withdraw to the truce lines demanded by the UN mediator.

That at last enabled the President to concentrate on cracking the Berlin blockade. While the American-led airlift continued, the United

States invoked the aid of Secretary General Lie and Herbert V. Evatt of Australia, that year's Assembly president, to try to persuade Stalin that the Soviets could not hope to push the United States out of Berlin. The blockade finally ended on May 12, 1949, but the airlift had to be continued until September 30 to keep feeding the two million Berliners and supplying them and their industries with coal.

So it developed that the Israelis, for all their daring in setting up their new state in the face of strenuous Arab opposition, were able to stave off repeated attacks that might have crushed them had the great powers not been preoccupied with the larger issues of a threatened Communist domination of the European continent.

At the very least, it gave the Israelis time to build up their strength against future attacks by the Arab states, which were not long in coming. What the Israelis had achieved was a country, about the size of the state of New Jersey, fronting on the eastern Mediterranean Sea, with little more than a million people at the outset. About half its southern area, the Negev, was desert; along the eastern boundary, the Jordan River, there was almost constant movement of Arab infiltrators despite all the precautions taken by border guards. And the same was true of the northern frontier with Lebanon.

This was a country that would for a long time lead a precarious existence—as the most realistic of its founders, Foreign Minister Moshe Sharett, freely admitted. I recall a mass interview he gave to us UN correspondents soon after the declaration of Israel's decision on May 14, 1948, to become a nation. Everything went along smoothly until somebody in the back of the room at the old skating rink at Flushing Meadow posed a question that went something like this: "Mr. Sharett, the last time there was a Jewish state, it was under the Maccabees about two thousand years ago and it lasted almost two hundred years. How long do you think this one will last?"

Quite seriously, Sharett responded at once, "I'll settle for two hundred years."

On that sober note, the first mass conference of the new foreign minister of Israel ended. In the years to come, when he became prime minister, he may have changed his view and extended his forecast, but nothing could blot out my memory of that exciting night at the end of the

Special Assembly. It helped make 1948 far more important to me than any imaginary crisis projected for 1984.

As for American-Israeli relations, President Truman said it best in a letter to President Chaim Weizmann of Israel on the first anniversary of the partition resolution, November 29, 1948:

> I was struck by the common experience you and I had so recently shared. We had both been abandoned by the so-called realistic experts to our supposedly forlorn lost cause. Yet we both kept pressing for what we were sure was right—and we were both proven to be right. . . .
>
> What you [in Israel] have received at the hands of the world has been far less than what was your due. But you have more than made the most of what you have received, and I admire you for it.

On May 11, 1949, under American sponsorship, Israel became the fifty-ninth member of the United Nations. It was at last the realization of the dream of Chaim Weizmann, Moshe Sharett, and all the others of the little group of devoted Zionists who had given their lives to what had, as President Truman said, once been thought of as a lost cause.

Through the intercession of Professors Clark and Baker, I resumed teaching the General Studies class in journalism in 1949 after my return from the Paris Assembly. This time, even though I still considered myself at a disadvantage as a teacher, I found the diversion from newspaper work to be interesting, even challenging. Since my class continued to meet at night, I was able to handle it without much trouble along with my UN correspondence for the *Post*. And both Professors Clark and Baker continued to be encouraging.

Professor Clark told me several times, when we reviewed my classwork now and then, "Don't worry about not having teaching experience. You seem to make something happen in a classroom." Just what, I never was quite sure, but I continued with the routine I'd worked out for myself—as little lecturing as possible and as much practical work as I could crowd into my weekly ninety-minute meeting with my students. I had stayed on by request after my first night's experience in 1948.

Like any other teacher in a field that was more or less professional, I had the undoubted advantage of being able to pass along my daily experiences in the coverage of news to a number of young people who seemed to be interested in world affairs, whether or not they meant to be practicing journalists. Also, I was able to give them current assignments in writing about specifics that were in the news, together with weekly criticism of their work.

All told, I think I still learned more from them, in many ways, than they learned from me. Toward the end of 1949, Professor Baker suggested to me that I could be asked to fill a professional vacancy at the Graduate School of Journalism, if I was interested. And that gave me quite a turn, because it meant leaving almost twenty-five years of newspaper work at a time when I was traveling the international circuit and thoroughly enjoying it.

When and if the offer came, Dorothy and I would have to make a decision based on the assumption that I could qualify as a teacher at the university level. But could I? The question, surely, could not be answered theoretically.

9 ★ LAND OF PROMISE

When Dean Ackerman asked me to see him at Columbia in the spring of 1950, I was prepared for almost anything except what actually happened. Our meeting in the school Joseph Pulitzer had endowed began well. The dean offered me a Columbia professorship with tenure, the university's retirement benefits, and help in finding a university-owned apartment. It was much more than I had expected, so the first reference to the pay for this glorious approach to academe came as a shock to me.

As I told the dean, once I'd pulled myself together, the stipend was so modest that it would mean a $5,000 a year cut from my *Post* salary—and newspaper salaries in those years, while improved, still were not overly generous. The dean was apologetic, but he said it was the best he could do and suggested that I might want to continue with my night teaching at the School of General Studies to make ends meet.

That wasn't particularly attractive, however. I told him that I'd like to think it over, consult my wife, and give him my answer after my forthcoming assignment—a flight to Israel to do a series of articles for the *Post* on the new nation and its problems. He agreed, told me to take my time, and assured me he'd interview no one else for the professorial vacancy until I returned from Israel.

When I left the Graduate School of Journalism that day, I no longer worried about whether I would be able to function as a journalism professor. The problem now was whether Dorothy and I could afford the intellectual luxury of academe without investing our savings to keep body and soul together.

I did not know then whether the dean was offering me the going rate for Columbia University professors or hedging his bet by proposing the lowest possible salary if it turned out I couldn't function as a teacher. In retrospect, I suppose his motives consisted of a bit of both, even though he was effusive in his compliments about my work in General Studies, which he'd heard of from Professor Clark. And Ackerman also reminded me that he could not think of another instance in which a working journalist had been offered a Columbia professorship without passing through all the lower academic grades.

Dorothy wasn't disturbed by the projected cut in income. And next day, while I was at Lake Success, she set out to explore the neighborhood in Morningside Heights for a suitable Columbia apartment. As luck would have it, Professor Clark's wife, Mary, knew of a fine five-room Columbia apartment on Morningside Drive that was available; to make sure that it would be ours if we decided to move from our one room and kitchen in Brooklyn, which we still occupied five years after World War II, Mrs. Clark saw to it that Dorothy would have first call on the vacancy.

It was my first lesson in the privileges that could be counted on for faculty wives, something that sharpened Dorothy's interest. And although she assured me she would be able to manage on the reduced income in academe, she did not press me to accept the Columbia offer until after the trip to Israel.

It was difficult for me to make up my mind just then to leave workaday journalism. Regardless of all the ups and downs of newspapering, I believed I'd miss the excitement and the swiftness of change. After all, I'd been doing it for nearly twenty-five years. Whether teaching would satisfy me, always provided I'd qualify for the work, I still did not know.

That was the mood I was in when I set off for Israel in the early summer of 1950, hoping that my experiences in the Middle East would divert me. They did, but not in the way I'd imagined. For at first sight on the auto ride from Lydda Airport to Jerusalem, this new country still bore the scars of its war of independence on every side. Far from resembling the Biblical Promised Land of milk and honey, this was a place of rusted barbed wire, abandoned vehicles, and whole areas desolated by war.

I suppose I might have called it a land of promise, perhaps, but even that was a shaky first impression of a country that was still partly occupied by foreign troops, although it proudly professed to have beaten off the aggressors. Along the fifty-mile route to Jerusalem, however, the auto I was riding in had to take detours to avoid a part of the route that still was occupied by Arab soldiers under the terms of a truce that had been signed in February 1949.

We passed damaged villages, collapsed bridges, abandoned slit trenches and emplacements where guns had once been installed. I was told there had been desperate fighting in this general area because it represented the outer line of the defenses of Jerusalem.

Once I arrived at the outskirts of Jerusalem, however, the brutality of the 1948 fighting came home to me forcefully. Not more than a quarter mile from my small room at the King David Hotel, Jordan's British-trained Arab Legion still occupied the Old City. And on the roof of the hotel, I was told, Israeli riflemen remained on guard against Arab incursions. Whether I liked it or not, I was to sleep on the edge of what had been a battle zone and might again be the scene of combat.

This was scarcely what I'd expected. Deeply disturbed over what I had already seen, I lay awake for some time in my dingy hotel room and wondered at might-have-beens. If this was to be the refuge of persecuted Jewry after the Holocaust, none of them could be sure of a secure future. Nor could there be any assurance that the persecutions of Jews or other minority peoples who cling to their beliefs could be halted without more fighting, there in what was called the Holy Land.

The reality of an embattled Israel already had blotted out the hazy notions I'd entertained on the thirty-hour flight from New York City to Lydda Airport that I would find, at last, a new nation where at least some of the refugees from terror and persecution would be secure. At first glance, there did not seem to me to be a refuge here in Jerusalem. And I thought of the sacrificed life of Uncle Simon in a Nazi death camp; of the despairing little girl in Vienna who had cried at my departure and murmured, "Nim mich mit"; of the cantor who had escaped from Germany and sung "Die Lorelei" on a radio station in New York City to begin life anew in a strange land.

Was this here in Jerusalem, I wondered, the best the world could do to provide a haven for innocent victims of persecution? Could there be no greater assurance from a global peacekeeping organization that the people of Jerusalem, a city thought of as holy by three religions—Christianity, Islam, and Judaism—could go to sleep at night without worrying what the morrow would bring?

From what I had seen already, the future of Israel was manifestly uncertain. Here, in this city of perhaps 250,000 people at the time the Israelis had to fight and win their independence, no one could be sure that terror, persecution and sudden death did not lurk around the corner. Over its 3,000-year history, this city had been ravaged by conquerors many times, sacked by brutal victors at least four times with many of its inhabitants put to the sword. It could happen again. In this dark mood, I fell into a troubled sleep.

When I awoke next morning, the sun was shining brightly, people were out in the streets going about their workaday lives, and I felt better. Yes, the Arab Legion still remained on patrol in the Old City outside my hotel window, and the Israeli guards of the Haganah continued on guard on the roof.

After a hasty breakfast, I determined to see Jerusalem by myself on foot and without a government escort to judge the damage and the future for myself. In my first two hours, I saw signs everywhere that buildings had been either razed or renovated after the brief but ugly war for freedom that these people had to wage against their neighbors. Those structures that had not undergone major damage, with few exceptions, bore telltale scars of shrapnel bursts and bombing.

What heartened me, however, was brushing up against the people themselves. In the streets, I heard the babel of many languages other than Hebrew and Yiddish (a riotous combination of Hebrew and the native language of the speaker, as a rule)—English, German, French, Turkish, even Russian and other Slavic tongues. There were few beggars. Mostly, on the streets and in the shops, the people of Jerusalem were going about their business. As nearly as I could judge, they dealt mainly in shekels, the modern version of the country's ancient currency, although I saw dollars, British pounds, and French francs change hands as well. The shelves in the bakeries and other food shops seemed filled, the occasional café or restaurant appeared not to lack for customers, and the general stores, too, seemed to have a decent amount of trade.

Of the homes in Jerusalem I could not be so sure, however, because I had little access to them. From what I did see, it seemed out of the question to me that anybody in the city proper, with its largely Jewish population, could be living in the comfort of, say, an average American home, let alone anything approaching luxury. And as for the Old City, the poorest part of Jerusalem, being mainly occupied still by the Arabs, the few glimpses I had of that quarter made an even more dismal impression.

So here in the Holy City, as I saw it, there were two societies living side by side without any intermingling except with hostility, sometimes even brutality. When they were forced to converse, for example if Arabs were dependent on Jews for food and services, they got along together but grudgingly. What struck me forcibly was the way the words "Arab" and "Jew" were pronounced by the respective opponents of each people—as if even the words themselves were a curse. It followed that both Israel and Israel's neighbors were not then ready for peace in the Middle East, nor would they be for many a year thereafter.

My view of the countryside was much more favorable. During that early period of Israeli freedom from British control, despite the ever present danger of Arab guerrilla incursions or worse, I traveled by car from north of Dan to south of Beersheba without encountering either violence or despair, except in the camps of displaced persons where Arabs were being kept pending their absorption in nearby Arab lands.

To me, it was a nagging question whether the Arabs had deserted their villages in what was now Israeli territory of their own free will or whether they had been driven out because of the fighting. I never did get a clear response, because these Arabs were embittered and their Israeli hosts were suspicious—and neither trusted the other. But as nearly as I could determine, what happened at the outset of this particular war, once Israel declared itself a nation, was due mainly to the mistaken strategy of the Arab leadership.

In daily and nightly broadcasts in Arabic, mainly from Egypt, the highest Arab religious leader, the Grand Mufti of Jerusalem, Haj Amin el Husseini, had warned his fellow Arabs to flee for their lives. Other clerics of his faith and disposition had taken up the campaign to panic the Arab dwellers, evidently as a paramilitary measure to block roads, spread confusion, and thereby hamper the defenses hastily thrown together by the Israeli army.

But the strategy backfired. When the Arabs fled, they lost their homes, their farms, and virtually all their possessions. The Arabs who stayed put, especially in the Old City of Jerusalem, were seldom harmed, so I was told, except when they were caught in murderous cross fire between the contending forces. And so, this new nation still maintained a large Arab population of several hundred thousand in displaced person camps, in the few farms and homes outside the Arab quarters in cities like Jerusalem, and in collective settlements elsewhere on Israeli territory.

However, since that lightning defensive war of 1948, fully 400,000 Jews had emigrated to Israel from Europe, North Africa, and what the British called the Near East (Middle East to Americans). Thus, the vacant Arab villages soon were populated with these newcomers who were, for the most part, trained through manner and disposition to work on the land. So I came to find that fully a quarter of Israel was given over to agriculture even at the outset of its rebirth as a nation.

What I was not prepared for was the extent of the collective use of the land by the farming population and the frequent establishment of collectives for industry and for the general marketing of products in the cities. To an American, this process of socialization seemed at first glance to be a dubious prospect at best, given the wide variety of peoples and languages in the various collectives for marketing and farming. However, after a time, I came to understand that collective work in the Jewish communities outside Israel had been the general practice except in America and much of western Europe.

This was how most of these people—the settlers who had first come to Palestine under British rule and those who had followed since the war for independence—were accustomed to earn their living. And that, too, was why I found so many hard-working farmers laboring in their agricultural collectives without complaint over the rather strained manner of their existence. This, after all, was now their land, and they knew perfectly well that their lives would be whatever they could make of themselves.

This was as true of the city dwellers as those on the farms, as I realized when I came to visit such thriving cities as Tel Aviv, Haifa, Ramla, Rehovoth, and Petach Tikva. Let me illustrate by detailing a visit to a prosperous former Arab village, Ein Karem, in the Judaean Hills near Jerusalem, which was totally occupied in 1950 by a Jewish farm collective. The place was clean and well kept, I thought, whether the people lived in the impressive stone houses (once the property of richer Arabs) or in the humbler dwellings of mud, plaster, and stone of the poorer folk. To me, at least, there was no doubt of the productivity of the farm from the well-tended vineyards to the green fields. The food served at a meal I shared with them during my visit to the collective was well cooked, solid, and unpretentious, and there was plenty of it including meat, stacks of sliced brown bread with plum or peach butter, and vegetables culled from the fields.

I was struck, too, by the youth collective that was run in several places, including a former Arab mosque. The children—many of them orphans whose parents had died in Nazi murder factories, plus others from nearby families who couldn't care for their own—were being educated entirely in Hebrew. I was told that they picked up the language quickly, within a few weeks at most, regardless of the language of their parents.

Many of the boys I saw were at work as carpenters, turning out toys. The girls either repaired clothes and furniture indoors or worked in the vegetable and flower gardens nearby. Like all else that was the product of the collective, much of the stuff not designed for home use was sent to the cities. As for exports, except for citrus fruits and such specialties as diamonds and textiles finished off by experts who came to Israel as refugees, little money could be earned from them in 1950. Imports still were many times as great and much more expensive.

Where, then, did the money come from to keep this desperately needy country afloat? Mainly, except for whatever could be borrowed by the government, the hundreds of millions of dollars that came each year from organized American Jewry sustained the new state in its neediest and most formative years. As many a government functionary conceded to me, Israel could not have survived had it not been for the stout-hearted youth who made up Israel's crack fighting force and the generosity of the Jewish community in the United States.

If the farm collectives were important to the new Israel of 1950, the city dwellers—the eager consumers who formed the bulk of the population—were the very backbone of this new land. What the Israelis themselves had to say about their cities actually set the tone of much of urban life, a kind of folk wisdom that ran much as follows:

"When you see Jerusalem, you will see the past both of the Jewish people and of many others as well. If you want to see Israel of the future, go to Haifa and you will find a lot of things that are new now, even to us. But for the present, you must take the time to stay in Tel Aviv because it is commercially by far our most important city. And as Tel Aviv goes, so goes Israel for the present."

Like all generalities, there was some truth in this, but there was also a lot of wishful thinking. What I found in Tel Aviv was a noisy, bustling, small-scale replica of a combination of New York and Viennese life, if such a thing is possible! Even though Tel Aviv had perhaps a total of about 300,000 people when I first saw it, there was a lot of New York's vitality about it on the streets and in the shops. But there also were so many coffeehouses in the Viennese manner, where people could lounge and read newspapers and magazines, that the business section outwardly presented a curiously split personality. I could not make up my mind during a hasty visit if Tel Aviv was for real, as the saying goes, or whether it presented merely an illusion of a commercially important city. The next century will tell that story better than the present, always provided the Israelis can hold out against the pressures of the hostile 40 million Arabs in the lands surrounding their own.

It's still true, almost without special emphasis, that the continued support of the U.S. government, both within the United Nations and outside it, will be even more crucial to Israel's existence in the future than it has been in the past.

When I returned to New York from my wanderings in Israel, the *Post* published a special section of the paper on my findings—the last direct report I was able to make from the land itself. I decided later that summer, with Dorothy's approval, to continue with my experiment as a combined educator-journalist by accepting the Columbia professorship. We moved from Brooklyn then to the Columbia apartment on Morningside Drive where Professor Clark and his wife were neighbors.

Between five-day-a-week classes at the Graduate School of Journalism, a weekly night undergraduate class in General Studies, and a weekly seminar for no more than four or five graduate students at a time at the United Nations, I had all I could handle as a very new and eager but untrained professor. Now, instead of daily dispatches, I turned to doing books on matters that particularly interested me—and it followed that the Middle East in general and Israel in particular continued to hold my attention.

It was under these circumstances that I noted the changes in the Israeli position and those of the hostile neighbors of the Jewish state, particularly when either the United States or the United Nations (usually both) assumed an active role in the continued clashes between Israeli and Arab interests. The following brief summation will illustrate how drastically involved these relationships have become in the most important single issue confronting the world today—global atomic war or peace.

There was a fragile truce between Israel and its Arab neighbors following the 1949 armistice in the war for independence. But hostilities broke out again seven years later, following repeated Egyptian provocations. The British and French forces joined the Israeli army on October 29, 1956, in a punitive attack during which the Israelis took and held Egypt's Sinai Peninsula. A UN Emergency Force (UNEF) separated the combatants after nine days of fighting and enforced a cease-fire on November 6, 1956.

More Arab raids ensued, however, during the next decade. And on May 19, 1967, Egypt's Gamal Abdel Nasser made the fatal error of seizing both the Sinai Peninsula and the Gaza Strip along Israel's Mediterranean coast. In the Six-Day War, the Israelis—alone, this time—took the Sinai back again, booted Egypt out of the Gaza Strip, expelled Jordan from the Old City of Jerusalem and the West Bank of the Jordan River, and grabbed the northern Golan Heights from Syria. The fighting ended on June 10, 1967, with UN intervention.

That truce lasted until October 6, 1973, when Syria attacked Israel to try to reconquer the Golan Heights, from which Arab raids on Israeli territory had been frequently conducted. This was the Yom Kippur War, so named because the Syrians began it on the Day of Atonement, the holiest day of the Jewish year when most of Israel was at prayer in the nation's synagogues. But the Israeli army, alert as always, recaptured the Golan and crossed the Suez Canal to attack Arab positions there until another UN cease fire began on October 24, 1973. A UN peacekeeping force then took hold once again to separate the combatants.

Out of interest aroused by my 1950 series of articles on my month-long visit to Israel, I had followed such events as these in my Columbia seminars at the UN for graduate students for almost a quarter of a century, but my time at Columbia now was running out. And although I continued to conduct my seminars at successive teaching assignments elsewhere, I no longer was able to keep in such close touch with American/UN relations in the Middle East. Instead, the Vietnam War and the Asian Pacific generally became the center of my successive studies for the Council on Foreign Relations, the Ford Foundation, and other organizations.

Still, it was fascinating to watch the always hesitant development of American efforts to create a better relationship between Israel and its Arab neighbors under nearly all the Presidents of the latter 20th century.

The first major Arab state to make peace with Israel was Egypt under Anwar al-Sadat, who signed an accord with the Israelis on March 26, 1979, and was rewarded with the return of the Sinai Peninsula although Israel still retained the Gaza Strip. Two years later, however, Israel found it necessary to launch a pre-emptive strike at another Arab state, Iraq, which then was conducting its first nuclear experiments for military purposes.

Next came the onset of a new flood of Jewish immigration from Gorbachev's Soviet Union, permitted and encouraged by his well-nigh helpless government, that was expected to add at least a million Jewish refugees to Israel's population. Such massive immigration strained the resources of the Jewish state and also made its Arab neighbors exceedingly nervous, except of course for Egypt. For the rest, peace with Israel still was a sometime thing, and the PLO, the Palestine Liberation Organization, still was tied to Soviet policy.

Even so, the deep strains within the Arab world continually emerged to confound the policy of the Arab League and the PLO of unremitting hostility toward Israel. This was exacerbated when Saddam Hussein's Iraq boldly attacked and absorbed oil-rich Kuwait on the Arabian peninsula beginning August 2, 1990. Because of the threat to the flow of Arab oil to the United States, President Bush touched off the Persian Gulf War on January 16, 1991, in which the Iraqis were forced out of Kuwait by an air bombing that lasted until February 21 and was succeeded by a four-day ground war. Israel then took direct hits from Iraqi missiles but, out of respect for the U.S. position, did not respond in order to help maintain Arab support for the attack on Iraq.

Once President Clinton took over in 1993, one of his first acts was to authorize another air attack on Iraq's espionage station in Baghdad which had been suspected of plotting to murder George Bush while he was President. And meanwhile, Israel and the PLO already were negotiating in secret for the beginnings of what Israel hoped would be a lasting peace between them—something that would have been unthinkable in the turbulent years in which Israel had so often fought for its life. That effort came to a head in the White House Rose Garden on September 13, 1993, when the PLO's Yasir Arafat and Israel's Prime Minister Yitzhak Rabin shook hands after the signature of a draft peace accord in the presence of President Clinton and some of the key officials on both sides.

Both America and the world at large realized all too soon that the conservatives on both sides were not ready for peace when a series of fatal attacks among Palestinian Arabs and Jewish settlers were meant to unhinge the process through which the Israelis were yielding Jericho on the occupied West Bank of the Jordan River to the PLO and also withdrawing from the Gaza Strip. But somehow, for all the shakiness of the effort to set up a viable self-governing Palestinian territory within Israel, the two sides managed to continue their effort through the first year of their projected five-year timetable for peace.

There were many in the United States who were willing to predict boldly, in print and on the air, that the effort would fail and the Arabs and Israel once again would be arming for more wars, that Arafat would not rest until he had seized all of Jerusalem for the capital of the PLO, that the Israelis would have to banish the Palestinians from their nation for self-preservation. And yet, the interest of the United States in a peaceful Middle East is so dominant today, and is certain to increase in importance in the next century, that more wars east of the Nile could become an unmitigated disaster for all concerned.

It was for this reason that I maintained my interest in the Middle East's peace negotiations and the usefulness of the United Nations when it often seemed to the vast majority of Americans that both were doomed. The consequences of such a failure were too dismal to contemplate then or later.

A little less than a year later, extending the fragile peace process, King Hussein of Jordan and Prime Minister Shamir signed another White House peace agreement in the presence of President Clinton. The President also expressed hope of a similar accord between Syria and Israel.

Nevertheless, frequent attacks by extremists continue in the Middle East and elsewhere to try to derail the peace process.

10 ★ AFTER FIFTY YEARS

In light of the demise of the League of Nations after only twenty years between the two world wars, it is heartening to those of us who believe in sustained international relations to look back on a half-century of the United Nations.

Toward century's end, for all its dithering and frustration during the Cold War and to some extent thereafter, the world organization may still be groping for its proper place in world affairs, but it has grown to a membership of almost 200 nations large and small. It cannot very easily be wished out of existence now by its conservative detractors abroad and the reviving isolationists at home.

After the Cold War, the UN tried to be a worldwide peacekeeper in Somalia and Bosnia-Herzegovina as well as in a number of smaller conflicts without having the kind of political, economic and military organization that would have been able to function effectively. And the lamentable results after the initial humanitarian effort to feed the hungry ended, in effect, cost it support in the United States, Western Europe, and elsewhere.

It was in Rwanda, however, that Secretary General Boutros Boutros Ghali finally lost his temper and railed against the failure of UN's members to rush troops at once into a bloody African civil war. The peacekeepers he finally recruited came mostly from African nations.

This wasn't what Franklin Roosevelt and Winston Churchill had in mind when they agreed to the first broad draft document on January 1, 1942, that bound the United States, the United Kingdom, and twenty-four other nations (with more added later) to a fight to the finish against the Axis. The President had changed the title "Declaration by the Associated Powers" and substituted the words "United Nations" throughout. Churchill not only approved. He also quoted Byron's "Childe Harold":

> Here, where the sword United Nations drew,
> Our countrymen were warring on that day!
> And this is much—and all—which will not pass away.

That was the beginning of the UN, which was ratified in San Francisco four years later at the organizing conference for the successor world organization to the League of Nations. In addition to the UN's great sponsors, who gave it name and substance, Trygve Lie, the first Secretary General, also was important in preserving the new body from suffering the fate of the League.

His most important supporters included Eleanor Roosevelt, and Prime Minister Indira Gandhi of India, Assistant Secretary General Andrew W. Cordier and Ralph Bunche, the Palestine case mediator; Herbert V. Evatt, Carlos P. Romulo, and Lester B. (Mike) Pearson, three General Assembly presidents at various times; and other influential individual delegates such as Sir Alexander Cadogan, Alexandre Parodi, and Golda Meir.

Through every crisis in the formative first seven years of the UN, Lie and one or more of these leaders were most active in either intervening to halt a war or averting one. And on Lie's own devoted staff, he had Andrew Cordier, Tor Gjesdal, and Wilder Foote who helped him time and again to stave off a UN failure or even a complete collapse. Thus was the pattern set for those who followed the big Norwegian—especially Dag Hammarskjold of Sweden, whose services ended tragically in 1961 in a plane crash while he was on a peace mission in Africa. Had he lived, he might well have added to the luster of his accomplishments, recognized by a posthumous Nobel Peace Prize.

At a time when the Cold War had made mortal enemies out of the United States and the Soviet Union, Secretary General Lie became the indispensable go-between who managed somehow to maintain contact between the two fiercest antagonists in the UN. Had he not been able to do so, through miracles of diplomatic management, I have no doubt that, along with several hundred of my fellow journalists on the UN assignment, I would have had to report the end of still another world organization dedicated to peace. Between the implacable opponents—the Soviet Andrei Gromyko and the stolid Vermonter, former Senator Warren R. Austin, the chief American delegate—there was little "give" in the crises of the UN's opening years. Both had strict instructions from their governments, which they followed with vigor and sometimes poisonous invective. And neither, to my knowledge, ever made a suggestion, privately or publicly, that might in any way have eased the burden of the man in the middle, the Secretary General.

These were intermediate roles that often were filled, cautiously and privately, by such delegates on the Western side as Cadogan of Britain and Parodi of France (among others). In crises like the Berlin blockade, for example, Evatt of Australia, then the General Assembly president, was invaluable as a mediator. And Mike Pearson, too, had both the diplomatic skill and the courage to handle such assignments, also being recognized while he was an Assembly president for his various roles in difficult situations requiring mediation. It should never be forgotten that one of the most energetic and distinguished mediators on whom Lie had to call, Count Folke Bernadotte of Sweden, was assassinated while he was on the job. And the same thing might well have happened to the gutsy American, Ralph Bunche, who abandoned the safety of a diplomatic role at UN headquarters to take up where Bernadotte had left off. The testimonial to Bunche's success, too, was the award of a Nobel Peace Prize.

Perhaps the most difficult of all Lie's operations while Secretary General was the negotiation of a cease-fire in the Korean War in which the United States and fifteen other UN members opposed the Communist forces of North Korea backed by Communist China. Here, no single mediator could have done the job. A UN Commission also became useless, because the Communist side seemed to take the position that the UN, too, was the enemy.

In effect, therefore, Lie himself had to be the mediator. He put up with a lot of abuse, a spate of lies by the Communist side about Americans engaging in germ warfare, and understandable bitterness on the American-UN side. But as Lie wrote in his annual report for 1952:

"The UN has sought and should continue to seek in all ways to reach a reasonable and fair armistice agreement without sacrifice of moral principle. . . . Until there is an armistice, it is the part of wisdom and duty under the Charter (of the UN) for Members to carry on the fight . . . and to do so with a more equitable sharing of the burdens."

When the armistice was finally achieved in 1953, a few months after Lie's retirement, what he said was, "Korea proves that aggression does not pay."

Beyond such developments as these and others during the various wars of the latter part of this century, Lie's greatest achievement as Secretary General was to maintain the UN's headquarters, temporary or permanent, in the United States. Perhaps it is mainly because I am an internationally minded American that I believe a UN headquarters in Europe would have undermined hope for effective world organization among a large section of the American public and that American membership remains crucial to the UN.

In any event, I was well aware, at the time of the argument about whether to leave the UN in New York or shift it elsewhere, that people in whom I had great confidence—such as Secretary of State Dean Acheson—were all for a European headquarters for the UN. Of course, New York was uproarious, dirty, noisy, bad-mannered, pushy, and terribly expensive—all complaints I often heard from many delegates—but to my mind this was where a world peacekeeping organization belonged if it cared at all about bidding for American support.

Although Lie probably would not have made much of my particular argument for a permanent American headquarters, he insisted from the outset of his work as Secretary General that New York City should be the home of the UN. And fortunately for the world organization, he had his way. Strangely enough, in so doing, he never alienated Soviet support at critical times in his long tenure. In fact, as his first five-year term was about to end in 1950, the U.S. State Department was pleasantly surprised when news came from Moscow that the Soviet Union would support no candidate other than the incumbent, Trygve Lie. And so it was ordained, although Lie himself informed the Big Five—the permanent Security Council members—the United States, the Soviet Union, France, Britain, and China—that it would be out of the question for him to complete a second five-year term.

Whenever discussions for a successor to Lie took place in the Security Council, formally or informally, it became standard procedure to consider the qualifications of the most prominent among Third World delegates, Carlos Peña Romulo, the articulate Filipino who had already served as a president of the General Assembly. Although he was a perennial favorite of the United States and other Western powers as well as a number of Third World countries, he was invariably knocked out of contention by the Soviet Union. It never seemed to bother him. He was also a favorite among the people of the UN press corps because he had been a journalist before he became a diplomat and had won a Pulitzer Prize while the Philippines was an American possession. More than once, when all other sources were closed to us on important breaking stories, I can testify that it was Romulo who saw to it that we knew what was going on behind the scenes and why certain positions were being taken. This is not to give the impression that Rommy was a tipster or that he leaked material to the press corps about which he had been sworn to secrecy. He was too principled for that; to the best of my knowledge, while I was a reporter operating against world-class competition and later in my weekly UN seminars at Columbia, he never played favorites among the reporters—and that included his fellow journalists from the Philippines.

What particularly recommended Romulo to the United States, I believe, was his World War II service as an aide to General Douglas MacArthur during the siege of Bataan in the early stages of the war, and as the radio "Voice of Freedom" from Corregidor in the last stand these against Japan. It was then that he won his military title of Brigadier General. Earlier, as editor and publisher of the *Philippines Herald,* he had received his Pulitzer Prize for foreign correspondence in 1942, based on dispatches published in 1941 before Pearl Harbor in which he had sounded a warning against Japanese intentions in the Pacific. It was the theme of his findings after a tour of the Far East of trouble centers from Hong Kong to Batavia. I have tried to preserve a reminder of his work as a soldier-journalist—his description of life during the Japanese siege of Corregidor when he walked into the Malinta tunnel there on New Year's Day:

"The smell of the place hit me like a blow in the face. There was the stench of sweat and dirty clothes, the coppery smell of blood and disinfectant coming from the lateral where the hospital was situated. . . . I stood there gaping, bewildered and alarmed by the bedlam going on about me. This was the final refuge of a fortress we all had assumed had been prepared and impregnable for years. Now that disaster was upon us, soldiers were rushing about belatedly installing beds and desks and sewage drains and electric lights."

Just before Corregidor fell to the Japanese on May 6, 1942, MacArthur was evacuated with his staff, Romulo among them, on direct orders from President Roosevelt and all proceeded by PT boat and airplane to Australia to renew the fighting from that vantage point. Having known the face of war at firsthand, as the tough-minded Filipino observed so many times afterward during his career as a diplomat, he was bound to spend much of the rest of his career as one of the strongest advocates for peace.

This was what made him so valuable to Trygve Lie, who tried in vain to bring about his election as Secretary General, and caused him to be so widely respected at the UN for the rest of his days. After serving as the Philippines' foreign minister, he died in 1986.

What Andrew Cordier accomplished at the UN as Lie's strong right arm among his Assistant Secretaries General is not as well known for a number of reasons, the primary one being that he was the top American in the Secretary General's immediate staff. To be sure, Byron Price, as the Assistant Secretary General in charge of maintenance, also had major responsibilities, as did other Americans among his associates. But I believe it was Cordier who continued to be the strongest American voice in the Secretary General's inner circle for as long as he remained at the UN.

Being an American, he was obviously excluded from consideration as Secretary General when that office became vacant with Lie's retirement. The same thing happened to Mike Pearson, as a Canadian and Britain's foremost candidate for Lie's successor, when he was nominated and knocked out of competition through a Soviet veto. Cordier took a different tack, retiring to become dean of Columbia University's School of International Affairs and, later, president of the university and a continued influential presence in the international community.

During the span of my experience at the UN, I was always impressed by the prestige and authority that radiated from the presence of two completely different world leaders, Eleanor Roosevelt and Indira Gandhi. Next to Trygve Lie himself, I am sure that both the American

I have a few words with President Harry Truman.

Interviewing Bernard M. Baruch, U.S. delegate to the UN Atomic Energy Commission.

A conference with General A.G.L. McNaughton, Canada's delegate to the UN.

Andrei Gromyko of the Soviet Union tries an argument on me as a reporter at the UN. From my expression, I am not sure he is on the level.

and the Indian were indispensable to the survival of the world organization in its most trying period.

What Mrs. Roosevelt contributed, to a greater extent than any other American except her late husband, was her faith in the absolute necessity for American membership in a world organization dedicated to peace. It is for this reason, I am certain, that she became a member of the U.S. Mission to the United Nations from the outset and also exercised her unique influence within our own country as a leading member of the American Association for the United Nations.

I'm not sure how far her loyalty to a world organization extended, that is, whether she thoroughly believed in our membership in all the UN specialized agencies, including some in which almost everything American was under continual attack. I never had a chance to discuss it with her. Nevertheless, I often wondered if she would have approved of the Reagan administration's decision to withdraw from the UN Educational, Scientific and Cultural Organization (UNESCO), in which the United States almost from the outset had to face continual attack by the Soviet Union and its allies. I may not have favored all the points of the Reagan policies in world affairs, but I thoroughly approved of the UNESCO withdrawal and even undertook, by request, an extended speaking tour abroad arranged under State Department auspices to explain our position.

Whatever Mrs. Roosevelt may have thought of UNESCO in her years at the UN, she did not hesitate to denounce Soviet Premier Nikita S. Khrushchev when he came to the UN and, in her words, "tried to destroy it." She wrote:

"There was a time at the outset when people disillusioned by the League of Nations could scoff at the idea of another world organization designed to work for the peaceful settlement of international disputes. But that time has passed. Today we are seeing more and more clearly that it *can* work, that it *does* work, and it will be increasingly effective if we back it with all our strength. After all, it is because it is an effective organization that Mr. Khrushchev has been so determined to destroy it."

Although Mrs. Roosevelt invariably showed sympathy for India's struggles to maintain its position as the world's largest democracy, she was reserved in her estimates of the Indian leadership as long as the Indian national policy was to show greater consideration for the Soviet Union than the United States. Nevertheless, in 1962, Mrs. Roosevelt did undertake a lengthy trip through India at the invitation of Prime Minister Jawaharlal Nehru, the father of Indira Gandhi, his eventual successor in the highest office in their country. Mrs. Roosevelt wrote:

"We must face the fact that in the years after the war [World War II] our popularity took a terrible tumble in India, as it did throughout the Arab countries. Having shaken off the domination of one foreign power, they are understandably determined not to fall under the influence of any other. . . . In addition, we have against us their feeling that because our skins are white we necessarily look down on all peoples whose skins are yellow or black or brown. This thought is never out of their minds. They always asked me pointedly about our treatment of minorities in our country."

Being much more a diplomat than a journalist, despite her years as a syndicated columnist doing "My Day" for a number of newspapers, Mrs. Roosevelt seldom made a great point of India's relationships with the largest Communist powers, its neighbors the Soviet Union and China. Nevertheless, it was a question that invariably came up whenever Indira Gandhi appeared in New York City, either at the UN or at some diplomatic function.

Not that Mrs. Gandhi either looked or acted or talked like a Communist representative. On the contrary, in her beautiful silk saris and mink coats, her small slender figure was the envy of many an American hostess. No one could doubt, looking at her on such occasions, that she could dominate the politics of her own country to such an extent that she was invariably referred to, even by her opponents, as "The Lady."

However, in the last of many interviews I had with her—on a hot midsummer's afternoon in 1970 in her private office at Parliament House, New Delhi—she argued vehemently that the Soviet-India relationship was "grossly exaggerated." As usual, she repeated her assurances that she was not anti-American but that India, because of its geographical position, had to pursue a policy of "even-handedness" toward the neighboring Soviet Union and Communist China. And yet, when she made reference to American support of Pakistan, there was a touch of bitterness in her voice.

Despite her sensitivity on such matters as these, she remained deeply committed to the cause of world peace through the United Nations. Perhaps this was due in large measure to the idealistic outlook she had inherited from her father, but regardless of the origin of her belief there is no doubt she meant it. At no time in the many years that I knew her as a reporter did I ever detect a trace of wishful thinking about Indira Gandhi. She was a no-nonsense politician in her own country and a world leader while abroad with a large following in Third World countries.

It was for these reasons that her support for the United Nations remained important, along with that of others like Trygve Lie and Eleanor Roosevelt whose views so often differed from her own. Through them and others—the people of the UN—the world organization was able to survive its earliest crises. As a result, following the end of the Cold War with the collapse of Communism and the Soviet Union, the UN became a more important global force against military aggression.

In a very real sense, it made possible the American-led UN coalition that wiped out Saddam Hussein's atomic experiments and long-range weapons in 1990–91. It was a step toward a new world order in which the UN and kindred regional organizations in the Americas, Europe, the North Atlantic, and eventually the Pacific must all continue to play an important part.

After fifty years, the cause of international peace and security can neither be laughed at, mocked, or forced out of existence through a resurgent isolationism in the United States, born out of sheer frustration with the complications of peacekeeping more than anything else. No one has ever contended that it was possible to create peace merely by waving a magic wand. It is a sometimes painful, often expensive, continuous effort that must be maintained by the leadership of nations, great and small, with clear-headedness and patience and, above all, faith that war one day can be banished from the Earth.

PART 3

Back to Academe

11 ★ NEW TIMES ON MORNINGSIDE

I can't pretend that it was easy to separate myself from workaday journalism after twenty-five years to become a Columbia University professor. And yet, for a short time at least, Dorothy and I had a sentimental feeling of homecoming about our return to Morningside Heights in the late summer of 1950 when we moved from Brooklyn to our new Columbia apartment after five years at the UN, in Washington, and abroad.

It didn't last long. Once the fall semester began for the sixty-five graduate students in the Class of 1951 at the Journalism School, I had more than enough to do. And so did Dorothy, who was caught up soon enough in the faculty wives' routine of teas, receptions for visiting dignitaries, and formal dinners for recipients of university honors and other people of importance to the university.

As for myself, despite several years of once-a-week night classes, I was completely unprepared for the complexities of life at Columbia, both socially and professionally. The teaching load in itself was more than I'd bargained for—classes in newswriting, editing and makeup, crusading journalism, critical writing; a seminar in Washington and Foreign Correspondence; and a day at the UN with four or five students at a time. Also, to maintain family solvency, I still kept my night class for beginners.

Then, there were student papers to read. In one summary from my diary that first year, I noted that those critiques covered more than a hundred papers each week of varying length, content, and competence—twenty-five or thirty from the newswriting class, thirty-one from critical writing, twenty-two from Washington and foreign correspondence, four or five from the UN, and twenty-one from my night class.

Another factor I had not counted on was the contribution every faculty member was expected to make to university life. That part was easy at first—membership in a faculty committee that was appointed to resolve a dispute between the Graduate School of Business and the School of General Studies over the latter's proposed offering of a business degree. Beyond that, I had a pleasant surprise—an invitation to join a University Faculty Seminar on Peace in which some of the outstanding figures at the UN also participated.

Altogether, I thought I was fully justified in begging off when my colleagues in the university faculties wanted me to serve on various committees that were forming to promote or oppose the expected candidacy of the president of Columbia, General Dwight David Eisenhower, for President of the United States in 1952. This was one academic pitfall I was able to avoid, regardless of my background as a former political reporter, and I was duly thankful.

As I learned quickly enough without too much experience in campus politics, nothing is less rewarding than a furious political debate at the university level over a presidential campaign. And that was particularly true at Columbia once it became clear that General Eisenhower was being pressed to make the presidential run for 1952 as a Republican. The faculty's Democrats, as might be expected, were outraged.

As early as March 1952, in my second year at Columbia, I noted in my diary: "Truman says he isn't running for re-election. As of now, it seems nothing can stop Ike from becoming the next President of the United States."

The General had come to Columbia in 1948 after retiring from his Army command. Having publicly forsworn any ambition just then to make a run for the Presidency, something Truman had wanted him to do, Ike had seemed content with university life. One of my oldest friends in the news business, Bob Harron, who was for many years the director of public information for the university, often told me that Ike and Mamie had hoped to stay at Columbia for the remainder of Ike's active career.

Of course there was a certain amount of opposition to Eisenhower as a university president on the Columbia campus between 1948 and 1950, before Dorothy and I arrived, but by all accounts it was minor. At any rate, Bob Harron once again is my authority for the belief that Ike and

Mamie thoroughly enjoyed themselves at Columbia. Even when the Columbia College newspaper, the *Spectator,* criticized the General, he professed to be amused. True or not, this was the situation when President Truman in 1950 drafted Ike to organize the military command of the newly formed North Atlantic Treaty Organization (NATO).

So it developed that, at just about the time that Dorothy and I moved into our Columbia apartment at 90 Morningside Drive, the Eisenhowers left for Paris from their Columbia home three blocks away. Thomas J. Watson, Ike's friend on the board of the university's Trustees, was reported to have assured him that the Columbia presidency would remain open for him pending his return, and so it was. But when he and Mamie came back to 60 Morningside Drive in the summer of 1952, the circumstances were quite different.

By then, he had become the Republican nominee for President and was waging an active campaign against the Democratic nominee, Adlai Stevenson, beloved of many Columbia academics because he could quote from the literary classics with charm and grace. At any rate, those of us who were the Eisenhowers' neighbors on Morningside Drive saw them more often during the 1952 Presidential campaign. In fact, when Dorothy and a friend went to the Army-Columbia football game that year at Baker Field on the northern tip of Manhattan, she reported proudly that she had sat next to Ike and Mamie in the wooden grandstand while the little Lions held the Cadets from West Point to a 14–14 tie.

Regardless of campus political sentiment, Ike really didn't have to run much of a campaign against Stevenson. If anything, the so-called egghead vote proved to be more of a handicap than an advantage to the Democratic nominee. On election night 1952, Ike's political landslide became so evident by 7:30 P.M. that even my student editors concluded they could wrap up their election extra without hanging around until the last votes were counted.

Like most of the editors and broadcasters that night, the students showed sound judgment. In the popular vote, Ike had nearly 34 million to Stevenson's 27 million; in the Electoral College, the count stood at 442 to 89, a sweeping victory for the General. It also marked the last rites for the New Deal, which was buried under the great weight of the Republican victory.

Not long afterward, Grayson Kirk became the president of Columbia by unanimous action of the university Trustees, having served as vice-president and provost during Ike's relatively brief tenure. A year later I also was selected for a new job at the university, which lightened my academic load and considerably relieved my financial problems. As Dorothy murmured to me, once she had learned to appreciate the shifting currents and influences of life in a great university, "Isn't Columbia wonderful?" Truly, it was.

This was my next adventure in academe:

While I was concluding my fourth year as a university professor in 1954, Dean Ackerman confided to me that he would be retiring a year hence and would propose me as his successor in the administration of the Pulitzer Prizes. It was something I hadn't expected, and I wondered, quite naturally, whether the members of what was then the Advisory Board on the Pulitzer Prizes would accept the dean's recommendation.

I needn't have been concerned. Both the dean and Dick Baker, who was to become acting dean on Ackerman's retirement pending the selection of a permanent replacement, kept reassuring me. And as the annual meeting of the board approached in late April 1954, the dean briefed me on the work of the respective juries in journalism, letters, drama, and music that the board was to consider. He also helped me draft a suitable agenda for the board's session with the jury reports (it actually took two days in the 1950s)—a document that was distributed in advance to the second Joseph Pulitzer, the board chairman; Grayson Kirk as president of the university; and the rest of the board's membership.

At that juncture, the board called itself "advisory" because the university Trustees, in theory, made the final determination in voting the prizes. In reality, the Trustees received the board's report so late that they could do nothing other than accept or reject the board's recommendations. Consequently, there was ill feeling among at least some of the Trustees about the extent of their responsibility for the awards, given the short time they had to consider the board's recommendations.

So much for the advisory part of the board's duties. In practical terms, with few exceptions in my experience, its decisions became final.

Even though the dean had had me do much of his preparatory work for the board's 1954 session, he handled its secretarial chores on the first day but had me replace him for the second and final day of the meeting. Having introduced me to Chairman Pulitzer, the dean retired from the room and left me at the mercy of the board.

The second Joseph Pulitzer, favored son of the donor of the prizes and the school, was still active as editor and publisher of the *St. Louis Post-Dispatch*. His colleagues around the horseshoe-shaped table in the American Press Institute Room of the Journalism Building's first floor were working newspaper executives and columnists except for President Kirk, a distinguished historian before he took over at Columbia. It was he who had insisted on Pulitzer's chairmanship.

I found myself at the chairman's side with the agenda folder before me and the jury reports and exhibits on the table but waited for him to open the meeting. Instead, he turned to me, smiling, and said, "Please proceed, Mr. Secretary." Puzzled, I asked, "How do you wish me to proceed, Mr. Chairman?" Everybody else seemed amused.

I remember glancing at President Kirk, seated across the table from me, for a clue, but all he did was to nod in encouragement. Frankly, I didn't know whether I was to ask for Divine guidance, make a short speech, or submit a formal motion of some kind.

At that point, Chairman Pulitzer helped me out. He pointed toward his eyeglasses with the index and middle fingers of his left hand and explained, "I do not see as well as I should, Mr. Secretary, so I must ask you to announce each item first and summarize the relevant jury report for our consideration. Then I shall take over as chairman to direct the discussion, but you must examine and count the vote for each prize, then go on to the next item. Do you have any questions?"

"No, Mr. Chairman," I said, enormously relieved, and proceeded as directed without further embarrassment—except for one piece of poor judgment, when I attempted to argue with the formidable Arthur Krock of the *New York Times*. As I recall, it was a matter of little consequence and had no bearing on the outcome of the prize discussion except that I repressed my urge to display further differences of opinion with any other board member.

At the conclusion of my services for the day, Chairman Pulitzer excused me just before the board went into executive session, saying, "I think you took hold very nicely, Mr. Secretary." I understood that my future as secretary of the board and administrator of the Pulitzer Prizes would be decided behind closed doors, which understandably made me nervous.

I needn't have been. Later that day, Dean Ackerman came to my office to notify me that the board had accepted me as its Secretary and the prize Administrator and had recommended a suitable pay increase from the Pulitzer Prize fund. He notified me that I would be responsible, until further notice, for preparing for subsequent board meetings, jury appointments (subject to the board's ratification), and other details of the business of the awards.

For April 23, 1954, I wrote in my diary:

"Sometimes you have good days. Today was one of the best I've ever had.... It was a good day for the dean, too. He enjoyed it.... I never was so surprised in my life."

That day, too, was notable for the dedication of Room 301, in which the board eventually would meet, as the World Room in honor of the defunct Pulitzer newspapers in New York, the morning, evening, and Sunday *Worlds*. This was an entirely new story because it involved the acquisition by Columbia of the stained glass Statue of Liberty window that had been in the World building's lobby.

At Dean Ackerman's request, I had been trying for some time to acquire the Liberty window for Columbia as a memento of Joseph Pulitzer's services to the nation. My first notion was a fund-raising drive, which Herbert Bayard Swope endorsed by agreeing to serve as chairman. But at just about the same time in the spring of 1953 the current owner of the building, Leonard Shankman, offered conditionally to sell the window to the university for a nominal sum.

However, a few days later, the City's Real Estate Board moved to have the building condemned by the Board of Estimate so that it could be razed to widen the traffic approaches to the nearby Brooklyn Bridge. That left the Liberty window decision to City Hall, where I still had friends, with the result that the mayor's office agreed to let the university remove the window free of charge once the condemnation proceedings ended.

Both Swope and I were relieved, and the fund-raising drive ended. On March 9, 1954, concluding negotiations with the mayor's office, we were able to remove the window from the World building and store it, pending the construction of a suitable frame in which it would be installed in the World Room. The event was memorialized in press releases from City Hall, grateful comment from Columbia, and pictorial coverage in the city's major newspapers.

Just before the Advisory Board met in the World Room in advance of dedication ceremonies for the newly installed window, I had to deal with another crisis.

An observant student who had been taking pictures of the window came rushing into my office with prints that showed the stained glass replica of the Statue of Liberty was holding her torch high *in her left hand*. Now this kind of thing, in the era of Senator Joseph R. McCarthy Jr.'s witch hunt for Communists in leading universities, had to be taken seriously. As the student commented, looking at his prints of the window, "Do you think we'll be accused of putting up a subversive Statue of Liberty?"

Heavens, no! The dean and I called in the workmen, explained that the window had to face inward rather than outward, and thereby were able to restore confidence in a Statue of Liberty that correctly bore her torch in her right hand. And so, after the conclusion of the Pulitzer Advisory Board meeting in the World Room on April 23, 1954, Mayor Robert F. Wagner became our guest of honor at Columbia's dedication of the Liberty window with President Kirk, Dean Ackerman, and the Pulitzer board's other members in attendance. Such, too, were my professorial duties at Columbia.

As a new hand on the campus, I expected to be pressed into service for odds and ends of university business. The decision of my joint General Studies/Graduate School of Business Committee to permit General Studies to offer a doctorate in business studies was one result. My appointment to the executive committee of the Eisenhower-endorsed American Assembly at Arden House was another. However, I considered membership in the university-wide Peace Seminar to be a major privilege, because I was able to listen once a week to Professor Philip C. Jessup and other experts in international relations. The membership I was offered as a result on the Council on Foreign Relations came under the same heading.

What really surprised me was an unsought appointment, temporary in nature, to serve as a special consultant to three Secretaries of the Air Force in the Eisenhower administration, two of whom became Deputy Secretaries of Defense. On the basis of my military experience in World War II, I hadn't thought of myself as a temporary occupant of the military holy of holies, the E Ring at the Pentagon, but that is what I was asked to do from time to time while Ike was in the White House between 1953 and 1962.

To be perfectly honest, I was flabbergasted when I was asked to prepare a report on the Air Force information services soon after Ike left Columbia to take up residence in the White House. I was given to understand that the report was considered necessary because the Department of the Air Force, like its brother military services, had been dealt a sharp cut in its budget (about $5 billion) in line with a Congressional drive for military retrenchments. And while I wasn't told that I was to seek out unnecessary information activities in the Air Force, I had to assume that that was the purpose of my projected report.

Quite frankly, I didn't believe myself qualified, but both Dean Ackerman and President Kirk seemed to think I should make the effort, provided it didn't interfere with my regular duties at the university. So I went to Washington, D.C., at the beginning of my summer vacation in 1953 after receiving a telegram from Harold E. Talbott, then Secretary of the Air Force, saying he wanted to see me. When I saw him on June 5 at the Pentagon, I told him flatly that I didn't believe I was the best man for whatever job he had in mind for me and preferred to spend the summer in Aquebogue, Long Island.

Secretary Talbott insisted, however. He told me it was my duty to serve (which was news to me!) and disclosed incidentally that I had been recommended by Herbert Bayard Swope. I temporized, trying as best I could to take a little time for reflection before plunging into an entirely new line of work. He did reluctantly give me a few days to make up my mind, after which I returned to Columbia with the set notion that neither the dean nor President Kirk would approve, which, I hoped, would get me off the hook.

I was wrong. President Kirk told me the Air Force proposal was both exciting and a challenge and gave me the necessary go-ahead but twice told me forcibly that he did not want me to leave Columbia. I assured him that I had no intention of doing so and repeated my pledge to Dean Ackerman, after which he suggested that, out of fairness to myself, I ought not to accept a summer-long commitment but confine myself to temporary service as a consultant.

The upshot was that I spent the first part of the summer at the Pentagon as a special assistant to the Secretary of the Air Force. After spending about a month talking to people in the Air Force information services and their superiors, the military commanders, I produced a report and thought I had fulfilled my obligation. However, the Secretary had me in once again in the presence of two of his chief civilian assistants to undergo a rigorous cross-examination on both my findings and recommendations.

After that, the Secretary asked me to stay on as a consultant, but once again, I told him I had to get permission from Columbia. What I wanted to avoid, no matter what, was a situation in which I was held accountable for my Columbia commitments and also for whatever duties the Air Force assigned to me. I was only partly successful. During the 1953–54 university year, I was summoned to Washington several times for consultation, addressed the Air War College, attended several Air Force conferences, and finally, on April 14, 1954, was asked by Secretary Talbott to become the civilian chief of Air Force information services.

What may have motivated him then, I believe, was the falling Air Force enlistment rate after the Korean War settlement. But whatever his reason, I had to tell him most respectfully that I could not break my Columbia contract even though I appreciated the honor of being asked to serve. He then named a new one-star general as his military information chief, whose first duty it was to try to increase the attractiveness of the Air Force as a career for ambitious young men. Equally important (and this was something on which I agreed to help) was planning the new Air Force Academy, which began with my visit to the proposed site in Colorado.

Even though Secretary Talbott resigned in 1955 in connection with charges before Congress that he had had a conflict of interest between his official government duties and his business interests, I still was called to the Pentagon from time to time thereafter for the rest of the Eisenhower administration. The succeeding Air Force secretaries, Donald A. Quarles and James H. Douglas Jr., also had problems with their military information services, but gradually (I believe) I may have helped them find competent professionals in uniform to handle the job. One of the best, whom I admired, was a West Pointer who also had a Harvard law degree, Air Force Colonel Syd Fisher.

And with that, I became an Air Force alumnus.

In retrospect, I suppose I should not have been surprised at the conflicts within the Pentagon and other factors I had to deal with at one time or another. It reminded me very much of a story a general officer once told me about the Inchon landing in Korea, when he was speeding ashore with his troops in a landing ship/tank (LST). The driver, a frightened GI, was rocking back and forth under fire, and he cried out at one point, "Sir, they're shooting at us!"

The General answered, "What in hell did you expect, son? Chimes?"

12 ★ ON JOURNALISM

Early in my Columbia experience, a student at Joseph Pulitzer's school wrote a long paper about her admiration for the donor in which she identified him throughout as "Robert Pulitzer." This outrage, as our dean called it, was not committed in one of my classes, but in common with other members of the faculty, I heard about it from the dean when he lectured us on the importance of teaching our young charges to get their facts straight.

After a certain amount of meditation, the dean decided that the same lecture could well be repeated for the benefit of the entire student body, and this he proceeded to do. I am sure the students were properly impressed because all of them, including the offending student, listened to the lecture with becoming solemnity. And after I returned to my office, the culprit, a small, rather frightened young woman, came to see me, probably because she had heard that I had something to do with the Pulitzer Prizes, and asked:

"Didn't I spell Pulitzer right?"

I also remember another small, rather frightened young woman, in an early class I conducted in newswriting, who always seemed to tense up whenever I stopped near her to look at her copy. I never could understand what she had to fear from me, even if I am a six-footer, because she was a first-rate student. Also, her identification of public figures in the news was beyond reproach, so much so that I'm sure she never gave the dean nervous palpitations about her spelling of Joseph Pulitzer. And while I do not know what ever happened to the author of the paper about "Robert Pulitzer," her fellow alumna became the governor of one of the original thirteen states of the American union.

I have long since concluded, from these and other examples of professional training among some 5,000 students, spread over well-nigh forty years of teaching experiences at Columbia and elsewhere, that it is impossible to forecast the development of students' careers based on their classroom performances. And I have given up trying.

From the brooding introvert who suddenly decked a fellow student at a Christmas party at the school and became a famous broadcaster, to the quiet young man who rose to the head of the world's greatest wire service, the accomplishments of the students I knew at Columbia and elsewhere have invariably aroused my admiration. But neither I nor any other teacher who sees students for perhaps a semester or two at most can take credit for their successes; nor can we be charged with their failures unless we happen to be accessories before or after the fact.

It is with this caveat that I preface my writing about professionalism in journalism late in the century on the basis of a considerable career in the field both as a working newspaperman and teacher. Considering that the handling of the unexpected is a very basic part of the routine of the journalist, both in the print and electronic media, I would also plead that no rule, except perhaps in the field of libel, can be regarded as engraved in stone. And even in libel, occasionally, both the stone and the engraving thereon can be overturned to add to the confusion of the multitudes.

This is the greatest problem in handing down judgments in the field in which everybody from the town council in Ho-Ho-Kus, New Jersey, to the President of the United States consider themselves experts. So far as I know, expertise in the professionalism of the breed does not exist at the current writing. And I doubt that it ever will as long as the raucous voices of democracy continue a basic part of the American heritage.

This is the very heart of the First Amendment to the Constitution of the United States.

There are a few things a teacher can and should do, certainly at the university level, to help beginners over the rough spots that everybody experiences sooner or later.

I remember an enterprising student in one of my classes, a few years after I came to Columbia, who had decided for some peculiar reason that heaven and earth would fall if he did not obtain an exclusive interview with Anthony Eden, then the British Foreign Secretary and certainly one of the handsomest foreign secretaries in all British history.

Fortunately for me as one of the student's instructors, I learned by happenstance of his project and invited him to my office to chew over the matter. As I soon discovered, my young man's plans were astonishingly like those of many an imaginary pulp-paper journalist in the detective magazines. With becoming modesty, he mentioned his intention of disguising himself and following his quarry around the UN until he could pose as a fellow diplomat and strike up a conversation in, say, the delegates' lounge, the delegates' dining room or, in a dire emergency, the room marked FOR MEN ONLY.

There were a number of other fanciful proposals to which I listened with a show of interest because I liked the young man's enterprise even if, for understandable reasons, my confidence in his judgment was somewhat limited by circumstances. Finally, as I recall the incident, I suggested to him as casually as I could, "Have you ever thought of going in the front door?"

This seemed to be confusing to him. I elaborated: "Maybe, if you approach Mr. Eden at the UN or elsewhere and ask him if you could talk to him for a few minutes as part of your student experience, he might very well oblige you."

The student seemed stunned by this scarcely novel notion of procedure. He protested that he would be sent about his business in short order. I argued that most politicians, and Secretary Eden was one, preferred to talk to almost anybody, including students, rather than face up to the sometimes embarrassing questions of professional journalists who could, if they wished, publish or broadcast his opinions at length before he was ready for them to do so.

The young man was dubious. However, the longer we talked, the more receptive he became to my proposed procedure. And at last, he agreed to try to seek the interview as I'd suggested, properly identify himself, and stay out of the gents' room as an unsuitable site for his colloquy with one of the elite members of the UN diplomatic corps.

Of course I hadn't the faintest idea that Foreign Secretary Eden actually would sit for a one-on-one meeting with my student, much less discuss the foreign policies of his government with the aspiring journalist. All I was trying to do was avert either frustration or embarrassment, possibly both, for a well-meaning member of one of my classes.

Both my student and I had a stroke of luck.

What happened created both pleasure and satisfaction for all parties, including Foreign Secretary Eden. As my student related his adventure later, both for the benefit of his classmates and me, he noted that the newspapers had carried a story, several days after his interview with me, about Eden's meeting with the Secretary of State in Washington, D.C. Thereafter, a few inquiries by telephone at the British press office in New York gave my aspiring reporter a basic schedule of the Foreign Secretary's movements, including the time of his expected arrival by train at Pennsylvania Station in New York City.

Instead of waiting at the station, the young man boarded the train at Newark, hoping to locate Secretary Eden, and quickly identified his compartment. In response to a knock, Eden himself opened the door, whereupon the student requested an interview as part of his graduate work in journalism at Columbia University. During the short ride to Penn Station, the two talked together amiably, and even though the interview as such was scarcely world-shaking it was—from the student's point of view—eminently satisfactory.

Upon leaving, he was so delighted that he burst out, he later confessed, with thanks for what he considered a scoop. To that, Secretary Eden replied with diplomatic finesse, "I congratulate you and wish you many more scoops." I wish I could guarantee the same results for every student who undertakes such a self-inspired assignment, but that isn't precisely the way the system works.

All I could do for my student's classmates was to suggest that, as a matter of professional procedure, it could never hurt to try the front door first. And second-story work could also be dangerous if it developed into a misunderstanding between journalists and their sources, especially those who travel with armed escorts.

It should be perfectly evident, as well, that allowance has to be made for the sometimes astonishing quirks of editors and broadcasters who assign people on their staffs to seek out news sources for the edification or entertainment of the public. Consider, for example, the plight of the *New York Times* reporter who had interviewed a new and sexy young soprano before her performance as Carmen in a New York opera house, and who was so impressed that he brought back a picture of the lady. To his dismay, the picture editor rejected the photo, saying, "Too sexy." Whereupon the reporter suggested hopefully, "But Carmen is a sexy opera, isn't it?" The grumpy answer was, "Not in the *New York Times.*"

Possibly, there may be a few more quirks at that great newspaper than there are elsewhere in news offices (including those of broadcasters), but all editors have quirks, and reporters, whether they like it or not, must be duly appreciative. That, too, is a part of the problem of professionalism among journalists.

It is somewhat easier, I suppose, to appear to be a businesslike professional in handling police and court assignments, especially in criminal cases, than it is to work in the more complicated fields (for journalists, at any rate) of domestic politics and diplomacy at the international level. There are, after all, legal procedures that usually apply to journalists—as well as officers of the law from police to judges—in the coverage of crime; moreover, violators can be held in contempt of court, which is not worth risking except in extraordinary circumstances.

In politics and diplomacy, by contrast, whatever rules there are appear mainly in journalism textbooks and may be phrased, within my experience as the author of such works, at the convenience of these involved. These procedures, briefly summarized, include a broad understanding between the principals of the various meanings of "off-the-record" (do not use), "for background only" (do not disclose the source), "use in paraphrase" (no direct quotes) or "on the record" (everything goes). The key thing is that the reporter and the news source understand each others' definitions and adhere to them. The first time I discuss these matters with students or talk about them to an uninformed public, there is often a lot of head-shaking over the notion that important people would trust a mere reporter with something they did not want the public to know or give a reporter permission to use a fact without disclosing the source. Even greater concern is often voiced over the prospect of unauthorized "leaks" of important information for one reason or another.

On the other hand, some remarks made in public by newsworthy figures are truly worth publishing or broadcasting, such as Winston

Churchill's reply, during one of his political campaigns, to someone in the audience who shouted at the great man, "I would rather vote for the devil than vote for you." The candidate responded, "If your friend is not interested in running for public office, would you consider voting for me?"

Naturally, politicians in every land and under almost any known political system like to be pictured at their best in the news media, no matter what the circumstances, but become exceedingly virtuous and claim to be misrepresented or misunderstood if they are victimized by bad breaks in the news. And here, frequently, charges of ethical misconduct arise against the working journalist who may have had a difference of opinion with various sources over what may or may not be used.

I remember discussing the problem in the 1950s with a high government official at the Pentagon during one of a number of Congressional inquiries into the withholding at the Federal level of news that some in the press believed the public should have. The federal official conceded that one of the principal complainants, J. Russell Wiggins, then executive editor of the *Washington Post,* had a certain amount of justification on his side. But at the same time, the official could not help voicing suspicions of press motives, which was just about what I expected. In such cases, it is very difficult, and sometimes impossible, to bring about an accommodation between press and government people, mainly because one seldom trusts the other in marginal instances of what is to be made known and what is to be withheld.

Then, too, in questions that so often arise over an unauthorized disclosure of information—the "leak," as it is called, for purposes ranging from vindictiveness to personal publicity—all sides profess to be painfully virtuous and denounce the "leaker." But except in rare cases they do nothing else to disturb the practice. I do not know how to legislate, much less enforce, a code of conduct on such matters that would be agreeable to all concerned in an open society.

The issue, bluntly put for the journalists as well as their sources, is, "What price professionalism?" It still begs for an answer.

My own attitude more or less parallels that of the old Yankee catcher, Yogi Berra, one of baseball's greats, while he was rooming with Dr. Bob Brown who was patiently wading through *Gray's Anatomy* as a preface to entering a medical career. Finally, one day, Brown slammed the book shut and cried out, "I've finished it!"

To which the ever-patient Yogi asked, "How did it come out?"

When everything is in the clear and big news is breaking, I've found that students are often on a par with practiced professionals in delivering information in bulk. The problem in such procedures is to determine what it all means, which is what editors want most to know, and sometimes the pros are no better at it than the novices.

The problem of locating the most likely successor to UN Secretary General Trygve Lie after his resignation late in 1952 illustrates the difficulties of producing news in bulk. The day after Lie's announcement, I took my graduate seminar in foreign correspondence to the UN and turned them loose on the unsuspecting delegates to report on the leading candidates for his job. Within a few hours they had interviewed everybody from Dean Acheson to Andrei Vishinsky, Anthony Eden to Mme. Vijaya Lakshmi Pandit of India, and come up with an enormous list of names including those of the leading candidates: Carlos P. Romulo, the U.S. favorite; Mike Pearson, the British candidate; and Nasrollah Entezam of Iran, the French candidate. There were a lot of others, too, including a Mexican, a Lebanese, a Belgian, and a Swede.

The students' reporting fairly well paralleled that of the seasoned UN correspondents, but they did not take the precaution of using their findings in such a way that the reader, listener, or viewer would know their information was inconclusive. Some of the less experienced professionals, too, went overboard in predicting the election of one or other of the more prominent candidates.

The eventual selection was a Swede but not the one that had been touted at the outset of the UN's search, Eric Boheman. The right Swede turned out to be Dag Hammarskjold, a choice that delighted Secretary General Lie and taught my seminarians a lesson in the gathering and display of news in bulk. Their reporting was faultless, I told them in analyzing their work, but what they did with it was something else again. If it was any comfort to them, they also realized they were not alone in trying to report the choice of a UN Secretary General as if it were a horse race in which all bets had to be put down before post time. Hammarskjold,

With my Columbia students at the UN interviewing Secretary-General Dag Hammarskjold.

More student interviews, this time with U.S. delegate Henry Cabot Lodge, Jr.

Criticizing a printed page layout for an apprehensive student.

A new Soviet delegate, Yakov Malik, tries an argument on me while two UN staff members are amused at the tableau.

as a late entry, finished far ahead of the contenders who were first off the mark.

After it was all over, a rather mournful-looking Yugoslav journalist told me he had followed the work of my students with great interest although he doubted such practical training would be possible in his country. Of course he was right. Everything in Yugoslavia then, as in the Stalinist Soviet Union, was determined in secret by its Communist leadership without the inconvenience of dealing with a free press.

Throughout my twenty-six years at Columbia as a teacher, it was easier for me to deal with my early classes, mainly those in the 1950s and early 1960s, than it was with the larger classes thereafter. When I worked with sixty-five or seventy people during the first and most exciting part of my teaching experience, I knew nearly everybody and even today remember most of the names and faces of those who were in my classes. Later, when the roster of graduate students each year increased to as many as 125, with perhaps another score or more in various separate professional programs, I couldn't hope to work with all of them.

I make the point to explain why so many of my reminiscences involve my earliest classes, especially those between 1951 and 1960 and particularly 1951 and 1952, when so many of my former students became lifelong friends. If I was at all effective as a teacher, I believe it was primarily because I enjoyed working with young people one-on-one in the classroom. For me at least, lecturing to a great mass of faceless students in an academic atmosphere made me distinctly uncomfortable. And I have no apologies to offer for that.

Still, after becoming an emeritus professor at Columbia and going on to teach at other universities for periods of anywhere from one or two to as many as six years, one of the great attractions in this quite different experience was a return to small classes and one-on-one teaching. I suppose the main reason for my preference is that this is how I learned the news business both before and during my student years. It also accounts for my insistence on conducting my night class at Columbia's School of General Studies for many years after I no longer needed the extra money to remain solvent.

What my students thought of both the advantages and disadvantages of a one-on-one relationship with their instructor is something else again. I remember working for a journalism dean after leaving Columbia, a first-rate professional who had been a former student, who recalled both his surprise and his pain in a writing class when I suddenly ripped his copy paper from his typewriter and retyped his story to show him how the work should be done. Others have confirmed such behavior as one of my teaching excesses.

In retrospect, my behavior seems cruel and unusual, even to me. But I still am at a loss to explain what else I could have done to show how and why news must be handled quickly, crisply, and on the spot. As some deskman whose name I have long forgotten once shouted at me years ago when, on 7 A.M. rewrite, I was dreaming of how to begin a two-paragraph piece based on an incomplete police report: "Get going, you! Go with what you've got!" To which a latter-day student added, with equal grammatical disregard, when I tried to jar him into immediate action, "And if you ain't got much, it's too damned bad." Through such methods as these, I fear I may have interfered with the aspirations of many a student who wanted to be a novelist, dramatist, or poet. In extenuation of my faults as a teacher, I would plead that I tried as best I could to advance the training of the next generation of journalists in an open society at home and abroad.

There were many times in academe when I had to work under great pressure, something I thought would be impossible in the leisurely processes of teaching. However, the dramatic events of the last week of October 1962 proved me wrong. For in that period, the seventy-five or so members of the Columbia journalism Class of 1963, their instructors, and I all had to face up to the possibility of an atomic war with the Soviets.

During much of that tense month, there had been fairly reliable reports out of Washington, topped by some colorful language in the U.S. Senate, suggesting that something deadly serious was going on in Fidel Castro's Cuba. But until the night of October 22, 1962, when President John F. Kennedy went on national television to announce an air and naval blockade of Cuba, the nation scarcely realized that the Soviets were bent on installing atomic-tipped missiles on the island only ninety miles away. Hal Hendrix of the *Miami News* published the first hint.

In my diary for the next day, I noted that the students and instructors in my weekly newswriting class were jittery—and with good reason. All of us were concentrating on the probable Soviet reaction to the blockade Kennedy had ordered. The little historical exercise I had prepared for October 24, the seventeenth birthday of the UN, aroused little interest, although I tried to persuade the students to concentrate on rewriting my fact sheet.

On the evidence of my diary entries for that week, it was no go. What we always tried to do in that class was handle the students in small groups, seven or eight to an instructor, for a three-hour session at their typewriters in our big second-floor newsroom. But that day and the next, all eyes and ears were on the wire service machines that clacked away in our wire room, with bells sounding on and off for bulletins and flashes to give the alarm for new developments.

The issue was whether Premier Nikita S. Khrushchev, from Moscow, would challenge the United States by sending aircraft or ships to run the blockade. Having some knowledge of the mood in the Pentagon at first hand from my own experience, I knew perfectly well that both the Strategic and Tactical Air Commands were on alert, as were the Navy's combat aircraft on their big carriers, lying off the Cuban coast.

In my diary for those tense days, there are entries that capture the mood of the crisis better than anything else I can write now.

"It's like a fantasy, which it is not. . . . Prepared Associated Press copy to show the students how the story was being handled nationally. . . . Students were jittery, expecting the Russians to try to run the blockade and getting shot down. . . ."

October 25: "We let a Soviet tanker through our Cuban blockade . . . a screwy, impossible day when a lot of things were happening. . . . [And at last, relief during that weekend] The Cuban war is over. . . . Khrushchev said he would remove the missiles and bases, Kennedy said he would call off the blockade. The UN is being called into session, Castro has piped down and the status quo is restored. . . ."

Subsequently, although I could not wedge the entire 1963 class into the UN sideshow Khrushchev put on following the Cuban crisis, a few of the class did manage to observe the Russian's peculiar behavior. However, I have no recollection that any of them were able to describe the garish scene with the completeness of that sometime journalist and member of the U.S. delegation, Eleanor Roosevelt, who wrote: "Mr. Khrushchev banged his shoe on the table, he shouted, he interrupted, he behaved hysterically and with gross bad manners. . . . One result of Mr. Khrushchev's attack on the Secretary General was the tremendous tribute paid to Dag Hammarskjold in the vote of the UN special session. The adopted resolution passed 70–0 with a number of abstentions."

I shall have to leave it to the surviving members of the Class of 1963, now three decades out of school, to judge the effectiveness of their training in the handling of global emergencies such as the Cuban crisis and the UN session that followed it. Among them are editors and publishers, including the president of a large and powerful American newspaper group; a number of present and former Washington and foreign correspondents; university people and government civil servants; the editor of one of the two dominant national news magazines; and an erstwhile candidate for a presidential nomination.

On my own part, this was one of the two heart-stoppers of the 1960s that I wish I could have handled with greater understanding as a teacher. The other was the assassination of President Kennedy in the following year when I was on sabbatical leave and nowhere near a classroom. I doubt if any description of that scene in mere words could have had the impact on the nation that the few moments of television footage conveyed when the cameras caught Jacqueline Kennedy crying over the body of her husband in the back of their open limousine that November 22, 1963, in downtown Dallas. It was this tragic scene recorded by Merriman Smith for United Press International and a sorrowing nation that won him a Pulitzer Prize in 1964.

13 ★ CONFLICT ON CAMPUS

Everybody I knew at Columbia assured me that it couldn't happen to us. But it did.

That morning of May 1, 1970, when I reached our campus and saw a red flag flying from the mathematics building, I knew we were in for it. The student riots that had been sweeping through every major university and a lot of smaller ones finally had caught up with us.

Why Columbia?

I'm still not sure. Of course the Vietnam War was unpopular, but that had been evident for years. In the early 1960s, long before the war had reached its peak, there had been scattered but ugly incidents on campus that had been linked to the earliest anti-Vietnam protests.

I remember being summoned to an emergency meeting of the University Council to deal with a student riot in the late spring of 1965, in which our Navy ROTC was prevented from marching by an aroused band of protestors. I wrote at the time in my diary: "We tried to cool off the administration. If the university executives get defiant and start cracking down, they will only play into the hands of the protestors. It takes me back to 1933."

Only this wasn't 1933 and the bottom of the Great Depression. Moreover, even if some of my colleagues suspected Communist influences were at work behind the anti-Vietnam movement, something that had been so clearly evident in our economic crises of 1933, I doubt very much that our students during the Vietnam War were reacting to some fiendish undercover plot hatched in Moscow.

No, this seemed to me to be a continuation of the antiwar rioting that began at Columbia College and spread to the rest of the campus. There was no particular symbolism to May Day except that on April 30, as my diary pointed out, President Nixon had ordered an attack on Cambodia and I'm sure the students realized, as all the rest of us did, that this would prolong the war. But I also believe that the season had something to do with it, too, because the academic year was almost over and it was, from the students' point of view, a time to blow off steam on almost any pretext. Nixon had given them one.

From then on, in Vietnam as well as in the nation's capital and on many a university campus including our own at Columbia, everything in that ill-starred war led straight downhill into the bottomless pit of national recrimination.

By a curious combination of circumstances, as early as 1955, I had come across our leaning toward involvement in Vietnam without realizing it at the time. What I was concerned about then during the Eisenhower administration was the difficulty of separating emotion from reason in the formulation of a realistic American defense policy in the Pacific. We had only then just begun to emerge from the drawn war in Korea and hadn't really gotten over the enormous sacrifices the nation had had to make in the Pacific conflict against Japan in World War II.

In that year of 1955, at any rate, I was bound across the Pacific and had stopped off at Pearl Harbor. I recall how moved I was when I stood for the first time on the planking over the wreckage of the USS *Arizona*. Nor could I dismiss the memory of Pearl Harbor from my mind entirely as I continued with what turned out to be a six-week, 20,000-mile survey for the U.S. Air Force broadly covering the area bounded by Hawaii, the Philippines, Taipei, and Japan. My report dealt with our problems with the peoples in the countries we had bases in at the time.

What I found was that, except in Hawaii and in Taipei (the Chinese Nationalist refuge from their triumphant Communist foes), we were regarded with the mistrust and suspicion attached to an occupying power. Vietnam then was not yet an important consideration in our strategic approach to an all-Pacific defense because President Eisenhower, in the previous year, had rejected the French plea for American armed intervention in southeast Asia.

Consequently, it did not seem to matter to the American public that the Eisenhower administration (already in 1955) was spending enormous sums of money to bolster neighboring regimes in Laos and Cambodia.

The figures I was given at the time showed that American grants to the Cambodian government of Prince Norodom Sihanouk had topped $366 million beginning in 1954. And in Laos, the bill at the time was for economic assistance for King Savang Vatthana $328 million, with another $200 million or so for military aid.

It follows, as I realized when our military commitment to Vietnam actually began, that neither President Eisenhower nor President Kennedy had leveled with the American public on what they really were up to in southeast Asia. In 1954, Ike was asking Ngo Dinh Diem in South Vietnam how the United States could "assist Vietnam in its present hour of trial." And Kennedy, without any public announcement, had put 3,200 American military personnel in South Vietnam by the end of 1961, his first year in the White House. Many more were yet to come, although I couldn't have anticipated that in my 1955 report to the Secretary of the Air Force.

What I did do in 1955 and in subsequent reports on the "limited war" in the Pacific area was to emphasize the increasingly critical views of peoples near our bases on the East Asian perimeter, including the Philippines where young men in the former American territory were taking to the hills to oppose their own government and ours. To say the least, our outlook in East Asia was cloudy, although I could scarcely guess at the extent of public disenchantment at home once the Vietnam War took form.

The most I thought of, six years after that first expedition to the Far East, was to warn my faculty colleagues at Columbia, during a staff luncheon, not to expect too much of our Asian graduate students who then formed about 10 percent of our enrollment. War on the Asian mainland involving American air and ground forces was bound to put them in a difficult position, and it was my belief, therefore, that we ought to anticipate at least some critical attitudes toward the United States.

What actually did happen was that the Asian students, being strangers within our gates, were much less outspoken against the war than their American colleagues.

Altogether, my contact with the Vietnam War, once it escalated, was much closer than I had bargained for as an elderly ex–World War II type. In various capacities, I made three trips through Southeast Asia in the 1960s and early 1970s and twice came within range of the shooting in Vietnam.

In the summer of 1964, when Dorothy and I arrived in Saigon for the first time, I was on a research project for the Council on Foreign Relations and was invited to lunch by the newly appointed American commander, General William C. Westmoreland, who wasn't at all backward about predicting a vastly enlarged war that would take in neighboring Laos and Cambodia as well as Vietnam. He told me then, "The only way this war can be won is to fight one campaign in all three countries."

I must say I was greatly impressed. But when I returned to our hotel, the Caravelle, I found that the lobby had been bombed by a Vietcong soldier. Both Dorothy and I might well have been blown up with the furniture had we been there at the time. It considerably cooled my enthusiasm for the Westmoreland doctrine of victory.

Later on during that visit, I flew north to Kontum with General Westmoreland and saw even more dismal prospects of a victorious war for American arms. Most of the countryside then had been seized by the Vietcong guerrilla forces even before the massive entry of the North Vietnamese army. The South Vietnamese soldiers evidently were no match for the rebels. It was clear enough even at that early stage in the war that we would have to either pull out or bomb North Vietnam and fight the war with American ground troops as well.

When Dorothy and I returned to Saigon a second time, in 1970, on another Asian book project (this one for the Ford Foundation) while I was on sabbatical from Columbia, the war still was not being won, even though we had moved in with a half million or so ground troops and tried to use air power against North Vietnam and Cambodia, the sanctuary for the Vietcong. Nothing seemed to work right for us in that war.

Still, looking back in my diaries for that period, I can see very little evidence that I was aware early on that the outcome might be seriously affected by the growing disenchantment of the American public—and particularly of the university students of draft age. I still put greater stock in the old-fashioned military doctrine that wars are won or lost on the battlefield. The importance of the devastating public role in that conflict came to me only with the passage of years, even though I worried from the outset over the alienation of the native peoples near our Asian bases. With hindsight, this myopic view can best be documented from a few random entries in my diaries.

April 21, 1964: "At the State Dept. in the a.m., I heard Secretary Rusk at top form explain why we weren't rushing into new foreign policy ventures. The current line, he said, is paying off too well in the light of Soviet-Chinese quarrels. Next, to the White House rose garden and heard President Johnson speak with the fervor of an evangelist of his foreign aid programs. He strode about hatless and coatless in the damp, cloudy atmosphere."

However, there is no record that either I or anybody else that day asked the President or Secretary Rusk about the reason for such slow progress in the Vietnam War and the rising clamor from General Westmoreland for more American troops and American air power. To continue with another entry:

"May 22, 1965: The all-day Orvil Dryfoos–sponsored conference at Dartmouth, this year on what Europeans think of us. . . . European and American journalists stood together against the academics, government and CIA types. The academics hated it, the journalists tolerated it. . . ."

In few words, the critical European view of the American performance in Vietnam was becoming an embarrassment at home and few of us knew what to do about it. Nor did the White House or State Department. Then came this:

February 21, 1966: Saw Bill Moyers, LBJ's press secretary, and told him about our 50th anniversary dinner at Columbia to celebrate the Pulitzer Prizes on May 10, 1966 and our invitation to the President to be the main speaker. Moyers promised to help."

Moyers couldn't deliver, despite his goodwill. Probably because of the multiple Pulitzer Prizes that already had been bestowed on American correspondents critical of the Vietnam War, President Johnson never replied to the invitation to address the Pulitzer celebration. Although it was evident by then that the public opposition to the war was rising and student antiwar demonstrations had begun, the enormity of the protest movement had yet to be felt. LBJ, Rusk, and Westmoreland still were going by the book and fighting the war on the battlefield without paying attention to the home front.

I had been trying meanwhile to bring the feeling of war into the classroom. One of the first to come to my newswriting class for a news conference was the newly appointed South Vietnamese ambassador to Washington, an eloquent and combative little diplomat named Vu Van Thai.

Just before the opening of the 1965–66 academic year, I had heard him make a fervent plea for understanding before a meeting of government and academic Asian specialists at Wingspread, Frank Lloyd Wright's gorgeous conference center at Racine, Wisconsin. The specialists were impressed, so I thought it might be worthwhile for him to come to Columbia, and he agreed.

To his surprise and mine as well, Ambassador Vu's news conference at Columbia fell flat. The Class of 1966 gave him a cold reception, which represented quite a difference in point of view between the new generation of journalists and their elders in government and academe.

Nevertheless, despite rising student protests against the war elsewhere in the United States (with minimal responses at the time on the Columbia campus), I kept news conferences and lectures going about the Vietnam War in both my newswriting and my foreign correspondence classes. It was the big story. It merited the interest of young professionals.

With the help of our School of International Affairs, and Professor Philip Mosely in particular, all the arguments as well as the background on the conflict were thoroughly ventilated. But the result continued to be awkward for both the students and myself. The news conferences with specialists produced little response; much of the written work, although professional in scope, showed little interest and no spark.

It was apparent that everything about the Vietnam War, even the work of the young correspondents in the field who were so critical, seemed unappealing to the students, my own and others elsewhere. I suppose they all wished mightily that this inconvenient war would just go away. (Probably, by that time, Messrs. Johnson and Rusk also would have been greatly obliged to see it disappear.) But wars have a habit of hanging on—and that was the unpleasing aspect of this one.

Finally, it occurred to me that a working war correspondent who came to the classroom might make a difference in the kind of instruction I was trying to present—the practical work of a reporter in the field. My opportunity came when Harrison Salisbury of the *New York Times,* a Pulitzer Prize winner in 1955, came home from a controversial assignment in Hanoi, North Vietnam, early in 1967. Because he was an old friend and already under criticism for reporting from the enemy side, he agreed to come to Columbia immediately. And that, I thought, was a break for the students.

I introduced Harrison briefly, explaining that he had been the first and to date the only American who had gone into enemy territory after the massive American bombing raids on the North Vietnamese capital. He had arrived by air in Hanoi on December 23, 1966, from Vientiane by courtesy of the International Control Commission and had remained there until mid-January. The immediacy of news interest in Hanoi was beyond question, for American bombers had flown over the city as recently as December 13 and 14.

To quote from my diary on his appearance:

"Harrison Salisbury came to my newswriting class and made an eloquent defense of his reporting from Hanoi but conceded that it would have been treason had Congress declared war on North Vietnam. Our students gave him a very cool reception."

Although I have never pretended to be expert at reading the student mind, I would suspect that the coolness was not so much toward Salisbury personally as an almost total lack of interest in anything about the Vietnam War.

At any rate, the veteran correspondent was submitted for his second Pulitzer Prize that year by the *New York Times* but lost out to John Hughes of the *Christian Science Monitor,* whose reporting from Indonesia was both important and less controversial.

Even so, an unbiased reporting jury of five editors voted 4–1 for Salisbury that spring. But in the Pulitzer board's deliberations, despite Chairman Pulitzer's championship of his cause, Salisbury lost to Hughes 6–5. And at the meeting later of the university Trustees, the board's decision was upheld by an equally close vote. Thereafter, Turner Catledge, the *Times*'s managing editor, accused the board of voting on political rather than professional grounds.

I have stressed the differences between the students and their peers because I believe it accounts, to some extent, for the overwhelming opposition the students led all over the country to oppose the war in 1968, directly after the success of the enemy's Tet (Lunar New Year) offensive beginning January 31, 1968. Student strikes against colleges and universities spread across the nation with the realization that all President Johnson's forecasts of victory had been a sham.

There was trouble at Columbia, too, with campus guards and city police being called to restore order after student rampages. It was costly to the university in more ways than one, for President Kirk retired soon afterward at age sixty-five and Dean Barrett left the Journalism School, as well.

In an effort to restore order across the country, President Johnson halted the bombing of North Vietnam except for border areas, proposed peace talks, and announced he would not be a candidate for reelection. Temporarily, there was a "war moratorium," as the students called it; some of us in the Columbia faculty, myself included, held our classes outside our building for a few days that spring at the request of the students. It was refreshing, but it did little good, for the war continued.

President Nixon tried to be reassuring at first when he succeeded LBJ in 1969. He told the American people that he was for "Vietnamization" of the war, meaning that the North and South Vietnamese were to do most of the fighting and American troops gradually would be withdrawn. He made good on his pledge of withdrawing a majority of the 535,000 American ground forces, the peak of the American commitment. But suddenly, he reversed course, widened the war to Laos and Cambodia, and let it be known that he would destroy the sanctuaries of the Vietcong in both neighboring countries. So American forces went into action once again, along with South Vietnamese and a minor group of Cambodians who joined the anti-Communist action. In my diary, date of April 30, the entry reads: "Nixon's order to U.S. troops to attack in Cambodia was a terrible shock tonight." That was when the campus riots flared anew. To make matters worse, jittery National Guardsmen shot and killed four protesting students on May 4, 1970, at Kent State University in Ohio. And from then on, it was hopeless at Columbia as well as a lot of other universities. It was impossible to maintain academic discipline.

Of the nation's 2,550 colleges and universities, according to the Carnegie Commission on Higher Education, 21 percent closed down, 4 percent called police to halt riots, and 57 percent in all suffered from organized student dissent in varied forms. Too late, President Nixon recalled the American forces from Cambodia and let the native troops struggle on alone, there and in Laos.

But the damage had been done. After that, there was little hope for anything constructive to come out of the American participation in the conflict. The best we academics were able to expect was that sufficient order could be restored on our campus and others to permit us to continue teaching for the 1970s.

For Dean Andrew W. Cordier of the School of International Affairs, who had become acting president of Columbia after Grayson Kirk's retirement, it was a risky situation. But he stuck it out in his interim role, was rewarded with a year as university president, and then returned to his own school in 1972 in favor of Dr. William J. McGill. However, no sooner had Dr. McGill taken office as Columbia's president than more trouble erupted when the American bombing of North Vietnam was resumed in force. During these demonstrations, I was in the middle once again because they occurred during the Pulitzer Prize judging and the students threatened to close us down along with everything else on campus.

First of all, the antiwar demonstrators occupied four campus buildings beginning April 24, 1972. Dr. McGill patiently obtained court orders to force a reopening of the buildings, which did not include the Journalism Building for the time being, and personally served them on the student strikers. By the end of the day, all four were reopened temporarily. But overnight they were reoccupied and the harassed president had to call the police.

This time, rather than start a pitched battle, the students vacated the buildings on their own accord. But by nightfall, all four—and a fifth—were seized. On April 26, I wrote in my diary: "All the excitement about Columbia is outside the campus. Here, things are fairly quiet even though five buildings are still held by the strikers.... Anyway, we are surviving."

I was warned that there would be a disruption of the Pulitzer Prize announcement, but nothing happened. Although I took precautions by moving my usual meeting with the reporters off campus, we were undisturbed. All the buildings finally were reopened, the last being Hamilton Hall at 5:45 A.M. on May 1, 1972, and the Pulitzer announcement went off that day as scheduled. For a few days thereafter, our students among others refused to attend classes as part of their antiwar protest, their "war moratorium." But after a while, they wearied, and we resumed a shaky schedule of classes, final examinations, and awards to close the academic year at Commencement. Our experience, so I was told, was fairly typical of what had happened in other colleges and universities.

No matter what the White House did after that, Vietnam was marked down as a losing cause. At the end, on April 29, 1975, the few remaining Americans fled Saigon in disorder just ahead of the takeover by a vanguard of the North Vietnamese army and the Vietcong. Saigon became Ho Chi Minh City, despite the efforts of four American presidents to avert so shamefully complete a disaster to American arms.

The only winners in this country, in a sense, were the student strikers, but even that was debatable as subsequent events demonstrated. Our new dean, Elie Abel, seemed to derive a certain amount of satisfaction thereafter in stressing the difficulties that students would have in obtaining jobs in our field during periods of economic downturn. I suppose he couldn't be blamed.

14 ★ "I TREAD THE WORLD"

The transition of the working journalist to more enduring pursuits is often likely to span the entire rainbow of emotions ranging from joy to pain. Regardless of how the changeling may twist and turn to adjust to a new environment, new options, and new challenges, the problems are real and must be faced with a certain amount of resolution.

This was the mood in which I shifted from a quarter century of daily newspaper work to the supposed atmosphere of reflective calm on Morningside Heights among the academic elite on the Columbia campus. At last, so I thought, I would have time to devote myself entirely to reading, writing, teaching—and especially to the publication of a few books of more or less enduring quality.

But it wasn't to be quite that easy.

Although I could scarcely compare my situation toward century's end to the position of the late editor of the *Brooklyn Eagle,* Walt Whitman, in his transition from workaday journalist to poet in the middle of the nineteenth century, something of Whitman's reflections struck a responsive chord in me. And this was particularly true when he sang:

It is ended—I dally no more,
After today, I inure myself to run, leap, swim, wrestle, fight . . .

I henceforth tread the world, chaste, temperate, an early riser,
    a gymnast, a steady grower,
Every hour the semen of centuries—and still of centuries.

I will follow up these continual lessons of the air, water, earth,
I perceive I have no time to lose.

Poetic musings weren't likely to create a stir within me, however, much as I clung to this poet's *Leaves of Grass* and shared his enthusiasm for music, theater, the oddities of human nature, and travel to far-off places. But, like many another journalist in every age and every land from the time of Herodotus, the father of history, I continued to feel the urge to express myself in whatever way was open to me.

All this may sound far too highflown for an ex-reporter who suddenly found himself in what was, occasionally, a more sedate university atmosphere. But this was how I felt and it was to lead to consequences considerably beyond my expectations.

My first books were workaday: an anthology with suitable commentary on some of the best of the Pulitzer Prizes in journalism, then a journalism textbook, which to my surprise went through five editions and was translated into a number of different languages including Arabic and Chinese.

If these modest works did nothing else, they at least gave me the confidence to continue writing, which every writer needs. However, I recall how much I hesitated before I tried anything more ambitious in my earliest years at Columbia. True (as has been the case with many a youthful scribbler from time immemorial) I had batted out novels at a furious pace from the time I was old enough to hammer at the old Oliver typewriter my father brought to me as a child. But at Columbia, I couldn't very well take a chance on such youthful effusions, especially after being given the added responsibility of administering the Pulitzer Prizes.

No, what I thought of continuously in my first productive years at the university was a critical study of foreign correspondence that would by no means be limited to the United States. My aim originally was to reflect on the impact of major developments in foreign affairs on the body politic—and vice versa—as seen through the sometimes clouded lens of the reporter. However, the ambitious nature of the undertaking made me continue to hesitate.

What finally happened was that I confided my hopes, desires, and frustrations to a sympathetic auditor, Grayson Kirk, soon after he assumed the university's presidency following General Eisenhower's departure for the White House and after I began handling the Pulitzer Prizes.

That, of course, had not been the purpose of our conference, which had to do with the Pulitzer awards, but I simply took a chance afterward by imposing myself on him.

At once, I thought I was in trouble. For although President Kirk listened patiently to my projected research into the annals of foreign correspondence, he made no immediate comment. Indeed, when he sent me on my way back to the Journalism Building, I thought I'd annoyed him unduly with a personal problem. I was wrong. Several days later I received a note from him, which I still have and which I still occasionally take from its file and reread in moments of discouragement over the literary process. As a professional historian and scholar of consequence, he wrote, "I feel strongly that a history of foreign correspondence would be well worth the time and study that would go into it. . . . I would encourage you by all means to go ahead with it."

The date was January 28, 1960, ten years after I had left daily newspaper work and come to Columbia. Not long afterward, I began the first of several hundred interviews with working foreign correspondents I had known and associated with. In addition I wrote to many others. It became wonderfully fascinating to me because the reaction of most of my sources was so wholehearted, intimate, and rewarding.

The problem, as I soon realized, was that I had become so absorbed in that early part of my study that I had lost sight of the historical element in which President Kirk had been primarily interested. As with far greater works of consequence, regardless of form and content, my first attempt at a meaningful book had suddenly developed a life of its own and was about to get out of hand.

What to do? Very little, except to follow my somewhat erratic star to see where it would lead me.

During this process, plus continued reading on the subject—both from the shelves of the Columbia University libraries and by the generosity of great newspapers that made their clipping morgues available to me—I realized I was permitting my enthusiasm for the present to overshadow the presumed glories of the past among the battling brigadiers of the press. How this would play with both the public and the reviewers concerned me, but I was blessed if I knew what to do about it. So I continued my book work along with my teaching and the special responsibility of the Pulitzer Prize administration and continued to hope for the best.

One summer's day more than a year later, in 1961, I discussed my problem with an old friend and fellow swimmer at Iron Pier Beach on Long Island Sound while Dorothy and I were vacationing in Aquebogue. My authority in this case was disinterested but impressive—the suffragan bishop of the Episcopal diocese of Long Island, Dr. Charles W. MacLean (who could if the mood seized him float on his back offshore while smoking a cigar).

At a time when Bishop MacLean was reclining on the rocky shore after such a floating exhibition, I outlined my predicament. Upon reflection, and several long pulls on his cigar, he became severe with me and demanded, "How can you justify a few snappy chapters on the background of foreign correspondence and some rambling observations on what is going on now, when you should be digging into the origin and evolution of the art, if that is what it is, and trying to read some meaning into it?"

Very well, I had my answer. One does not argue such matters with an Episcopal bishop or with a university president. Nor was I inclined to debate further with my editor at Columbia University Press, from which I had received a scholarly grant for the project. I took my lumps as an aspiring author, changed direction, and carried on.

By the end of 1962, my research, conversations, and correspondence with current foreign correspondents and their editors were reasonably complete. Despite all my doubts (and I had many of them), it was time for me to produce some reasonable approximation of a manuscript if I ever intended to achieve publication. I worked hard at it, finished a first draft within about six months and then went back over it to rewrite parts that needed clarification and remove others I thought I could dispense with. At last, lo and behold, the work was finished, presented with a timorous appearance of calm to the chief editor at Columbia University Press and, in due course, accepted.

I thought I was through, but once again much more remained to be done. First of all, I had to find an acceptable title for this new work. Not just anything would do; best-seller or not—and we all knew in advance that scholarship and not sales would be the test of this work's acceptance— its title did have to fit the book.

It sounds so simple-minded to reduce this process to a mere sentence in this narrative about the production of a serious work, but I was finally given to understand that titling a book was no mere mechanical consideration. We sat around my office in the Journalism Building late one afternoon—some of the people from Columbia University Press; my friend and colleague, Dick Baker; my secretary; occasionally a few students who came in to ask a question about *their* work who were permitted to stay while I finished mine. Looking at them all now and then, it seemed to me that the young people were as intrigued by this title-choosing process as I was.

After about an hour of general idea-bouncing back and forth, Professor Baker spread both hands upward in a gesture of heavenly appeal (in keeping with his training as a Methodist minister in Iowa) and asked somewhat critically, "Why not call it 'Foreign Correspondence'?"

Well! This may have been logical but—to me at least—it wasn't very exciting. Still, my editor was pleased. He pointed out to me that a book about foreign correspondence ought to have some reference to that in its title, otherwise the selective public interested in the subject might never find it. So at last, it was done. Completed. Finished.

Four years after President Kirk had recommended the research to me, the book was issued as *Foreign Correspondence: The Great Reporters and Their Times*. In a flattering front-page review in the *New York Times* Sunday Book Review section, a former foreign correspondent concluded that my work made "absorbing reading," but he added quickly, "One possible quibble is that he attempted too much."

Fair enough. I was perfectly willing to admit it for the sake of so positive a review in a newspaper that specialized in foreign correspondence. I wish I could add that a discerning public swarmed to the bookstores in New York and elsewhere and fairly tore my work from the shelves. That, alas, is much more likely to happen to more popular writers of books with either a romantic or a murderous flavor, take your pick. I had done enough of both in my younger years, mainly on tight newspaper deadlines, to last me a lifetime and couldn't have been paid enough to produce a book on either subject at my advanced time of life.

Fortunately, it wasn't necessary for me to do so to earn a decent living for my family. I wasn't writing in a highly competitive book market and my publishers, the people I wrote about, and the modest public that bought my work seemed satisfied with what I had done in my first real effort to produce a useful critical study of some consequence.

This had happened not when I was twenty-six and writing at a gallop to do a Parisian novel that began the night of the Four Arts Ball, but rather when I was sixty-two and considerably more settled in life. When the Parisian novel did come out in paperback long after I had forgotten it (which is another story entirely), it became a mild curiosity among my family and friends. One somewhat caustic editor even expressed the crude suspicion that I hadn't written it, which was a commentary of a sort on my progress or lack of it.

I have come by my liking for books about journalists and journalism honestly. And why not? Both have been a part of my life from the time at age seventeen I choked up as I was about to ask a question of the first American President who was close enough to me to act as a verbal sparring partner. Indeed, when the subject matter for a proposed book included foreign affairs as well as presidents and reporters, no one has ever had to twist my arm to persuade me to go to work immediately, if not sooner. Quite naturally, when the Council on Foreign Relations provided me with an imposing study group as background for my Asian book in the early 1960s, I jumped at the chance.

It was a lucky break for me in several ways. Having already agreed to work in the State Department's American Specialist program, the proposed tour—over 12,000 miles to seven nations, through thirty-five Asian cities, on my sabbatical leave—fitted in nicely with the council's program. What this trip actually amounted to, therefore, was a necessary conditioning exercise for my later meetings with the council's study group and for the book that eventually resulted.

All of us in the study group were poignantly aware of the problems that already had piled up for the United States in Southeast Asia, especially in Vietnam, but we could exert no influence there. Instead, our chairman, Philip Horton, focused our interest on the long-range prospects for improved American relationships with such major Asian powers as China, India, Pakistan, and Japan, as well as on the Soviet Union's mounting campaign to arouse greater opposition to us in each of those lands.

As a result, the council sent me on still another and even longer trip for four months, in the summer of 1964, to consult as many prominent Asians as I could on the sources of anti-American prejudice in their respective countries and to ask what could be done about it. We chose to call it an exercise in public diplomacy, especially as it affected the great newspapers and largely government-controlled electronic media in the area.

For me, in particular, it was a useful experiment. For in my graduate seminars at Columbia, I already was aware that a sizable number of future foreign editors and correspondents—both Americans and Asians—were taking their first steps in training for their specialties. That year of 1964–65 and the subsequent academic year, therefore, were crowded with weekly council study sessions, trips to the UN with my students, my other classes, Pulitzer responsibilities, and fairly regular visits to the White House and State Department in Washington.

All in all, it took me another four years to complete and publish the council's book, *Between Two Worlds,* which came out in 1967. After that, for my part, I was ready to call it quits for Asian-American relations for a while. But it didn't work out that way. *Between Two Worlds* won good reviews and several honors, including a distinguished service award from the Society of Professional Journalists, my second after *Foreign Correspondence*. Such reactions as these, I was given to understand, were the equivalent in academic terms of a best-seller on the broader public market.

I was satisfied. All I wanted to do now was handle my regular assignments—my classes and the Pulitzers—and try to reflect in my sixties on what I should do with the rest of my life. My chance for reflection didn't last long, however. The Ford Foundation invited me to undertake still another Asian assignment for a new book that would be centered on the directions being taken by Asia's non-Communist leaders.

With my acceptance, I worked on the new book for another four years, concluding with my next sabbatical in 1970–71. This time, Dorothy and I traveled around 50,000 miles, and I consulted all manner of people ranging from revolutionary student activists to heads of state. I also taught for limited periods at the East-West Center in Hawaii and the Chinese University of Hong Kong and puzzled over the shape of the new world order that seemed to be emerging in the Far East. The result was

New Era in the Pacific: An Adventure in Public Diplomacy, which was published in 1972.

After striving for much of my career to publish books that might have more than a mere transitory meaning, I now had much more than I could handle. After the first Asian book in 1967, I had published another book the following year called *The News Media: A Journalist Looks at His Profession.* Next, I had accepted a commission from the Knight Foundation to research and write a book about the uses of the First Amendment, *Free Press, Free People: The Best Cause,* which was in the final stages before its publication when I came home to do the second Asian volume.

In retrospect, I'm not quite sure how I managed to handle my classes, the Pulitzer Prize competition, and all the overlapping book projects without either a grievous mishap or a nervous collapse. I knew I had paid a high price in nervous exhaustion from undertaking too much work—a fault that dogged me through much of my career. Now I really wanted a breather.

But along came a Pulitzer Prize celebration on which I hadn't really counted. For in 1966, all of us at Columbia who had ever had anything to do with the awards had celebrated their fiftieth anniversary with a gala reception and dinner, to which the ticket of admission was a Pulitzer Prize. And now, in 1976, both Columbia and the Pulitzer board wanted to do something special to recognize the sixtieth anniversary of the prizes. And so, in due course, instead of being able to confine myself to my classes and related duties, I was asked in addition to prepare a history of the Pulitzer Prizes, well in advance of their sixtieth birthday.

My main problem with the Pulitzer history was that I could scarcely confine it to a recital of the known records of the awards, which my predecessors and I had compiled. There were, I suspected, things in the administration of the Pulitzers by my predecessors that either had been omitted from the record or hadn't been fully reported.

That meant there was still more research to do. And the most difficult question I had to answer was where and to whom I could apply to ensure that the many Pulitzer controversies over the years would be fully told this time.

All I can set down here is that I tried every living source within reach, sometimes came up with conflicting accounts of the way the same prize had been awarded, and then had to make an independent judgment of my own. At this late date I can only hope, therefore, that *The Pulitzer Prizes: A History,* published in 1974, told the story as completely and honestly as the current members of the Pulitzer board would have wished.

In any event, the Pulitzer history fulfilled a need. For the hundredth anniversary of the prizes, come the year 2016, the Administrator of that era should not have to do too much digging through old records to update the story of the awards as I presented it. Some of these files already were slowly dissolving in my time, and the memories of the surviving participants whom I interviewed often seemed shaky. With luck and good management, my history ought to survive.

Of the other books that I have done since, the one I hoped would make the greatest impression professionally, *A Crisis for the American Press,* received the least attention from the newspapers I had intended to help in 1978, the year of its publication.

The only news organizations that seemed to heed my somewhat subdued warning about the weakening of the First Amendment in our time were the Society of Professional Journalists, which voted me my third distinguished service award and still another for my teaching, and the Gannett Foundation, which awarded me a most welcome grant for further research on the subject. (My other three volumes were minor works—another textbook, another anthology, and the remaining curiosity of my experiences as a bookman, the paperback publication of the Parisian novel I had written in my twenties.)

Today, only a little more than a decade after the publication of the *Crisis* book, I would repeat my warning against taking the terms of the First Amendment for granted. Long ago, in 1922, William Allen White of the *Emporia* (Kansas) *Gazette,* put the position in trenchant terms:

"You say that freedom of utterance is not for time of stress and I reply with the sad truth that only in time of stress is freedom of utterance in danger. This state today is in more danger from suppression than from violence because, in the end, suppression leads to violence."

What we can anticipate is a greater effort to show that limits must be put on the First Amendment, which our colleagues in the law stress as essential to the preservation of the rule for a fair trial and that the charlatans of the far right would crush by all conceivable means. This movement is already far advanced, I believe.

With the number of daily newspapers in the United States already reduced by more than half, and with only a few two-newspaper cities remaining across the land, the defense of a free press is likely to be further weakened if greater inroads against the First Amendment cannot be checked. Like it or not, government-licensed broadcasters, with few exceptions, have little stomach for committing themselves to a fight for the public's right to free expression as well as their own. That effort will have to be made by the surviving champions of a free press.

As for myself, what I have done as I approach my ninetieth year is to complete a new edition of *Foreign Correspondence: The Great Reporters and Their Times,* which brings me full circle in my effort to produce an enduring work of consequence for a free press.

15 ★ LOOKING BACK

Had it not been for Joseph Pulitzer's $2 million bequest that made possible the creation of his Journalism School and the Pulitzer Prizes, neither education for journalism nor journalism as a profession could have taken shape as quickly as they did in this century.

Within the span of my lifetime, both have expanded in influence and stature in America. Although there is still a long way to go before public doubts about some of our excesses can be dispelled, I do believe we have progressed, mainly through the foresight of Pulitzer, Adolph Ochs, William Allen White, and a few other farsighted pioneers.

At the turn of the century, the feeling was general among journalists that experience was the only teacher and the only prize worth striving for was money. Much the same point of view had been prevalent early on in law and medicine when the first schools for lawyers and physicians were founded.

Journalists, so all but a thoughtful few insisted, had to be practical people who needed no ivory tower of learning to gather, process, and distribute the news. Such things, they said, could not be taught. But this, of course, was when print was king and electronic journalism, with its greater complications, hadn't even been imagined.

If Pulitzer was not the first to turn against this concept, I believe he was by far the strongest supporter of special education for journalists at the university level. And so it came about that he selected Columbia as a laboratory for that purpose, because it was, in a phrase current at that era, "on the main highway of events" in America.

In Pulitzer's negotiations with Columbia early in this century for the opening of a journalism school that he would endow, he wrote in the May issue of the *North American Review* in 1904 that what he wanted was an institution that would "exalt principle, knowledge, culture, at the expense of business if need be." As for the anti-intellectuals, with their mockery of higher education for professionals, he observed that the only position open to people by reason of birth was that of idiot.

In a famous passage, he wrote:

"What is a journalist? Not any business manager or publisher, or even a proprietor. A journalist is the lookout on the bridge of the ship of state. He notes the passing sail, the little things of interest that dot the horizon in fine weather. He reports the drifting castaway whom the ship can save. He peers through the fog and storm to give warning of dangers ahead. He is not thinking of his wages or the profits of his owners. He is there to watch over the safety and the welfare of the people who trust him."

He elaborated on his strong belief in the public service mission of the press when he wrote:

"Our Republic and its press will rise or fall together. An able, disinterested, public-spirited press, with trained intelligence to know the right and courage to do it, can preserve that public virtue without which popular government is a sham and a mockery. A cynical, mercenary, demagogic, corrupt press will produce in time a people as base as itself. The power to mold the future of the Republic will be in the hands of the journalists of future generations."

These were grand thoughts, imposing phraseology, for the out-at-the-seat-of-the-pants newspaper reporters and editors of the time. Their low financial estate was equaled only by the public's scathing disrespect of all but a few of the newspapers they produced. Reporters of the era were looked upon as untrustworthy vagabonds, most of them libertines and alcoholics. And their superiors sometimes evoked even less regard.

Pulitzer couldn't change such hostile attitudes overnight. Despite his eloquence and his bequest, his fellow publishers were cautious in the extreme. Few were as complimentary as H. L. Mencken, of the *Baltimore Sun,* who wrote: "The schools of journalism far surpass the old-time city rooms in the character of the recruits they enlist.... They do not try to make journalists out of busted lawyers, former whiskey drummers and unfrocked clergymen." Still, the new recruits seldom found warm acceptance in the newsrooms, if my own example can be taken as the norm, as I believe it was.

I have always appreciated what I was taught during my two last undergraduate years at Columbia, even though I had to work six nights a week on a tabloid to pay my way. Looking back on that experience, I appreciate how Professor Charles P. Cooper and his assistants helped me develop my work as a reporter. And I am indebted, as well, to others on the faculty—Allen Sinclair Will, Fraser Bond, and the libel lawyer, Harold L. Cross, who taught me an appreciation of the law and fine points of news work as they were practiced at the time. For my training as a copy editor, I am thankful to the inseparable duo from the *New York Times* copy desk, Theodore M. Bernstein and Robert Garst. And Professor Roscoe L. Conkling Brown was my mentor as a writer.

Yet, important though this professional instruction turned out to be, I found with the passage of time that the most important courses in my student years at Columbia were Director John Cunliffe's lectures (and heavy reading load) in English and American literature and drama. At the time, very few students—including myself—thought much of Cunliffe's courses; I believe I stuck them out, reading load and all, mainly because my classmate and first love, Dorothy Lannuier, was so impressed with them.

But when I became the Administrator of the Pulitzer Prizes, following my return to Columbia years later, both Cunliffe's lectures and the assigned readings in his courses gave me standards by which I was able to measure, with some degree of confidence, the various jury reports on which the Pulitzer board based so many of its awards. And at a personal level, my background in literature, drama, and music increased my enjoyment of the best of our time from O'Neill and Faulkner to George Gershwin.

If I have any criticism of the curricula in journalism schools in our universities today, it is that they take too little account of the broader cultural aspects of our life as a nation. For here, too, journalists usually have something to contribute beyond the daily grist of the news, and they should be given greater awareness of that responsibility as well as their purely professional duties as journalists.

If I may indulge in the luxury of self-criticism, this also was one of my faults after I returned to Columbia to teach.

Looking over the letters of appreciation that came from generous former students upon my reaching emeritus status, I realize that nearly all of them referred to some relatively simple bit of instruction that helped them as beginning journalists to resolve familiar problems in the handling of quick-breaking news. One former student thought it wise of me to refer him to the Manhattan telephone book for an easy way to reach an important news source who was elusive at his offices and clubs. (It worked.) Another remarked that I could write quickly and effectively the beginning of a complicated article that had stalled him. (And why not, after twenty-five years in the business?) Many others, both men and women, wrote to say how helpful it was for me to have pointed out that they seldom could wait for events to unfold in their entirety and would have to, in my own peculiar phraseology, "go with whatever got." (And if you didn't have much, hard luck, deadlines were deadlines.) Still another helpful reminder, for those who took the trouble to write, was my continual warning, "When in doubt, leave out." And in another bit of instruction, I blush because I continually used the misspelling of my own name by overeager students to hammer at the need for care and accuracy in the news. (It's still misspelled by experts.)

Granted, such criticism—along with my harder work of editing student copy—set a useful example of professionalism for newcomers to journalism, a valid and necessary teaching procedure. But with the blessings of hindsight, the emphasis on professional training for the people in my classes might well have been varied with more stress on the relatively few courses I offered over the years in cultural writing and criticism. Granted also that cultural journalism had not been my professional specialty when I came to Columbia as a professor; my performance as a reporter of foreign affairs, especially at the UN, had been by far my strongest point in a varied career. Agreed, too, that some students blossomed as critics of fiction and drama—and even of ballet—without any particular assistance from me. And a few graduates also publish books on such subjects, including some best-sellers.

For all that, if I had it to do all over again, I would make cultural courses obligatory in the training of journalists at the university level. Moreover, I have enough confidence in the work of my seminars in UN, Washington, and foreign correspondence to recommend that kind of training, as well, to those who aspire to eventual work in that field. I like the way a newsmagazine editor and former student described my teaching in that field once I retired:

"There . . . were times when tapping out a fast three or four takes on a Japanese election or a political shift in China seemed a breeze. Credit that to Cosmic Coverage, Mon Wed Fri, Prof. J. Hohenberg."

Cosmic Coverage? You bet! Expertise in political events in Washington, D.C.? For the present, it's desperately needed. More devotion to local events, too, could improve the reputation of the nation's news vendors. But, to revert to my own failings, all this cannot really make up for neglect in making available to the public a steady flow of news of cultural affairs, which determine—far more often than politics—the openness of many societies of our time, as well as their permanence. Witness the decline of Communism and the death of the Soviet Union amid continued pressure for conformity and secrecy among its people, which drove so distinguished a figure as Aleksandr Solzhenitsyn to take up temporary residence in rural Vermont until it was safe for him to return to the Russian successor state.

In world class journalism, as in cultural affairs, after all, there are times and places when you cannot "go with whatcher got."

Nevertheless, despite my faults, the glamorous part of life at a great university, together with my usually pleasant student relationships and classwork, helped keep me happy during my twenty-six years on Morningside Heights.

Once, when the International Press Institute invited me to be a discussion leader at a session in New Delhi, I took Dorothy with me as far as Paris (heaven, to her!) as the guest of Colonel and Mrs. Syd Fisher. Then, too, there were long Asian journeys for the Federal government, a summer's cross-country trip by car for us both, and several summer teaching assignments such as a much-appreciated session in Hawaii. Occasionally, too, I was able to arrange with Columbia to respond to invitations such as an American Assembly convocation in Shimoda, Japan, and a teaching seminar in Hong Kong (in English, save the mark!).

My regular visits to the UN with students and related trips to the

White House and State and Defense Department press rooms were always stimulating. And return visits by foreign dignitaries and American specialists in foreign affairs often enlivened both my seminars and the written assignments my students undertook (such as 1,500-word pieces for a ninety-minute deadline on the progress, or lack of it, of the Vietnam War or the cause of peace in the Middle East).

In my reporting classes, Columbia's prestige and a little arm-twisting on the side helped produce other distinguished figures in the city, state, and nation, who submitted to news conferences with student questioners, sometimes cheerfully, sometimes not. One session I'll never forget was with the Honorable John V. Lindsay when he was New York City's mayor. He arrived for a two-hour reporting class with a battalion of TV reporters and equipment, plus a few local newspaper stringers. The students had a hard time getting in a question or two because the professionals and I took up most of the class time.

But I was forgiven. I had tried.

After a few years, I learned it was a lot safer for instructional purposes to trust to Columbia's own specialists in politics, economics, and such crisis centers as the Soviet Union, China, and the Middle East. In return, when invited, I worked with those specialists in their own classes. And that, to me, was one of the best parts of the Columbia experience because sometimes, I am sure, I learned more from such encounters than some of my students did.

I don't want to gloss over the risks that are bound to exist in any college or university that border on substandard impoverished areas of most of the great cities of the land. Columbia had similar risks, although I must say that I didn't suffer from the near tragic experiences of some of my neighbors who were trapped, threatened, or robbed off campus.

The only time these risks hit home for me was on a freezing January afternoon in 1967 when a twenty-three-year-old thief boldly entered the Columbia Gift Shop on campus, operated at the time by faculty wives for the benefit of student scholarship funds, and pointed a sharpened wooden spear a foot from Dorothy's face.

When she was in good health, as she was then, she was absolutely fearless. And that day, without thinking of her own safety, she used both hands to thrust the spear aside and yelled to the only other person in the shop, another faculty wife, to phone the campus police. Then she rushed outside to organize a posse of students.

By that time, the thief had grabbed the other woman's pocketbook and fled, but he was caught by a city policeman after a seven-block chase. At the West 125th Street Police Station, the stolen pocketbook was recovered and the wooden spear was seized as evidence for the culprit's subsequent trial and imprisonment.

While no one was hurt in the incident, it was vivid testimony to an aspect of university life in New York and other big cities that is seldom called to public attention. However, neither then nor later did Dorothy or I let the risks spoil our enjoyment of the best of academe. And we never were bothered again.

As far as the Columbia journalism faculty was concerned, while I was a member we considered these and other university problems common to higher education throughout the land. But one that never bothered us in the least was the training of women and minority students generally for journalism in any aspect that interested a substantial number of them.

That was because the direction of Joseph Pulitzer's school was set by the first director, Talcott Williams. As a student, I remember hearing this intense little man with the snowy white hair and the walrus mustache telling my class how he had insisted on a substantial number of women students at a time when all save the most liberal papers would hire only a token woman or two. The evidence of his success was in the room before him that year, for in my class of 1927, 25 of the 65 students were women, 38 percent of the total. In 1974 and 1976, two of the last years in which I taught, that figure had gone up to 40 percent; 43 out of 107 students in 1974 were women, and in 1976 that figure went to 50 out of 120. I doubt if it has been any lower since, and in some years I would suggest that it probably was higher.

The women graduates of Columbia's J school have long since justified Williams's faith in them. They are, by century's end, well established in every field that once belonged exclusively to men, including war correspondence, racket busting, editorial direction, and executive leadership, and are in dominant posts in politics and education (including a woman dean of the Columbia Graduate Journalism School). Nor has Columbia been alone in advocating equal treatment of the sexes. Toward century's end, I know of no J school in America that dares practice sexual discrimination openly.

Encouragement for the admission of minorities for journalism education, too, was implicit in the terms of the Pulitzer agreement with Columbia that established the J school. For with the annual selection of three Pulitzer traveling scholars for study abroad, beginning in 1913, something more than encouragement for foreign reporting obviously was intended. The Pulitzer school could scarcely send its graduates to Latin America, Asia, or Africa and still bar from admission the children of immigrants representing these minorities or the immigrants themselves.

The first dean, Carl Ackerman, was especially active in recruiting qualified Latin Americans and Asian Americans; later, there was some progress, as well, for the admission of more qualified African Americans. In the "foreign legion" of students from outside our shores, I enjoyed working with some uniquely qualified students of smaller minorities, including Arabs and Koreans. The one student we admitted from the Soviet Union, I was given to understand, came to us because the Department of State asked the faculty to give him favorable consideration.

The difficulty with most domestic minority applicants as well as those from abroad is that an Ivy League education has always been expensive; today, for that matter, it is an even greater drain on both individual applicants and their families. The problem has been resolved in part by the American Press Institute (then at Columbia and now in Reston, Virginia) and the Nieman Fellowships at Harvard, whereby private funding generally can be arranged for professional applicants.

Something like this might be at least a partial solution for the training of larger numbers of qualified minority and foreign students who don't have the money to quit work for a year to undertake advanced studies in specialties such as the reporting of science, economics, and foreign affairs. On the basis of my own experience and of others I know, I am well aware that a certain number of minority students and a scattering of foreigners do turn up at Columbia and elsewhere, but I am sure that their finances are extremely limited. Or so it appears to me at this writing, at any rate. As always in academe, progress comes in fits and starts, and sometimes there can be a certain amount of backsliding, too. As far as journalism education is concerned, I am sure that we can do better, not only at Columbia but elsewhere in America as well. In the next century, with the increasing development of electronic journalism and computer technology, great changes lie ahead.

PART 4

The Pulitzers and I

16 ★ PROBLEMS AND PRIZES

My first problem as administrator of the Pulitzer Prizes began with the death of the second Joseph Pulitzer on March 30, 1955 at the age of 70. Until after his funeral in St. Louis, nothing could be done about replacing him as chairman of the Advisory Board which was about to meet and I was acting as secretary for the first time.

On the motion of Arthur Krock of the *New York Times,* an outgoing board member, I circulated a mail ballot to the other board members to vote on Krock's nomination of Joseph Pulitzer, Jr., the late chairman's oldest son and the new editor and publisher of the *St. Louis Post-Dispatch,* as the board's new chairman.

Next, because it was necessary to replace Krock as well so that we would have a full membership plus a new chairman, President Kirk suggested Turner Catledge, the *New York Times*'s managing editor, as the quickest available new member. That choice, too, was approved by another mail ballot, virtually on the eve of our two-day meeting.

Otherwise, I was prepared but shaky, wondering how I would get along with the new chairman. I'd circulated all the jury recommendations, had all the available exhibits ready for inspection, and had drawn up an agenda for the third Pulitzer's approval.

I needn't have worried. Chairman Pulitzer and I consulted by phone before the meeting, so that both of us knew fairly well what the controversial choices were likely to be when we assembled on April 28 in the American Press Institute's conference room at the Journalism Building.

The drama jury's choice of the Clifford Odets play *The Flowering Peach* was debatable for several reasons, the most important being that it hadn't attracted either overwhelming critical acclaim or enthusiastic audiences. It was, in brief, the story of Noah and his family aboard the Ark, done in a dialect that was immediately familiar to a native New Yorker like myself. Another New Yorker, Lester Markel, had already dubbed it "The Greenberg Pastures," which didn't help it perceptibly.

There was, however, another play, Tennessee Williams's *Cat on a Hot Tin Roof,* superb if depressing theater, which the jury hadn't seen at the time its report was due. It had been a hit from the outset with Burl Ives and Barbara Bel Geddes as the stars. It caused the drama jury to revise its original report so that, when the board assembled, the recommended drama award was for the Williams play. As a result, I suggested that at least two board members should see it and report their views on the jury's change of front.

But the main problem, in my judgment, continued to be the fiction prize. Long before I'd had anything whatever to do with the Pulitzer Prizes one of the bitterest criticisms of its annual awards had been its disposition to ignore the work of such American masters as William Faulkner and Ernest Hemingway, among others, until late in their careers. In Faulkner's case, he had never been so honored and his latest work, *A Fable,* even though not his best by any means, had been passed over by the fiction jury in favor of a first novel about the hunting of the buffalo, *The Last Hunt,* by Milton Lott, a thirty-one-year writer who was little known to the public. It did seem to me that at least one member of the board, Hodding Carter (like Faulkner a Mississippian), would have ample ground for protest if he chose to make an issue of the matter of Lott versus Faulkner. Anyway, without consulting Carter, I did suggest to both Chairman Pulitzer and President Kirk that we had a problem. And so it turned out.

Fortunately for me, the third Joseph Pulitzer and I got along tolerably well from the outset. Despite our differences in personality, training, and professional outlook, I can't recall we ever had a serious disagreement in the twenty-two years we were together on the Pulitzer board.

Certainly, at that first meeting when it counted the most, his views as chairman and mine as the board's secretary blended together so favorably that the meeting went smoother than I had anticipated. He followed his father's procedure whereby I prefaced each prize discussion with a summary of the issues, if any; after that he took over, to try, without undue haste, to bring the board to a prompt decision.

The first five journalism awards were quickly ratified by accepting the choices of the respective juries. Then, with the editorial prize, the board took the third choice of the jury rather than the first. In editorial cartoons, the board's selection was in favor of D. R. Fitzpatrick of the *St. Louis Post-Dispatch,* a previous winner, as a tribute to the second Joseph Pulitzer (and in the discussion his son, the chairman, quite properly abstained). Again, in the case of the photography prize, the board took the jury's third choice rather than the first.

Then the fireworks began. With my summation of the fiction jury's failure to recognize William Faulkner, Hodding Carter—as expected—made an eloquent argument in favor of overturning the fiction jury's position, and he carried the board with him. It was, he said, no disrespect to a first novelist to bestow a long-delayed honor on Faulkner for *A Fable.* Being at the outset of his career, so the argument went, Milton Lott would have years ahead of him to win his own prize.

I suspect that not too many board members had read either *A Fable* or *The Last Hunt,* for a very good reason—there was comparatively little time for all the required reading between the board members' receipt of the jury reports in all areas and the two-day Pulitzer board meeting. But at last, the membership did do simple justice to Faulkner without much argument against the views of his champion, Carter.

In the case of the drama award, by unanimous agreement, it was decided to put that matter over until the morrow, when two board members would report on *Cat on a Hot Tin Roof* and give their views of the revised drama jury report. The rest of the board's business that day was completed with comparatively little discussion.

On the morrow, Chairman Pulitzer, President Kirk, and I met with the rest of the board in the university's trustees' room to decide the drama award. Both board members who had seen the Williams play the night before spoke in favor of adopting the jury's revised report, which was the way their colleagues voted without argument. The board thereafter affirmed its decisions of the day before, adopted the phraseology I'd written as a formula for each prize, and reappointed me as administrator and board secretary.

All that remained was for me to prepare the minutes of the 1955 board session for the approval of the university trustees. Their meeting, by statute, came on the first Monday of each month during the academic year, in this instance on May 2, which gave me Saturday and Sunday to wrap up my Pulitzer duties for 1955.

Although I knew quite well that the trustees had the power to withhold a prize voted by the board, as well as to approve it, that hadn't happened to date, and I never gave it serious consideration at the time. But I did know that previous members of the trustees' board had never been satisfied merely to be rubber stamps for the Pulitzer advisory board. Manifestly, since the complete report of the board meeting and its actions on the prizes could not have been known to the trustees in advance of their May 2 meeting, that, in effect, was the position in which they found themselves once again for 1955.

Since President Kirk was the only Pulitzer board member who was at the trustees' meeting, and since the university's information department had prepared all the Pulitzer press releases by the time the trustees met, all I had to do that Monday was to wait for word from the president's office that the trustees had acted favorably. Then, I could give the information office permission to release the results and begin thinking about next year.

Knowing that the trustees' meeting was set to begin at 3 P.M., I calculated that I could expect the release to come from Low, the president's office, by 3:30 P.M. But that time came and passed without developments. Consequently, I became increasingly nervous but had no way of knowing what hitch had developed. Almost another hour passed before I finally was given word to release the advance texts as they had been prepared without change.

Why the delay until 4:22 P.M.? Simply put, the reason given me was that the Trustees had to wait for a quorum before they could vote acceptance of the prizes. At the time, I treated the whole business as humorous relief, which was a great mistake. There would come a time when the Trustees would pose serious objections to an automatic endorsement of a controversial award voted by the Advisory Board.

But that time was far distant.

The reactions to the announcement of the Pulitzers that first year are worth noting. It is not because they set a precedent in any sense but rather because the way the awards were received demonstrated to me anew that I was deeply involved in something that, for better or worse, had a powerful hold on public opinion in America. Take the case of the investigative reporting prize, which aroused no debate within the board and went almost routinely to the editor of a small Texas paper, Roland Kenneth Towery of the *Cuero Record,* for exposing a scandal in the veterans' land grant program in his home state. On a hunch, undoubtedly based on a leak from someone familiar with the jury verdicts, Edward R. Murrow had television cameras ready that Monday afternoon in the office at the *Cuero Record* for the first flash about Towery's prize. Thereby, Murrow caught the instant reaction—the surprise, the tension, and the exultation that made Towery's appearance that night on the Murrow show, *See It Now,* so memorable.

Anthony Lewis's reaction was quite different. He was then a reporter on the *Washington Daily News*, and he was applying for a job at the *New York Times* that Monday in May but had just been told, "So sorry, no openings," when he learned he had won the prize for national reporting, the first of his two prizes in the field. It may not have made much difference to the *Times* but it meant a great deal to Tony Lewis, who eventually wound up as an op-ed page columnist for the newspaper.

The "also-rans" became a problem for me, particularly the reactions of the distinguished fiction jurors who had been overruled. One of them vowed to write Milton Lott a letter; another told me he was so upset that after hearing the news he worked vigorously in his garden for an hour in order to overcome his disappointment. I learned to my cost that a member of the journalism jury, a cherished friend of long standing, also took it amiss that he and his colleagues had been overruled—an experience that prompted me to be careful about risking a friendship to fill a vacancy in a Pulitzer jury.

On the plus side, I had a cheerful note from Arthur Krock, our retiring board member, who wished me well. And that, for the time being, was where my experience with the Pulitzer Prizes ended in 1955. Everybody else, including most of the prize winners, seemed to take the event in stride. For all the years that I served as a prize giver without vote, I never could be that relaxed. For me, handling my chores at the Pulitzers was like eternally writing for a deadline with only two or three minutes to go.

That kind of excitement had kept me in the news business for a lifetime. It also accounted for my fascination with the Pulitzer Prizes. Simply put, I liked working under pressure. It was what made me go.

I had a very special reason for trying to move the 1956 prizes to a speedy and satisfactory conclusion. The fall semester of the 1955–56 academic year coincided with my first sabbatical leave, and Dorothy and I already had planned an extended European auto tour during that summer and fall. President Kirk, as I learned upon inquiry, had no objection either to my sabbatical or to the plans I had made for it. As for Dean Ackerman, I knew that he had been under pressure to retire.

What remained, therefore, was the disposal of the Pulitzer Prizes, without any undue argument that might conceivably tie me up.

The letters, drama, and music reports came in on schedule and seemed to pose no problems at the outset. And in early March, the journalism jurors showed up and efficiently disposed of their work, including a recommended prize for Charles L. Bartlett of the *Chattanooga Times* for his disclosure of conflict of interest charges against Air Force Secretary Harold Talbott, which had led to Talbott's resignation the previous year.

That, however, had no effect on my standing as an Air Force consultant, because I already had other assignments from Talbott's replacement, Donald A. Quarles, and I had assured Secretary Quarles that I would be available provided I continued to have Columbia's consent for such work.

What did seem to me to be much more serious was a major issue that had been raised by the International Reporting Jury. It had recommended a Pulitzer Prize for a group known as the Hearst Team, which consisted of William Randolph Hearst, Jr., son of the first Joseph Pulitzer's bitterest foe, and his two associates, J. Kingsbury Smith and Frank Conniff. They had been cited for their exclusive series of interviews with the leaders of the Soviet Union in Moscow.

Having worked for Hearst in New York, I thought I was in much the same position as any voting member of the Pulitzer board who was even indirectly involved in a recommended exhibit. Such conflicts were resolved with the retirement of the affected member from the room until after a decision had been made.

It turned out differently for me, however, as secretary of the board because Chairman Pulitzer, to my surprise, led the board's members who were in favor of awarding a prize to the Hearst team. I had not discussed the position with him and realized, once the debate had begun, that it would only complicate matters if I now undertook to explain my position. I reasoned that I had best say nothing and keep strictly aloof from the proceedings. Which is what happened.

To quote from my diary on the first day of the two-day Pulitzer board meeting on April 26, 1956:

"The board fought about a Pulitzer prize for the Hearst team for most of the day and Joe Pulitzer and Bill Mathews finally won. So the headline will read: Hearst Wins a Pulitzer Prize! And I do not doubt that the elder Pulitzer and the elder Hearst, the bitterest of enemies at the turn of the century, will be whirling in their graves. . . .

"But that's not all, for Joe Jr. and Bill Jr. also are quite different. Joe is as liberal as Bill is not. Joe is Harvard and Bill is Stork Club. Joe collects art and Bill collects datelines. . . ."

It occurred to me that the fight might be renewed next day when the Pulitzer board reconvened to ratify its choices and take up any other business that remained. But nothing happened. The Hearst award, with all the rest, went into the record books and, so far as I can remember, there were no overturned jury verdicts that year.

As for myself, I had another pleasant surprise. Although President Kirk announced he was appointing Ed Barrett of *Newsweek* to replace Carl Ackerman, the retiring dean, he recommended my reappointment as the prize Administrator and board secretary, even though I had announced that I would be away on sabbatical leave from early June until January 31, 1957. It had seemed to me that a new dean also would be taking over these responsibilities, but it didn't work out that way even though my appointment at the time was on a year-to-year basis.

There were no arguments this time when the Pulitzer Prizes were announced on Monday, May 7, and a quorum of Trustees ratified all the awards without a peep, regardless of what some of them may have thought.

The Hearst team's performance, after all, had been strictly professional in Moscow, and it was on this basis that the prize was awarded. The only gripe, strangely enough, came from the sports writers who thought Red Smith, the much admired columnist of the *New York Herald-Tribune,* should have received an award for his life's work. As I recorded in my diary, "You can't please everybody."

For Dorothy and for me, there was a brief postscript. Although I had no part in the proceedings, Bill Hearst invited us to Toots Shor's bar on May 10 to celebrate the prize he had won with Joe Smith and Frank Conniff. My comment on the proceedings:

"We just stood around, had drinks (cokes for Dorothy and me) and talked and talked. Then we had a buffet supper and Toots said I added class to his joint. I only wish it were true. . . ."

I conclude the record of my first six years of teaching at Columbia with a final passage, written on June 1, for the end of the 1955–56 academic year:

"Drove to New York from Aquebogue. When we came to our apartment at 90 Morningside Drive, I found my passport and Air Force extended orders had arrived by registered mail from Washington. I couldn't understand either the orders or the reason for them, if any, which was a thundering surprise to me, for my passport bore visas for Saudi Arabia and Libya and a signed personal authorization from Frances Knight, the head of the U.S. Passport Office. Somebody sure wants me to go to these two places very badly. . . ."

However, I had promised Dorothy she would have her European auto trip. And since there seemed to be no emergency involving the United States in either Saudi Arabia or Libya at the time, I told her in good conscience that her trip would take precedence as promised. I never did make it to Saudi Arabia or Libya, and I never did find out why anybody at the Pentagon wanted me to go to either place.

That surprise seemed to me to be a fitting conclusion to my introduction to the Pulitzer Prizes. The Pulitzers would have more than enough surprises of their own for me in the years to come.

17 ★ FIGHTING WORDS

Most Pulitzer board meetings during my twenty-two years of service were models of decorous conduct. Voices were seldom raised. Differences were handled with tact and care. Hurt feelings usually were papered over with wan smiles and tut-tuts from the chair.

But for reasons I can't quite account for, the 1963 meeting was a lamentable exception. From the outset, almost everything seemed to go wrong. Even the third Joseph Pulitzer, who presided over the uproar that burst about him during his ninth year on the board, was sufficiently out of sorts to glare at those about him who were the most argumentative.

We had barely taken our places around the familiar oblong table scattered with books and exhibits when I sensed tension growing around me as I introduced the first subject for decision, the public service category in the journalism awards. In the light of what we know today about the divisiveness of birth control as a principle, I'm sure that few people will be particularly surprised that the same issue, posed by the Public Service Jury, caused a terrific row almost at once.

The problem, as it developed, was whether to award the gold medal for public service—the most coveted of the journalism awards—to the *Chicago Daily News* for its long and largely successful effort to make birth control information available to families on the Chicago public relief rolls (who were presumed to need it most).

What happened thereafter was an all-day wrangle, which halted, temporarily, then resumed between votes on the various other prizes based on jury recommendations. As the board's secretary, I considered that the best thing to do was to vote the birth control gold medal up or down and get on with other business, a point of view Chairman Pulitzer seemed to agree with. But when I called for a vote the first time, the result was a tie, 5–5, with other members abstaining. Allowing time for cooling off, votes on other prizes, and more birth control arguments, I proposed another vote on the gold medal, which still resulted in a tie, this time 6–6. Toward the end of the day, when everybody was tired, the *Chicago Daily News* was at last voted the gold medal for public service. But the citation was weasel-worded, and I confess that I did the weaseling, as follows:

"To the *Chicago Daily News,* for calling public attention to the issue of providing birth control services in the public health programs in its area."

Everybody around the table agreed to that, except Don Maxwell of the rival *Chicago Tribune,* who was still grumpy and voted "No" with a defiant flourish.

I suppose the board could have weathered that paper storm without further damage, if more arguments had not developed over two of the most cherished non-journalism prizes, one in drama and the other in fiction.

Don Maxwell was on the barricades again when I asked for action by the board on the drama prize, which a distinguished jury had proposed for Edward Albee's *Who's Afraid of Virginia Woolf?* To the *Tribune*'s editor, still huffy over the gold medal for his opposite number in Chicago's journalistic wars, the Albee drama was a "filthy play," and he was against giving it a prize. His colleague in Cleveland, Louis B. Seltzer, editor of the *Press* there, agreed in the course of a general rejection of any play that "reeks with obscenity" and "offends good taste."

The fight for Albee was based on the recommendation of the jurors—John Mason Brown, one of the best New York drama critics, and his academic colleague Professor John Gassner of the Yale Drama School. In their jury report, which Brown wrote, both experts agreed that this Albee work about four alcoholic characters, two women and two men, "is a study in hatreds and frustrations, of impotence and jealousy." They cited Albee for "summoning extraordinary interest and excitement in a play which is both overlong and weak in its pivotal point." Nevertheless, they recommended a prize for Albee as "a young man who, having already done much, will unquestionably do more and has just now done a great deal."

The board's majority, however, refused to go along with the jurors and voted no drama award for 1963, arguing that Albee's work did not meet the specifications for the award. In that year, it was to be given for an American play "which shall represent in marked fashion the educational value and power of the stage."

That, however, wasn't all the damage that was to be done to the list of distinguished jurors I had recruited—with so much effort, including appeals to the cause of American literature, because I had so little money to offer anybody on the roster either for judgments in journalism or for judgments in letters, drama, and music. One of the best juries I had ever assembled for fiction—Irita van Doren of the *New York Herald-Tribune* and John Barkham of the *Saturday Review of Literature*—had proposed a 1963 fiction prize for Katharine Ann Porter's novel *Ship of Fools*. But the Porter book at once ran into trouble, as had Milton Lott's *The Last Hunt,* because a novel by William Faulkner was also being considered.

Faulkner's novel, *The Reivers,* was his last, and his publishers had submitted it posthumously. The jurors saluted the great Mississippian by calling his novel "a sunny interlude (the last, alas) in the shaping of the vast Yoknapatawpha saga, in which Faulkner for once sounds relaxed, as though he were yarning to a circle of friends in that soft, elliptical drawl of his. *The Reivers* has been described as 'a perfect book for a last goodnight' and we agree."

Now I would be the last to argue, after a life-long journalistic career, that we supposedly tough and hard-bitten ink-stained wretches are in reality warm-hearted sentimentalists. And yet, in view of the circumstances and the accolade given to Faulkner by critics who picked someone else ahead of him, how else does one account for the board's immediate decision, almost without debate, to bestow on the dead novelist his last Pulitzer Prize for his last good-night?

At any rate, *Ship of Fools* was scuttled by a sentimental torpedo which, though hastily aimed by the jury, easily hit its mark.

The rest of the awards, mercifully, went off pretty much as planned, but the announcement of the prizes on May 6 hadn't been on the air for more than fifteen minutes when I received an indignant phone call from John Mason Brown announcing that he and Professor Gassner were resigning from further jury duty. I tried a weak joke, pointing out that no new jury appointments had been announced and he therefore had nothing to resign from. But this time, Brown was angry and determined. Although he recognized that he had not been reappointed (my poor little joke), he asked not to be reconsidered for jury service and explained:

"I do not challenge the right of the Advisory Board or the Trustees of Columbia University to ignore a juror's recommendation. It was with full knowledge of this right that I have served. But inasmuch as my recommendations have been disregarded twice since 1956, it seems to me that my usefulness to the Board has ceased."

In 1960, Brown and a colleague had recommended Lillian Hellman's *Toys in the Attic,* which was unceremoniously brushed aside in favor of a show most of the board's members had seen and enjoyed, *Fiorello!*—a folksy musical about Fiorello H. LaGuardia, a mayor of New York City in the FDR era. (Sheldon Harnick, the show's lyricist, reported later that the board's surprise verdict had made him solvent.)

Nevertheless, the board in 1963 took a licking in the press for its reversal of the Albee recommendation, especially when it turned out that at least one board member had rejected the drama without even having seen it. That piece of embarrassing information was disclosed when reporters polled the board by telephone after the news of the reversal became public.

As a result, the board came to an informal agreement, proposed by Barry Bingham, that no member should vote for or against any play he had not seen or any book he had not read. (This was in the era when the board was all male.) I do not doubt that the procedure has found merit among all members who have served since.

There was one other decision that year that also affected the drama awards of the future. The board decided to change the terms of the drama award to remove the "uplift" clause that had helped cause the trouble. The substitute provision for the drama prize read,

"For a distinguished play by an American author, preferably original in its source and dealing with American life."

I also made a change of my own at the time. Instead of using letters, drama, and music juries of only two members each, whose views were likely to be different at times, I obtained the board's permission to name three jurors in these categories. In journalism, I began using five people. I did not believe that there might be greater wisdom in numbers, what I did hope for was that tie votes for a proposed prize could be eliminated from the procedure of all juries, removing still another source of conflict among the board's members. That became at least a small advance toward assuring stronger jury reports.

While diverse views could scarcely be eliminated, and that certainly was not something I tried to do, the odd-numbered jury appointments did make for a few less fighting words in the discussion of the award process.

I do not want to give the impression that I was totally responsible for the selection of juries, however. What I did do, immediately at the end of one Pulitzer season with the announcement of the prizes, was to draw up a list of proposed juries in each category for the coming award period. While Grayson Kirk was the president of the university, he was always interested enough in any of my problems to see me as soon as possible and discuss them with me. That, too, was what he invariably did when I had my new jury listings and brought them to him.

With President Kirk's approval, therefore, the lists then went to the rest of the Pulitzer board members, to whom I also circulated a mail ballot. Over the years, I recall very few times that the university's president asked me to change any of my choices, and then it was only to make certain that we always had a number of new faces among those who, in fact, did determine most of the awards. As for the board members themselves, I don't remember a time when any juror on the first listing was vetoed in the consultation process.

The reason for the immediate selection of new juries was obvious enough. Books by the hundreds began coming in almost at once in the nominating process. New plays had to be seen. New music had to be heard. And as for the journalism jurors, they were given warning, with their appointment, that it was their duty to keep up with the developments in their particular area. To be sure, the journalism exhibits were bulkier and among the last to come in for judgment, so I could not send them out in toto. But what I did do, once all the entries were in, was to get up a catalogue in all categories for the information of both the juries and the board members. And after the juries made their selections in journalism by coming to Columbia in a group, usually during the second week of March, I was able to circulate reprints of key parts of each recommended exhibit to all board members along with the recommended non-journalism jury reports.

Eventually, once the prize results were announced, I also made public the names of the jurors who had served.

And yet, for all that, an Administrator's troubles only began when the jury reports came in before the key Pulitzer board meeting. In the case of the uproar in 1963, for example, I noted in my diary: "We'll get banged around for this one for sure."

And we were. But somehow we survived and tried as best we could to make adjustments in the system to eliminate possibilities of unfair or mistaken judgments. That, I think, was the least the board owed the American public in the annual judgments of the winning entries in the Pulitzer Prizes.

Despite all Columbia's good intentions as well as those of the Pulitzer board, we could not solve the very real problems of the American theater. In four of the six years between 1963 and 1968, no award was made for a "distinguished play by an American author, preferably original in its source and dealing with American life."

On the basis of the reactions at the time, I do not believe it was the fault collectively of the drama juries and the Pulitzer board that no award was made in that category for 1963, 1964, 1966, and 1968. For 1964, the only real possibility for an award would have been *Hello, Dolly!*—the musical (derived from a book) in which Carol Channing gave a magnificent performance. Chairman Pulitzer told me later that he'd have given her the award if it had been possible. For 1966 and 1968, the verdict against an award for a play also drew no serious opposition.

The more relaxed attitude after the uproar in 1963 is fairly evident in my diary notations for the Pulitzer board meeting and the announcement of the prizes for the subsequent year.

Of the 1964 board meeting, I wrote: "The Pulitzer board was good this year—no juries overruled.... There were no prizes in fiction, drama or music and a weak one in history, 'Puritan Village,' by a prep school historian.... I'm glad it's over. Every year is more difficult."

With the prize announcement on the first Monday in May following routine consideration of the Pulitzer board's decisions by the university's trustees, I made this comment:

"Pulitzer Day. At 3:23 P.M., the Trustees voted and some 70 or so people in the press corps dictated their bulletins by phone or returned to their offices with the press packets. The failure to award prizes in fiction, drama and music was accepted with relative calm and the usual big play. I went home at 5 P.M. and didn't have a call all night. Of course, some reporters called jurors, board members and others to see if there'd been any skullduggery but they found none."

The only unfavorable part of the news follow-up came with the discovery by a *New York Times* reporter that the winner of the history award was jobless. But that circumstance was something that wasn't quite in my line, so I didn't worry about it. It was, as it turned out, the particular concern of the laureate in history for that year. What I had to do was to get up my jury lists for the forthcoming year and, following their acceptance, prepare for another sabbatical journey, this time to Hong Kong and East Asia in connection with my book project for the Council on Foreign Relations.

Once that was done, Dorothy and I took off. But always, during my Pulitzer service, I had to be aware that I still was responsible for the operation of the Pulitzer office at Columbia whether I was at home or abroad. It did make a great difference in my life and the lives of those around me.

There were no fighting words over fiction at any time in the 1950s and 1960s that could be compared with the almost continual arguments about the drama awards. In the decade between 1954 and 1964, for example, the prizes were passed twice (1954 and 1964) and twice again in the 1970s (1971 and 1974) without perceptible displeasure that amounted to much. The difference was that none of the prizewinning works between 1954 and 1975 are still being read. Mainly, they included the last works of major writers of that generation, best-sellers of a particular year, or fiction that may have been current at the time but was quickly forgotten.

There was nothing in those two decades to compare with the artistry of Edith Wharton or Willa Cather, the enduring values of John Steinbeck's *The Grapes of Wrath,* the phenomenal popularity of Margaret Mitchell's *Gone with the Wind,* or the adaptability to the theater of

James Michener's *Tales of the South Pacific*. Fiction in America, clearly, had gone into a quiet decline from which it still has not fully recovered toward century's end.

By contrast, despite all the arguments the drama prize touched off, there is no doubt that it helped stimulate the growth of a distinctive American theater. The awards gave encouragement to such major dramatists as Eugene O'Neill, Robert E. Sherwood, Maxwell Anderson, Tennessee Williams, and Arthur Miller. The prize also glorified a distinctive American art form, the musical theater, as it was displayed in the music of George Gershwin, Richard Rodgers, and Leonard Bernstein among others, plus the theatrical wizardry of Oscar Hammerstein II and George S. Kaufman. The decline of Broadway as a showplace, it seems to me, came from causes other than the genius behind the rise of the living theater in America and the public recognition it evoked through the Pulitzer Prizes.

Although there were some at Columbia, particularly among older faculty people, who believed that all the argument over the drama prizes was bad for the reputation of the university, I never thought that this was necessarily so. On the contrary, I believed it to be inevitable that strong-minded people, in taking the measure of a powerful art form of national importance on an annual basis, were bound to disagree at times over the merits of its chief performers. Had the Pulitzers been awarded for work that aroused little public interest, they would not have lasted even a decade, let alone advance confidently toward their first century, as is the case today.

Drama, in fact, was only the beginning of the clash of diverse opinions over the annual awards. With the passing years, some of the most violent public disputes over the prizes involved three national crises: the Vietnam War, the publication of the Pentagon Papers, and the Watergate scandal that led to the resignation of President Nixon. Each of these issues put the free press clause of the First Amendment to the severest test by pitting the full force of the Federal government's displeasure against the actions of a strong and determined press. And each also involved a Pulitzer Prize, awarded for uncovering wrongdoing at the top of the nation's governance.

I also would cite some early arguments over what seemed like an entirely innocuous academic award, the Pulitzer Prize in biography, as an almost certain indication of the shape of things to come.

18 ★ AMONG MY SOUVENIRS

Whenever I am asked whether my Pulitzer experience was dull, and that still happens sometimes, I pull a small book from the shelf just above my writing desk—one of the cherished souvenirs of my times at Columbia.

It is my autographed copy of John F. Kennedy's *Profiles in Courage,* which won him a Pulitzer Prize while he was a Senator from Massachusetts and which thrust me into the middle of a furious argument with the columnist Drew Pearson. Pearson had charged that the book had been ghostwritten, an allegation Kennedy denied, and thereby caused my superiors at the university to ask me to undertake a quiet investigation.

The fuss that resulted was a further demonstration (if one were needed) of the hazards of prize-giving. For those who are inclined to believe that the art of biography is a consummate bore, the uproar over the Kennedy book—and a few others before and after it—are more than sufficient evidence to the contrary.

Kennedy's *Profiles in Courage* had been my first experience with the divisiveness of biography as a literary exercise. Until that time, to be candid, I had taken that category on the Pulitzer list pretty much for granted. However, as I soon discovered, that had been a capital error.

An expert jury in biography had not even recommended the Kennedy book for a Pulitzer Prize in 1957. When it was thrust upon the board at the annual meeting to decide finally on the awards for that year, the reaction of a majority of the board's membership came as a complete surprise both to Chairman Pulitzer and to me. Both of us had assumed that the board would accept routinely the recommendations of its distinguished jurors.

But among journalists, nothing ought to be taken for granted. And at the meeting that day—April 26, 1957—both the chairman and I had more than one surprise.

I am convinced to this day that Kennedy himself had nothing to do with the argument that ensued. I doubt if he had known anything more about the board's procedures other than the routine decisions of his publishers to submit his book for consideration in the biography category. Furthermore, I am certain that, as an author, he did not know in advance that the biography jurors had failed him. In fact, the jury report that year didn't even mention *Profiles in Courage* when it went before the board.

What happened then was this:

Dr. Julian P. Boyd, editor of the *Thomas Jefferson Papers* at Princeton, and Professor Bernard Mayo of the University of Virginia, the biography jurors that year, had picked as their first choice Alpheus T. Mason's biography of Chief Justice Harlan Fiske Stone, an eminent and authoritative work. As second choice, they had selected another highly regarded biography, James MacGregor Burns's tribute to Franklin Roosevelt, *Roosevelt: The Lion and the Fox*.

As has happened on occasion, a board member had other ideas and began arguing the merits of *Profiles in Courage*. Now this was at a time long before another President of the United States, George Bush, had made any hint of liberalism in politics seem like a criminal conspiracy against the American public, so the board's members—mainly Republicans—listened in respectful silence to their colleague, J. D. Ferguson of the *Milwaukee Journal*.

I must say Ferguson was most convincing. He spoke at length about the deep impression the young Senator's work had made on him and concluded: "I read it aloud to my twelve-year-old grandson and the boy was absolutely fascinated. I think we should give the prize to *Profiles in Courage*."

A few others around the table who had read Kennedy's book spoke up then. And while I can't swear to their political faith at the time, the incident having occurred more than thirty years ago, I would doubt there were any liberal Democrats of the Kennedy stripe among them. I don't remember that Chairman Pulitzer, the leading liberal at the table, had anything much to say in the ensuing discussion, which fascinated both of us.

Of course, it is true that Kennedy at the time had not yet emerged as a serious candidate for the presidency, a run that was three years away at the time. These were the prosperous Eisenhower years, and the board's conservatives, who were dominant, seemingly had nothing to fear from a Democratic interloper from Massachusetts who had just recovered from a serious illness.

In any event, political considerations were swept aside in the discussion about *Profiles in Courage*. When the vote for the book was tallied, it received a majority for that year's biography prize, and the result was so ordained and announced publicly in due course. Even the sometimes rebellious Columbia Trustees, who were in a cold war with the Pulitzer board just then, accepted the Kennedy work without a murmur.

Possibly, the position of the Kennedy book at or near the top of the best-seller list may have had some influence in the final decision but, to my knowledge, nobody made that a part of the argument in its favor. It seemed then to have won on its own merits.

The only raucous note in the public reaction to the award was sounded by Pearson in his weekly TV show some time later when he suggested that the book had been ghostwritten. That was what brought me into the argument, when I wrote to Senator Kennedy on January 7, 1958:

"I have just received several inquiries regarding Drew Pearson's remarks over the ABC Television network. Beyond answering them with a copy of a statement given to me by the American Broadcasting Company (a disclaimer of responsibility), I have taken no action and do not intend to do so. I thought you would like to know about this."

The reference was to the outcome of an unpublicized inquiry I had undertaken at the suggestion of my Columbia superiors into Pearson's charges, but I wrote the letter to Senator Kennedy on my own responsibility. He replied: "I am very grateful to you for your letter of Jan. 7 and the position you are taking as expressed therein. All of us regret that the situation has occurred—although I suppose it is not unusual either in the worlds of politics or literature."

He added in a handwritten note that he was seeing Pearson shortly and hoped the argument could be resolved thereafter. It was. Pearson delivered a typically ungracious retraction in his syndicated column, saying merely that Kennedy had been the author of *Profiles in Courage.*

It remained for Professor Burns, one of Kennedy's unsuccessful rivals for the 1957 biography prize, to point out that a Gallup poll after the prize announcement had produced a four-point rise to 45 percent in favor of Kennedy's chances for the next Democratic Presidential nomination. Burns concluded, not unreasonably:

"It seems possible that literary honors carry more weight with the public than has been commonly thought."

Accordingly, two years later, Professor Burns published his biography, *John Kennedy: A Political Profile,* which was used during Kennedy's successful run for the Presidency in 1960. So all turned out well for everybody, except Dr. Mason, the author of the recommended work on Chief Justice Stone in 1957. If anybody had a justified gripe against the biography category, he did. But like a well-mannered academic, he held his peace.

Five years later there was another biographical uproar when W. A. Swanberg's biography *Citizen Hearst* was rejected for a Pulitzer Prize because the Columbia Trustees overruled a judgment in the book's favor by the Pulitzer board. I still remember the mixed reaction of William Randolph Hearst, Jr., who hadn't liked the Swanberg portrait of his father to begin with, but who seemed to resent the Trustees' interference even more. "After all," he told me in an indignant phone call, "everything my Pop learned about journalism came right from Old Man Pulitzer." That book, too, is among my souvenirs.

What Joseph Pulitzer, Jr., thought of these sentiments may well be imagined, for he had taken the lead in obtaining a unanimous vote for the Hearst book from his fellow board members, only to find that the Trustees exercised their veto power (long since withdrawn). The third Pulitzer also had fought within the board to win the Pulitzer Prize six years before for "Young Bill" Hearst's team; but for all that, he never did say what his Pop had thought of the elder Hearst.

In the biography jury's deliberations, the *New York Times*'s book critic, Orville Prescott, had plumped for *Citizen Hearst* whereas Professor C. Vann Woodward of Yale had voted for the biography of Sinclair Lewis by Mark Schorer. Woodward's objection to the Hearst volume had been, as he phrased it, a serious doubt that it "measures up to the standards of the prize, certainly not those set up by recent selections."

The reference was to the "uplift" clause in the specifications for the award: "For a distinguished American biography or autobiography by an American author teaching patriotic and unselfish services to the people, illustrated by eminent example."

In my own notes made after the meeting, there is no reference to any discussion of the terms of the biography award. Nor did I or anybody else around the table have any suspicion of a Trustees' veto. Even if some Trustees had complained privately for years that they were being used as a mere rubber stamp by the Pulitzer Board, they had not to date done anything more about it. But the rebelliousness of the Trustees' membership was beyond doubt now.

True, the university's lawyers had warned the Trustees that they had no authority under the will of the elder Pulitzer to do anything more than accept or reject the board's selections (in other words, they could not substitute a choice of their own). In consequence, I had always followed my predecessors' procedure by having all the press announcements of the prizes written well in advance and held for release on the first Monday in May for the expected endorsement of the Trustees.

But that May 7, 1962, the usual script for the announcement dealing with the winning Hearst book wasn't followed. To quote from my diary entry that I wrote immediately afterward:

"It finally happened. The Trustees refused to honor the recommendations of the Pulitzer board for the first time in 46 years. I was in the middle as usual. Dr. Kirk told Harron [Bob Harron, the Columbia director of public information] at 3:25 P.M. that there would be no biography award but all others could be released."

After it was all over, I learned what had happened at the Trustees' meeting. When the Hearst biography award came up, a Trustee, unnamed, observed that the book didn't seem to tally with the terms of the award. There was no debate, not even much of a discussion, before the Trustees decided not to approve an award in biography for that year.

For Bob Harron, it was an immediate problem because he had more than fifty reporters and photographers waiting outside the Trustees' Room for the Pulitzer announcement. What he did was to ask his associates John Hastings and Nancy Carmody to revise the press packets to show that no award had been made in biography. And meanwhile, following Dr. Kirk's instructions, I notified the members of the Pulitzer board privately by telegraph that their Hearst book had been turned down.

The revised press packets were released at 4:23 P.M., the reporters with deadlines grabbed phones and began dictating the results to their offices without asking a question, and I thought the Trustees' action might possibly escape public notice if we were lucky. We weren't. The *New York Times*'s Peter Kihss began telephoning the Pulitzer board members as soon as he returned to his office and broke the story in next morning's *Times*.

"Quite a time!" I wrote in an added diary entry. "I did not sleep all the rest of the night after the Times's first edition hit the street with the Hearst story—too many queries, too much excitement."

As late as May 9, I was still on the firing line, writing in the diary, "Lots more rumbling about the denial of a prize for the Hearst book. I also received a lot of letters that had to go to the Pulitzer board. However, Ralph McGill [a member of the board that year] thought the whole thing was very funny. If I ever recover, I'm sure I'll think so, too."

Next day, at President Kirk's annual reception, the university's counsel and a Trustee finally confirmed for me that the Trustees, at their Monday meeting, had acted because they believed Hearst Sr. was not an "eminent example" worthy of having his life story honored with a Pulitzer Prize in biography. As for Dr. Kirk, he seemed to have taken the whole thing in stride.

To quote my diary for the night of May 10:

"President Kirk was in good humor about the Hearst thing. I'm glad it's all over and all turned out well. It could have been a disaster."

It is significant, too, that there were other biography reversals at the time and more excitement over the art among the academic and literary set, whereas there was relatively little comparable interest in the historians of the era, with few exceptions.

Although the university's trustees didn't figure in these additional biographical upsets, the Pulitzer board didn't hesitate to change or reshuffle their biography juries' recommendations. In a few cases, the Pulitzer board's membership also intruded on and changed a history award in order to accommodate a favored work in biography.

To show how the academic wind was blowing; a book by Margaret Leech, *In the Days of McKinley,* had been recommended for a prize by a biography jury in 1960 but was shifted instead to history for a Pulitzer award, and Samuel Eliot Morison's *John Paul Jones,* the biography jurors' second choice, became the biography winner. The history jury that was so rudely reversed consisted of the provost of Columbia University, Dr. John A. Krout, and Dean Roy F. Nichols of the University of Pennsylvania's graduate division, who had sought instead to honor Henry F. May's *The End of American Innocence* with a history prize.

Five years before, another biography jury had been as abruptly reversed to give a prize to a familiar figure in Washington, William S. White, for *The Taft Story.* After the reversal to honor the McKinley book, however, the biographical listing settled down, with a number of superior selections for awards, including the John Kennedy saga, as told by Arthur M. Schlesinger, Jr., in *A Thousand Days* (1966); George F. Kennan's *Memoirs* (1968); Joseph P. Lash's *Eleanor and Franklin* (1972); W. A. Swanberg's *Luce and His Empire* (1973); R. W. B. Lewis's *Edith Wharton* (1976); and Russell Baker's *Growing Up* (1983).

What had happened to American historical studies meanwhile? After the brilliance of historical scholarship in the first half of the twentieth century, as shown in the Pulitzer Prize listings, there were few occasions for excitement and jubilation among history scholars. Not many historians were able to create the kind of interest in the public domain that so obviously existed in the field of biography. With the exception of the reversal to honor Miss Leech, I recall no comparable fuss about any historical work through my own time and extending well into the 1980s.

Upon the death of an outstanding historian of an older school, Richard Hofstadter, a two-time Pulitzer winner, what seemed like a decline in American historical literature was mourned by another historian, Christopher Lasch:

"Our generation has seen too many brave beginnings, too many claims that came to nothing, too many books unfinished and even unbegun, too many broken and truncated careers. As activists, we have achieved far less than we hoped; as scholars, our record is undistinguished on the whole."

It is not too late to achieve something better, but it is no longer possible to be complacent about our accomplishments or the superiority of our own understanding of American society to that of the generation before us, whose finest historian was Richard Hofstadter.

Without really knowing why there seemed so much more vitality among biographers than historians toward the end of the twentieth century, it is my guess that the increasing recognition given by the Pulitzer Prizes to general nonfiction as a separate category had something to do with it. Merely to glance down the list of nonfiction prizes, beginning with 1962, is to jar one's realization of the apparent merger of the topical currency of journalism with the long-range view of the historian.

Whether this is good or bad depends entirely on one's sympathy for the difficulties of the historian and the greater thrill of pouncing on events as they are unfolding, the special skill of the journalist. But here, in general nonfiction, is recognition of the significance of events going back to those of the earlier part of the century. As examples, I would single out Barbara Tuchman's two prize-winning works, *The Guns of August* in 1963 and *Stilwell and the American Experience in China, 1911–1945* in 1972. Then, too, there is the monumental Hofstadter work, *Anti-Intellectualism in American Life*, a prizewinner in 1964; Frances FitzGerald's *Fire in the Lake: The Vietnamese and Americans in Vietnam*, a 1973 prize book, and Carl Sagan's *Dragons of Eden*, which won Pulitzer honors in 1978.

I cannot argue in good conscience that all these would have been equally worthy of a historical award, because I have no realistic basis for comparison. But I do contend that no one can reasonably draw an exact line between the proper domain of the historian and the encroaching advance of the journalist in dealing with current events. And the reverse, of course, is also true; more and more, we find that both historical and biographical studies are being affected by the forward rush of the journalist who not only reports on current events but also, all too often, dares to interpret their significance.

This may sometimes amount to nothing more than an awkward tapdance in the deep shadow of the stage of history, but the journalist—

being less inclined to yield to discouragement than the historian—continues to perform in that manner before a wondering public. This is what we must contend with today in our measurement of both the art of the historian and the work of the journalist.

It cannot be a source of wonderment, therefore, that studies in biography can be assessed with greater ease and appreciated by an ever-increasing public. It is the reason, too, that my copies of *Profiles in Courage* and *Citizen Hearst* still lie ready at hand near me—a continual reminder that biography ought never to be dull.

19 ★ THE PRIZES AND VIETNAM

Before I traveled to the Vietnam War front, all I heard were complaints from government bigwigs that the "goddam reporters are against us." And the gripes became even worse after the war correspondents began winning Pulitzer Prizes. Then, the pro-war people muttered, "The Pulitzers are against us."

Even at this late date, I think the complaints are worth examining. The Pulitzer Prizes, after all, were not established yesterday. And they are not going to vanish tomorrow, any more than the Congressional Medal of Honor is likely to dissolve suddenly.

What is basically involved here, I still believe, is something far more important than whether this or that reporter should have had a Pulitzer Prize. Or, indeed, whether the Vietnam War itself should have been fought against the advice of the first military expert (and President) of the war generation, Dwight David Eisenhower.

The issue, to put it bluntly, is whether the First Amendment really means what it says, that there must be absolute protection for the four freedoms in America: of speech, of press, of religious belief, and of the right of petition for a redress of grievances. This is what the Revolutionary War was all about: freedom. And this, basically, became the issue between the government and the press in Vietnam, with the Pulitzer Prizes in the middle.

From my vantage point, having seen the reporters in action in Vietnam more than once and known many of them later, I am satisfied that the laurels for fair and honest reporting both from the war fronts and the rioting campuses at home were properly distributed. My criticism is that some of the worthiest and most important contributions to the public interest in the conduct of the war were not tied to the authors by name.

In few words, I think twice as many reporters and news organizations could have been honored with Pulitzer Prizes in this font of democracy that we call America. We at Columbia should have done more, not less.

Let me lay to rest first of all the nagging allegation, which still crops up from time to time in literature produced for the various Vietnam anniversaries, that most of the Vietnam generation of American war correspondents turned out to be a bunch of wild-eyed radicals.

Not so. No wild-eyed longhair, frothing at the mouth, wrote this devastating critique on the conduct of the war in 1967: "The nation is over-committed, our resources strained, the treasury bare, inflation out of hand, and each of us must be prepared for an uncertain future of war, higher taxes and personal sacrifices for an indeterminate period."

The writer was John S. Knight, leader of the massive Knight (later, Knight-Ridder) newspaper chain, undoubtedly many times a millionaire at seventy-four years of age and still at the time a free and combative spirit in American journalism. For his major role in criticizing the conduct of the Vietnam War, he received the Pulitzer Prize in editorial writing in 1968—the year of Tet, the enemy offensive that broke the American combat lines across all that embattled land in southeast Asia.

One can call the roll of the correspondents in the field who received Pulitzer awards, as well, without finding any Communist-inspired critic, real or fancied, who was injudiciously battering away at the American war effort. Even so, the reporters were under continual pressure from military authorities in the field, as well as from critics within their own ranks, to tell the story of the war the way the White House and the Pentagon wanted it told.

I remember vividly the first time I came across this somewhat less than remarkable wartime phenomenon. I had just come from General William C. Westmoreland's headquarters in the summer of 1964, during my first trip to Vietnam, when I met a thin, mild-mannered, sandy-haired correspondent, Malcolm Browne, then chief of the Associated Press bureau in Saigon. Browne, with David Halberstam of the *New York Times*, had just won a Pulitzer Prize for himself and the AP for his work in the field, but he was still going about business as usual.

When I asked him what pressures he had been under in his prize-winning war correspondence, he smiled slightly and told me the story of the Battle of Ap Bac, long since a classic among war correspondents generally. Now Ap Bac was no Waterloo or Gettysburg, being just a bend in some dusty road leading from the Vietnam jungle, but in the early 1960s when the regime in Saigon was desperately bidding for more American aid and more arms against the Vietcong, almost any engagement was billed as a glorious victory. Only Browne, having talked to American survivors of the action, didn't think much of the victory claims and said so in his dispatch, which was carried on AP's wires.

Within a short time, an American admiral, Harry D. Felt, took Browne to task for belittling the government's claims at Ap Bac and warned him: "Look here, boy! You'd better get on the team!" Browne never did make it on the team, but after the war ended he became a science writer for the *New York Times*—something less than a radical preoccupation.

As for his co-winner, Halberstam, there is a story attached to his Pulitzer honor as well. On September 20, 1963, in an article an editor had dictated from his office, *Time* magazine created a sensation by charging that the Saigon war correspondents themselves had become a part of the Vietnam problem, adding, "They have covered a complex situation from only one angle, as if their own conclusions offered all the necessary illumination."

Halberstam was among the first to respond, saying, "What's been exaggerated? The intrigues? The hostility? It's all been proven. We've been accused of being a bunch of liberals but even that's not true." He further distinguished himself at another time by crumpling a statement from the American Embassy in Saigon, calling it a lie and refusing, publicly, to send it to his newspaper.

I wasn't surprised at all when I learned, first on a confidential basis, that President Kennedy himself had asked to have Halberstam removed from the war zone as a correspondent. What happened, I was told later, was that the President by chance met the publisher of the *Times*, Arthur Ochs (Punch) Sulzberger, and asked him in a seemingly casual manner if he had been planning to shift the argumentative Halberstam from Saigon. To that, the suave Punch responded, just as mildly, that the paper was quite satisfied with Halberstam's war correspondence. And that was that.

What the correspondent did after Vietnam was to be expected from a graduate of Harvard, Class of 1955. He wrote a series of best-selling books and did very well both critically and financially, which doesn't exactly tally with the attacks made on his character as a responsible journalist by the pro-war element during his Vietnam experience.

Another correspondent, with one of the longest service records in Vietnam, was a tough little New Zealander, Peter Arnett. He also worked with Browne in the AP office in Saigon and, with the photographer Horst Faas, also an AP staffer, won Pulitzer honors for his reporting from the battlefield while under fire.

I wrote about Arnett once as a small man "with the face of a cherub and the heart of a lion"—and that is how I still think of him as a latter-day journalist preoccupied with a less dangerous type of assignment. I recall that a Pulitzer Prize juror once told me that Arnett could have won a Pulitzer Prize in any of the long and difficult years during which he worked in Vietnam. He was picked in 1966, the fiftieth anniversary of the prizes. In my memory, he will always be a reporter's reporter.

The New Zealander's heroism was most marked when he rode from Da Nang to the battlefront in a supply helicopter that had been intended originally to act as support for a tank unit called Supply Column 21, near a spot in the Ia Drang valley, Van Tuong. But when the helicopter landed, its crew and its free-loading passenger found themselves trapped in the middle of a pitched battle with the Vietcong.

One American tank and three amtracs already had been destroyed. Three Americans lay dead in the field, with twenty-eight others wounded and the rest in a fierce firefight with the enemy.

It seemed to Arnett at that moment, as he later recalled, that nobody on the American side would emerge alive. But for six hours after the arrival of Arnett's helicopter in the middle of that bloody skirmish, the remaining Americans and their Vietnamese allies held out somehow against the Vietcong.

Then, at last, a relief column arrived and lifted the siege of the surrounded remnants of Supply Column 21.

There is an epilogue to the story, one typical of the American leadership in the Vietnam War. When Arnett filed his story to the Associated Press, he was astounded to learn that American Army information officers were denying that the Vietcong had triumphed over an American army column.

It was his own vivid camera shots, taken at the height of the fighting, that proved he had correctly—and heroically—reported what was later called the agony and death of Supply Column 21. It was this feat that won him his Pulitzer Prize—a magnificent display of fortitude, courage, and sheer professional know-how that was a credit to the survivors of that entrapment and their comrades who died fighting.

When the relief column blew up the remains of the disabled vehicles on the battlefield, they became a mute reminder of a tragic incident in a losing war, as the lone surviving correspondent reported it. Arnett did many another piece about the conflict in Vietnam, because he never was one to run away from a fight, but this was his finest.

Despite such gallantry in action, and so many other incidents like it by other Vietnam War correspondents, the complaints continued about "disloyal" reporters. A sample came from Marguerite Higgins of the *New York Herald Tribune,* who wrote at another time from Saigon, "Reporters here would like to see us lose the war to prove they are right." As events demonstrated, that had nothing to do with the loss of the war.

Four American Presidents, the Commanders in Chief, did their best to reverse our role in that unfortunate conflict, and all failed. Miss Higgins and five other correspondents had won a group Pulitzer Prize for her reporting on the Korean War.

Had it not been for an unemployed reporter, the massacre of helpless civilians in a Vietnamese village called My Lai might never have come to public notice. But the shootings by American troops under the orders of a superior officer did come to light when the first disclosures were made by the jobless reporter, Seymour M. Hersh, who won a Pulitzer Prize in 1970 for his work.

The jury that recommended him for the award wrote that his stories of the horror in Vietnam "shook the nation and had vast international repercussions." True enough: My Lai became a blot not only on the honor of the Army of the United States but on the credibility of the nation itself, in its shabby treatment of the people of a small Asian village caught in the middle of a war.

It was the effect of the war on America that I want to stress here, not the character of the correspondent involved, although Hersh's was and remains exemplary, as his conduct in the case demonstrated. But all the lying, deceit and double-dealing that marked what I call the Vietnam syndrome could not help reflecting on the character of the American government at that time and the worth of its pledges to honor its commitments to all concerned.

This is what was at stake when Hersh obtained a $2,000 grant from a small family foundation, then charged in his subsequent investigation that an Army platoon led by Lieutenant William L. Calley, Jr., shot to death more than a hundred Vietnamese civilians in a cruel and senseless attack in My Lai village (the Army called it "Pinkville") on March 16, 1968. To circulate his story Hersh had to rely on a friend who founded a tiny agency called the Dispatch News Service. And at first, only thirty-six newspapers headed by the Pulitzer family's *St. Louis Post-Dispatch* carried the story on November 13, 1969.

The cover-up then had gone on for more than a year, while the Army dragged out its court-martial inquiry in secret to consider its own charges against Calley, who had not then gone to trial. Eventually, he was tried and convicted by an Army court of killing twenty-two Vietnamese civilians, although he did succeed temporarily in overturning the sentence when he appealed to the civilian courts. However, on November 10, 1975, a Federal appeals court in New Orleans reinstated his sentence. By that time, Hersh had his Pulitzer Prize, a job on the *New York Times,* and a reputation as a first-rate investigative reporter.

The unanswered question to this day is what could possibly have motivated the Army to delay dealing with so sensitive a matter publicly when a jobless journalist, with little money and no influential friends, established the truth of the shocker at My Lai by the simple expedient of finding and interviewing some of the soldiers who had been disgusted with their orders to conduct a shooting spree among Vietnamese civilians.

That question remains an issue in the continual confrontations that have developed since between a free press and its government. This issue cannot be easily resolved as long as public officials believe it possible to use secretive methods in conducting the business of an open society. Eventually, one or the other will have to yield, and I can only hope that the loser will not be the free press.

I have reason for concern. Along with others who remember the Kent State tragedy, which climaxed the long and strained period of campus rioting over our military presence in Southeast Asia, I cannot ever again feel assured that a censorious public will always come down on the side of the free press.

The Vietnam War had been bad enough. But after almost a decade of fighting there, President Nixon had just told the nation that he was sending American troops into neighboring Cambodia to wipe out a haven that had been created there for the Vietcong guerrillas. It had long been the belief of his commanders that the war in Vietnam could not be won without extending it to Laos and Cambodia, and now, at last, they had sold this bill of badly damaged goods to a harassed President.

After Nixon's announcement on April 30, 1970, when violent student reactions began again at Kent State University in common with other campuses, the National Guard was called out to control the student rioters at Kent State. Storefronts had been smashed. People had been hurt. And a riotous crowd had stoned firemen trying to save the campus ROTC building after it had been set afire. There was no doubt that the situation was out of hand, and the presence of the guardsmen—as viewed by the state's governor on Sunday, May 3—was justified.

But what happened on Monday, May 4, was something else again. When the National Guardsmen first used tear gas, rioters began throwing rocks. Then the firing began and four students were killed. These were the circumstances as they were published in the *Akron* (Ohio) *Beacon Journal* on the basis of eyewitness accounts from the twenty-seven reporters and four photographers who had hurried to the scene to examine the casualties:

> Sandra Scheuer, 20, a sophomore from Youngstown, Ohio. She was walking to class that Monday afternoon when a bullet went through her windpipe.
> Allison Krause, 19, a freshman from Pittsburgh, Pa. The day before, she had placed a flower in the barrel of a National Guardsman's rifle. She was running across a parking lot with her boyfriend when the Guard began to fire.

Jeffrey Miller, 20, a sophomore from Plainview, N.J. Moments before he was shot, he was among a group of students who were taunting the Guard. A bullet hit him in the face.

William Schroeder, Jr., 19, a freshman from Lorain, Ohio. He was attending Kent State on an ROTC scholarship and was watching the demonstration when he was shot.

To add to the controversy that spread across the nation in the wake of the fatal shootings, the same paper obtained a confidential FBI report shortly afterward, which purportedly contended that the shootings had been unnecessary. And, bringing home the shock with terrible poignancy, twenty-one-year-old John Paul Filo's picture of a weeping girl kneeling over the body of a boyish victim circulated across the country after it was published in the *Valley Daily News* of nearby Tarentum, Pennsylvania.

There was no argument among either the Pulitzer Prize juries or the prize board when the *Beacon Journal*'s coverage and the Filo picture came up for judgment. Both the paper and the twenty-one-year-old photographer won Pulitzer Prizes. But what concerned me deeply was what I learned later when Bob Giles, the responsible *Beacon Journal* editor, wrote of a decidedly divided public reaction. The gist of his conclusions was:

"There were those who believed the student demonstrators had received exactly what they deserved and those who were quite ready to charge the National Guardsmen involved with murder. We believed it was vital for the Beacon Journal to be deeply involved in the quest for truth."

True, the adverse public reaction soon was overshadowed by greater events that took place in Vietnam itself. And true, as well, the Pulitzer board received no unfavorable criticism for its prize awards in the Kent State tragedy so far as I know. And, as a result of his insistence on getting at the truth about the killings of the four students and his courageous use of his staff and other resources at the *Beacon Journal,* Bob Giles was recognized within his own profession with promotion to editor and publisher of a larger newspaper, the *Detroit News.*

All this seems to point to eventual public acceptance of the press's responsibility to make the fullest use of its privileges under the First Amendment, in the event of any major failure of government to protect the public interest. And, I suppose, I should have thankfully accepted that conclusion instead of wondering, as so many other journalists did at the time, what would happen next to test this continual and never-ending struggle between press and government in an open society.

I did not have long to wait. On June 13, 1971, the *New York Times* broke the story of the long-secret Pentagon Papers, and the federal government moved through the courts to halt publication—a direct test of the validity of the First Amendment. Now, at last, the issue was joined.

20 ★ THE PRIZES AND THE LAW

The excitement over the Pentagon Papers case comes through to a new generation of journalists as a vague murmur toward century's end, but the issues it posed still remain troublesome.

This, in all probability, will continue to be the position in America for as long as there are differences between a vigorous and outspoken independent press and a government that seeks (by all possible means) to present itself in the best possible light before a free people. To maintain a proper balance between the two—press and government—will serve the public interest; but just how that is to be done will quite likely always be an open question.

At any rate, this was how I first reacted to the original government attack on the publication of the Pentagon Papers when the *New York Times* presented the opening articles, beginning June 13, 1971, under the byline of Neil Sheehan, a seasoned Vietnam War correspondent who had been the first to obtain them. Two days later, I wrote in my diary:

"The Attorney General of the United States went to court today for an injunction to stop The New York Times from publishing the Vietnam War documents it obtained from the Defense Department. Censorship of the worst kind. It can't last."

But it did last, which bothered me excessively as must have been the case with millions of other Americans beyond the *Times*'s own readership. For when the Federal District Court in New York granted a temporary injunction to Attorney General John N. Mitchell, who was acting for President Nixon, the *Times* had to halt publication of the documents that told the public for the first time how and why the country had been secretly maneuvered into the Vietnam War.

Top: A Pulitzer Prize Directorate in my time; (*left to right*) Joseph Pulitzer, Jr., chairman of the Pulitzer Prize Board; President William McGill of Columbia University; me next to him as administrator of the awards and secretary of the board. *Bottom left*: A critical vote at a Pulitzer board session when a prize is being decided; Norman Chandler of the *Los Angeles Times* is in front and next to him is Pulitzer. I am counting their votes and those of the others around the unseen part of the table. *Bottom right*: Dorothy and I are at a party for the Pulitzer Prize winners at Columbia in the late 1960s.

Outside our borders, friend and foe at once realized that a major struggle was in progress in the United States over the enforcement of the First Amendment—the key to the continuation of the United States as the world's oldest functioning democracy since the earliest ideal state in ancient Greece. This, in a few words, is what captured public attention at home and abroad.

One did not have to be a professor of Constitutional law in America to realize that any prior restraint on publication (or broadcast, for that matter) was an outright violation of Constitutional guarantees that all citizens had a right, short of a formal declaration of war, to know what their government was doing in Vietnam. Could it last?

There is no need to review at length all aspects of the struggle that ensued at this late date. It is sufficient to emphasize that, once the *New York Times* had to give in temporarily to restraint, the same source within the government that had supplied the papers to the *Times* now made them available to the *Washington Post* and other newspapers. The *Post* proceeded to publish them at once and, as a result, was also restrained temporarily from continuing to publish.

The source, Daniel Ellsberg, a member of the study group that prepared the Pentagon Papers at the direction of Defense Secretary Robert S. McNamara, was not at all bashful about announcing that he had given the documents to the *New York Times* and, later, to the *Washington Post* and a number of other newspapers.

The case was decided by a U.S. Supreme Court that was more liberal then than it became toward century's end following a number of conservative appointments. On June 30, 1971, the high court voted 6–3 that the press was right in putting the crux of the papers before the public. Justice Hugo L. Black wrote in a concurring opinion for the majority:

"In my view, far from deserving condemnation for their courageous reporting, the *New York Times* and the *Washington Post* and other newspapers should be commended for serving the purpose that the Founding Fathers saw so clearly. In revealing the workings of government that led to the Vietnam War, the newspapers did precisely that which the founders hoped and trusted they would do."

Fine words. But a closer examination of the Supreme Court's verdict broadly indicates that, had the government been able to show the nation's security had been endangered, the verdict might not have been so directly for the press. There seems, accordingly, to be an implicit warning in the high court's decision that prior restraint could yet be applied in such situations at some future time.

That, at any rate, was my own conclusion. In my diary for July 1, 1971, I wrote: "So the Supreme Court supported the *New York Times* and the *Washington Post* by ruling that the government had not proved the Vietnam papers were vital to national security. It wasn't a very clear-cut victory, after all, for the court obviously would have upheld the injunction if it had felt that national security had been endangered. It makes me very uneasy."

Ironically, I had just finished a new book, *Free Press / Free People: The Best Cause.* It was published that same year.

The *Times* people directly involved, especially the executives, have always contended that they would pursue the same course with the Pentagon Papers if they had to make the publication decision all over again. But I have often wondered whether my Columbia University colleagues at the time would take the same positions they adopted then in deciding Pulitzer Prize honors for any future case that raised similar issues.

If the high court's ruling was qualified, the way the Pulitzer organization threaded itself through this moral and legal labyrinth turned out to be downright tortuous. It was, by all odds, the most complicated situation during my service as the university's administrator of the prizes. And I marvel sometimes, considering all the differing points of view that had to be taken into account, that we were able to accomplish as much as we actually did.

To begin with, I was relieved when I saw that only one newspaper, the *New York Times,* had submitted an exhibit in contention for the highest Pulitzer award in journalism, the gold medal for public service. Having been the first to publish and to be temporarily restrained, the *Times* was given a clear shot at the gold medal by its competitors who had refrained from entering rival exhibits.

What the *Times* placed before the public service jury on its own responsibility was an exhibit consisting of the more than fifty full-size pages it had published serially in the Pentagon Papers case. Then, there was a companion exhibit for Neil Sheehan, the reporter who had obtained the documents and commented on them at length on the basis of his service as a Vietnam combat correspondent beginning in 1962. He was thereby nominated for a separate award in national or international reporting.

When the Pulitzer Prize juries assembled at Columbia on March 7–9, 1972, both *Times* entries were put together as a single exhibit, which the public service jury then unanimously recommended for the much-coveted gold medal—one for the paper, and presumably another for Sheehan.

The Pulitzer board, however, was by no means as unanimous at first. Joseph Pulitzer, Jr., the board's chairman, was the *Times*'s foremost champion, but the opposition, led by Vermont C. Royster of the *Wall Street Journal*, seriously questioned whether top secret government material like the Pentagon Papers should have been published by any newspaper.

At the height of the argument, someone asked to have Sheehan's name omitted—I am not sure who it was—but the objection was theoretically based on technical and not personal grounds. James Reston, the *Times*'s representative, was not in the room (and was barred anyway from being admitted to the discussion as an interested party), so that—regrettably— killed whatever chance Sheehan might have had for a reporting award that year.

The argument ended suddenly when another board member asked Royster if he'd have published the Pentagon Papers in the *Wall Street Journal* if they'd come to him first. He said yes, promptly, whereupon the members unanimously agreed that the public service gold medal should go to the *Times* for the publication of the Pentagon Papers, which is the way the citation was drafted.

That happened on April 13. But on April 30, at a special Sunday meeting of the Columbia Trustees, they twice voted down the award given the *Times* as well as another involving secret government papers, a document published by the columnist Jack Anderson that showed the United States had favored Pakistan in the Indo-Pakistan War. The Trustees, nearly all lawyers, were much more sensitive than the Pulitzer board about the government's "top secret" stamp.

As I later learned, President McGill prevailed on the Trustees to reconsider. Thereupon, both awards went through, but the Trustees issued a disapproving statement with the announcement on May 1, saying that "certain of the recipients would not have been chosen" if it had been their decision alone.

This statement opened wide a breach between the Trustees as the university's governing board and the Pulitzer board, which never was healed—something that everybody concerned with the awards had cause to regret.

The Trustees' problem was that they were legally bound, under the terms of the Pulitzer bequest, to limit themselves to approving or disapproving the choices of the Pulitzer board. They could not substitute their own prize selection for that of the Pulitzer board, which in the end led President McGill to threaten to resign at the Trustees' Sunday meeting. That was what caused them to reinstate the Pulitzer board's choices together with their own statement of protest.

The elimination of Neil Sheehan as an individual prizewinner, considering the value of his services in the Pentagon Papers case and in the Vietnam War itself, also was a disappointment to me and to most of his colleagues in the field, including some of his rivals. Although I never met him, I knew very well how bravely he had served both his news organization and his country from the time he went to Vietnam in 1962 as a correspondent for United Press International.

To my knowledge, in addition to missing out as a prizewinner in the Pentagon Papers case, he also might have qualified for a Pulitzer on at least one other occasion—and perhaps more. I am sure, as well, that at the very least he could have been cited along with the *New York Times* in the formula for the gold medal award in 1972, following a precedent set in 1960 when the *Los Angeles Times* and its investigative reporter Gene Sherman were named as gold medalists for their attack on the narcotics traffic in California.

When Sheehan finally did win the Pulitzer he had earned in Vietnam while only a few years out of Harvard (magna cum laude, 1958), it was not for war correspondence but for general nonfiction—his book about the war entitled *A Bright and Shining Lie: John Paul Vann and America in Vietnam*. The prize came to him in 1988 when he was fifty-two years old and no longer active in daily journalism.

I heard from him once after his departure from Vietnam when I wrote to ask him whether he shared the view of his *Times* editors who had pledged themselves to fight for their rights as citizens under the First Amendment if the government ever posed another challenge such as the one in the Pentagon Papers case. His reply:

"I shall feel just as strongly about the First Amendment until the day I die."

President McGill, Joseph Pulitzer, Jr., a representative of the Columbia Journalism School, and I agreed at a meeting on June 20, 1972, that the only possible solution to the almost continual strain between the Trustees and the Pulitzer organization was to ask the Trustees to divest themselves of their authority over the awards. Under the plan we worked out that day, once the Trustees stepped aside, the president of the university would announce the awards solely on the decisions of the Pulitzer board and its juries.

Once the Trustees accepted, it followed that the name of the governing body for the awards would become the Pulitzer Prize Board and the old designation, Advisory Board on the Pulitzer Prizes, would be discarded.

This was the note I wrote in my diary:

"President McGill, who would remain as a member of the Pulitzer Prize Board, undertook to carry out this negotiation with the Trustees. At the same time, we agreed to broaden the juries in letters, drama, music and art so that they would be drawn from non-conformist as well as conformist critics and scholars. We also agreed that we should try to be as venturesome in the arts as we are in journalism."

All this was easier said than done, as my own service during the next few years demonstrated. I would guess, without really knowing, that one of the principal reasons I was asked to stay on for two more years in both the Pulitzer office and my classrooms after reaching emeritus status in 1974 was precisely because the Trustees and the Pulitzer board still had their differences.

At any rate, when I agreed to remain on the job until I was seventy years old, I left myself wide open for another battering experience in the legal struggle over the prizes—Watergate. That classic of American journalism began breaking in the *Washington Post* before the dust had settled from the struggle over the Pentagon Papers.

Even at this late date, I am impressed by the speed with which the *Washington Post* moved to fix responsibility for the "third-rate burglary" in the Democratic National Committee's offices in the Watergate complex in Washington, D.C., before dawn on June 17, 1972. Fewer than seventeen months later, the evidence of President Nixon's culpability was so marked that I wrote in my diary:

"So now Time magazine has called on Nixon to resign. It is like *Osservatore Romano* calling on the Pope to step down. The Detroit News, New York Times and other papers are joining in this extraordinary demonstration. It is almost as if somebody had given the signal. But Nixon is at Key Biscayne, FL., and says nothing."

To me at least, the Watergate caper and the *Washington Post*'s role in smashing a criminal conspiracy that forced a President's resignation will always remain as the most extraordinary feat in the records of the Pulitzer Prizes in journalism.

21 ★ THE PRESIDENCY AND THE PRIZES

To the end of his days, Howard Simons always maintained in his near-sighted, mild-mannered way that the break against President Nixon in the Watergate case had been a colossal accident.

It was his view, and most newspaper people in the nation's capital agreed with him, that the *Washington Post* had been lucky to explode the worst Presidential scandal since Teapot Dome. And the paper had been even more fortunate, he murmured softly, that its investigation had forced Nixon's resignation.

This is how I best remember Howard's analysis—from our conversation one day years afterward in the *Post*'s newsroom during his tenure as managing editor:

"The whole Watergate thing was bizarre. It was a bizarre break-in at Democratic National Committee headquarters at Watergate. The White House reaction was bizarre—'a third-rate burglary,' they called it. And," here he sighed, as if he still didn't believe he and his boss, Ben Bradlee, had authorized so strange a circumstance, "we went with an investigation by two kids, one of whom we'd nearly fired [Carl Bernstein] and the other [Bob Woodward] with less than a year's experience as a reporter. It's no wonder the White House didn't take us seriously. . . . It was risky business."

This is the whole point about Watergate, or any other attack that pits a mere newspaper reporter against the awesome power of the Presidency—it really is risky business, which is why there are so few Pulitzer Prizes in the records at Columbia for *real* investigations of the White House.

To be sure, row upon row of White House correspondents may be seen on television on occasion at Presidential news conferences, dutifully taking notes. Some even ask a tough question now and then. But by and large, when the chips are down and the risks of questioning the conduct of the Presidency are very great, it would be madness for a reporter on the White House beat to take on an investigation of the nation's first citizen without authorization from the home office.

And it is no disgrace for an editor or a publisher to conclude that opposition to a Presidential action may best be taken with the least risk in the form of editorial opinion or a learned political column by the paper's White House analyst. As for television, the odds are even greater against a true investigation in a medium that must be licensed by the Federal government.

I do not wonder, therefore, that the White House of Richard Nixon came tumbling down through sheer accident, as Howard Simons conceded, because the *Washington Post* went with two green kids who produced the clinching evidence against a tough and powerful President. And it also does not seem strange to me, either, that most Pulitzer Prizes for national affairs are won for reportorial exploits in regional rather than national affairs, for disclosures affecting delinquent cabinet officials, at most, rather than a Chief Executive of the nation.

This is not to say that we must assume corruption in politics is a part of the problem at the White House in every administration. I don't believe that, and I doubt that many others of my ever-suspicious newspaper reportorial breed believe it. Nevertheless, in any open society, ours or others, experience has shown that corruption can be a problem. And the possibility cannot be excluded in administrations in which the President, however noble in character, cannot maintain leadership at all times.

The major instance of such transgressions in the Pulitzer files, aside from the Pentagon Papers and Watergate, is the Teapot Dome inquiry. In that case, despite the tremendous authority wielded by a Senate investigation of years' duration into the wrongdoing of a Cabinet officer whom even a President suspected, it was a newspaper reporter who produced the evidence that broke the scandal wide open.

The name of Paul Y. Anderson cannot be found on the always impressive roster of White House correspondents who are supposed to watch a Presidential administration day after day and night after night. Nor is he identified among the imperious Washington seers—the columnists and commentators who remark on the deeds, and sometimes the misdeeds, real or fancied—of our Presidents.

No, Paul Y. Anderson was just a local investigative reporter on the staff of the *St. Louis Post-Dispatch* when he was assigned to look into the strange case of the Federal government's lease of its oil lands at Teapot Dome, Wyoming, in 1922 to two private oilmen. Although President Harding publicly stood by his Interior Secretary, Albert B. Fall, that official was obliged to resign within a year under the pressure of a Senate investigation.

Still, nobody could prove that Fall had done anything wrong, until the *Post-Dispatch*'s Anderson charged four years later in a celebrated series called "Who Got the Bonds?" that Fall had been bribed by Harry F. Sinclair, one of the two oil promoters, with large sums in Liberty bonds. Fall was convicted at last and sent to jail; Sinclair also was jailed for contempt of the Senate; but the second oilman, Edward F. Doheny, was acquitted after a trial.

The Federal government finally moved, after President Harding's death in 1923, by canceling the Teapot Dome oil leases and forcing the resignation of the Attorney General and the Secretary of the Navy in addition to Fall. But had it not been for a reporter, the oil gang might have gotten away with a bare-faced raid on government oil lands.

Six years after Anderson was assigned to the Teapot Dome scandal, he won a Pulitzer Prize for reporting, but the award's tortuous phraseology discloses, I think, the mixed emotions of the Pulitzer board at the time:

"PAUL Y. ANDERSON, St. Louis Post-Dispatch, for his highly effective work in bringing to light a situation which resulted in revealing the disposition of Liberty Bonds purchased and distributed by the Continental Trading Company in connection with naval oil leases."

In a 1991 biography of the second Joseph Pulitzer, Anderson's managing editor in St. Louis, Oliver K. Bovard, is given part of the credit for the exposé, which is stated with greater directness as follows: "PAUL Y. ANDERSON, with important behind-the-scenes direction and support from Bovard in St. Louis, was chiefly responsible for the exposure of bribery, collusion and fraud which brought the downfall of those involved. For this he won a . . . Pulitzer Prize."

The passage of years does make a difference in the way the affairs of the Federal government are placed before the people.

In the *Washington Post*'s attack on the Watergate scandal, the key decision to take on the White House also was made at home, in the front office, with the publisher, Katharine Graham, and the top editorial executives, Ben Bradlee and Howard Simons, committing the paper to the risky investigation while all their rivals hesitated or backed off.

Some of the august members of the Washington press establishment were appalled at the *Washington Post*'s temerity. In the first cry of surprise over the attack on the Nixon White House, the pack ran with Ron Ziegler, the White House press secretary, who complained that "certain elements may try to stretch this beyond what it is." Also, Attorney General John N. Mitchell was even more self-serving, saying that the Watergate thieves hadn't operated "in our behalf or with our consent."

I remember one of the Washington correspondents saying at the time that the *Post* was "crazy to go with a couple of kids" and predicting, "Nixon is going to take the presses away from them before this is over."

I don't criticize the eminent journalist for his caution. In the same situation, I might have been just as standoffish. In fact, when the *Washington Post*'s exhibit came in for consideration for a Pulitzer Prize later, the letter over Simons's signature was so restrained it didn't even mention Richard Nixon by name, concluding:

"What started as a caper has become an ever-spreading tumor on the body politic reaching from just outside the Oval Office into the very mechanisms by which Americans conduct their public affairs. 'Watergate' as a euphemism is now more than just wire-tapping and breaking and entering. It is political espionage and sabotage, reaching into the highest echelons of government."

Do you believe it is any easier for a press establishment that is largely dominated by executives with Republican sympathies to take on Democratic Presidents? On the basis of the available evidence among Pulitzer Prize winners, I don't think so.

The *New York Times,* with its Democratic orientation at the time in its editorial and op-ed pages, became the bitterest critic of Lyndon Johnson's policies in the Vietnam War and did not hesitate to issue the Pentagon Papers, which discredited his and successive administrations that dealt with the war's problems. Still, in Democratic New York City, that was risky.

John S. Knight, very far from a flaming liberal at age seventy-four, frankly confessed in a column that helped him win a Pulitzer Prize, "As an opponent of our involvement in Vietnam since 1954, I have neither enjoyed criticizing three Presidents nor accurately predicted the tragic consequences of their policies."

And what about personal attacks on the Presidents themselves? These instances are rare, indeed, but I know of at least two Pulitzer Prizes that were given to reporters for such work (and the anti-Nixon awards were made over the objections of many of the Columbia Trustees):

> 1965—Louis M. Kohlmeier of the Wall Street Journal for his enterprise in reporting the growth of the fortune of President Lyndon B. Johnson and his family.
>
> 1974—James R. Polk of the Washington Star-News for his disclosure of alleged irregularities in the financing of the campaign to elect President Nixon in 1972.
>
> 1974—Jack White of the Providence (R.I.) Journal and Evening Bulletin for his initiative in exclusively disclosing President Nixon's Federal income tax payments in 1970 and 1971.

It was a long time before the *Washington Post*'s young reporters Woodward and Bernstein even came close to any major disclosure affecting President Nixon, however. But when they did produce tangible evidence linking the Nixon White House to the convicted Watergate burglars, some of his strongest supporters among the nation's press executives were appalled.

Moreover, the Pulitzer establishment at Columbia itself was divided on how far it was possible to go in attacking a sitting President. This was quite a change from the patronizing attitude that had been adopted toward Woodward and Bernstein's reporting directly after the Watergate break-in on June 17, 1972.

Indeed, after Nixon's landslide reelection victory in November 1972, the *Post*'s inquiry was generally regarded as a lost cause. It followed that when the Pulitzer Prize juries met on March 8–9, 1973, the public service jurors put the *Washington Post*'s Watergate inquiry third behind work on different stories done by the *Chicago Tribune* and the *New York Times*. When I asked why, one juror told me loftily, "Watergate is just a pimple on the elephant's ass."

But all at once, between the time the juries went home and the day the Pulitzer board met, Watergate blew sky-high. James W. McCord, a former FBI agent who had been involved with the five Watergate burglars, opened up in a bid for leniency before his sentencing judge, John J. Sirica, in Federal Court. He implicated, among others, John W. Dean III, counsel to the President. Dean in turn accused Nixon's two top aides, H. R. Haldeman and John Ehrlichman, of the cover-up. Nixon himself, shaken, invoked executive privilege to save himself. But it was too late, for the evidence was mounting against him.

By the time the Pulitzer board met on April 12, there was no question about who would win the gold medal for public service. The board reversed its jurors, voted unanimously for the *Washington Post* as the public service gold medalist and, for good measure, threw in an extra national reporting prize for the *Post*'s commentator, David Broder. Woodward and Bernstein were slighted by being omitted from the Pulitzer Prize citation as Neil Sheehan had been in the Pentagon Papers award to the *New York Times*.

However the Columbia Trustees may have felt privately, they did not try to block the prizes voted by the Pulitzer board on May 7. And now, the *Washington Post* and Messrs. Woodward and Bernstein finally won the nationwide recognition they had deserved from the outset. As for President Nixon, he may have believed himself safe—even if many of those about him now were either disgraced, facing trial, or convicted in the Watergate case—for he took to criticizing the Pulitzers. It gave him little satisfaction, for he soon was involved in a struggle to keep secret the White House tapes disclosing his part in this "third-rate burglary."

The end was in sight on July 24, 1974, when the U.S. Supreme Court ruled 8–0 that the President would have to yield the tapes. Between July 24 and 30, the House Judiciary Committee voted three articles of impeachment under which the President would have had to stand trial for misdeeds charged to him. And the House of Representatives then approved the committee report, 412–3. On August 9, 1974, Nixon resigned and his successor, Vice-President Gerald R. Ford, immediately gave him an unconditional pardon for all Federal crimes he had "committed or may have committed."

Thereby, Nixon became the only American President to quit high office under fire. By grace of his pardon, he lingered on for many years until his death in 1994 and occasionally was heard from in the unlikely role of an American elder statesman. It was scarcely the outcome that the ever-modest Howard Simons had anticipated when he told me what a colossal accident it had been that the *Washington Post* had been able to prove its case against Nixon.

Could it happen again? Not unless there is another venturesome and vindictive President who forgets the lessons of history. But even then, pitting a mere reporter against a President of the United States is a terrible mismatch that makes victory possible over the White House only through a fortunate accident.

That, too, is a lesson of history.

22 ★ WINDING DOWN

My last two years in the Pulitzer Prize Office coincided with the collapse of the American war effort in Southeast Asia and its aftermath.

It was not my happiest time, by any means, during the twenty-two years I administered the awards and served as the secretary of the Pulitzer Prize Board. This had nothing whatever to do with my impending departure from Columbia as an emeritus professor, for I already had several offers to continue teaching elsewhere. What bothered me was the prospect of the board's award of prizes for the coverage of the worst defeat for American arms since the War of 1812 when the British burned the White House.

Out of respect for the half-million Americans who had fought in Vietnam, as well as many of the young correspondents and my own students who had opposed the war, I tried as best I could to keep the Pulitzer Office out of the controversy. But now, with the end of the fighting, judgments had to be made—and fifty Pulitzer Prize journalism jurors came to Columbia on March 4, 1976, to begin the decision making.

The major argument, I was convinced, would be about the exhibits for two correspondents who had barely escaped from Saigon on April 30, 1975, just ahead of the victorious North Vietnamese troops and their Vietcong allies who seized the capital of defeated South Vietnam.

One was Keyes Beech, the veteran representing the *Chicago Daily News,* whose last dispatch began, "My last view of Saigon was through the tail door of the helicopter. Tan Son Nhut [the air field] was burning. So was Bien Hoa. Then the door closed—closed on the most humiliating chapter in American history."

The other that impressed me was the Associated Press's exhibit for its chief correspondent, George Esper, another veteran, who had sent this climactic bulletin at the end: "SAIGON (AP) - SOUTH VIETNAM HAS DECLARED UNCONDITIONAL SURRENDER TO THE VIETCONG, ENDING 30 YEARS OF WARFARE."

There was a third exhibit before the jurors that also warranted serious consideration, or so I believed. It was a *New York Times* submission for its veteran, Syd Schanberg, who also had risked his life to stay in Phnom Penh, the capital of Cambodia, when it fell to the native Communists on April 17, 1975, after a five-year war. Thereby, he had been able to gather indisputable evidence that a ruthless campaign of genocide already was under way by the conquerors—an 8,000 word article published by the *Times* on May 9, 1975, that began:

> Bangkok, Thailand, May 8—The victorious Cambodian Communists, who marched into Phnom Penh on April 17 and ended five years of war in Cambodia, are carrying out a peasant revolution that has thrown the entire countryside into upheaval.
>
> Perhaps as many as three or four million people, most of them on foot, have been forced out of the cities and sent on a mammoth and grueling exodus into areas deep in the countryside where, the Communists say, they will have to become peasants.

The implications in Schanberg's account that the conquerors had tortured, starved, and otherwise persecuted Cambodians by the millions were inescapable. That, too, had been a part of the cost of America's losing war in Southeast Asia.

It was with a feeling of despair that I wrote my last commentary on the conflict in my diary, remembering all the while how shabby and hopeless Saigon had looked on my last trip there in 1970—and how much worse it must have been five years later, both there and in Phnom Penh:

> All of us who were in Saigon knew as early as 1964—and maybe earlier—that the U.S. and its Vietnam allies couldn't win. We also guessed that the Communists would win one day but I doubt if we thought it would be as stunning a victory. So the last Americans now have been flown out of Saigon in a panicky rush. . . .

We never could have won without a world war (against the enemy's great protectors in Asia) but we were unwilling to risk it. So we lost, crying all the while that we could have won. Finis.

    Not all my thoughts were as gloomy that first morning of the 1976 jury work. For it was then that I received confirmation from the University of Tennessee at Knoxville that I would be the Meeman Distinguished Professor there for 1976–77—a chair named for Ed Meeman, an outstanding Tennessee journalist. After I had gone to Knoxville the previous spring with Dorothy to do a lecture series, by invitation, the negotiations for the Meeman chair had begun and now were successfully concluded.

I felt so relieved at the extension of my teaching career that I confided my good fortune to the Pulitzer jurors at our sixtieth anniversary luncheon, asked them to await the announcement from Knoxville before spreading the story, and thanked them for all the work they and their predecessors had done to make the prizes mean something in America. To my surprise, they stood and applauded, which was a nice way to bow out.

I already had asked Dick Baker to succeed me as the Pulitzer administrator, and he had agreed, subject to his acceptance by the Pulitzer board and the university (of which there was no doubt).

That afternoon, the international jury, after a laudatory reference to the two correspondents who had recorded the flight of the last Americans from Saigon, recommended that the 1976 prize for foreign reporting should go to Syd Schanberg for his disclosure of the peril facing millions of Cambodians with the Communist takeover in Phnom Penh. It was a worthy choice, I thought. At the very least, it averted the disagreeable business of seeming to celebrate the American defeat in Saigon with a Pulitzer award.

All in all, the journalism juries' selections that day and the next seemed to me to be superior to some in earlier years, so much so that I anticipated scant argument before the Pulitzer Prize Board. In fact, the only unpleasantness prior to the board meeting occurred when Joe Papp, producer of *A Chorus Line,* the drama jury's choice for a prize that year, refused to let us buy house seats so Joe Pulitzer could see the show before the board meeting. Papp needn't have been so chintzy. We were able to buy two fairly decent seats at the box office—the show no longer was a sellout.

It was such niggling annoyances that often had made me wonder why I continued to handle both a Columbia professorship and the Pulitzer administrative chores. But now, with the end in sight, it didn't matter to me any longer.

There was so little argument over the juries' choices in letters, drama, music, and journalism at the Pulitzer board meeting on April 9 that I had comparatively little to do other than hope Dick Baker would be accepted as my successor. He was, without any discussion, after which I looked forward to an early break for lunch and a chance to clean out my office later. But more surprises, all pleasant, awaited me as my diary demonstrates:

"My last Pulitzer board meeting. No argument on any prize. The board gave me a hand-illuminated scroll, a *festschrift* of letters from former board members and Lee Hills presented me with a 30-pound antique gold-plated plaque, which had etched-in signatures of all current board members memorializing my services. . . . At lunch, President McGill toasted me and I responded. I received a Pulitzer Prize Special Award. I felt as if I were being cremated in style and, despite everybody's good intentions, I was glad when it was over."

There was a modest bit of publicity about it in New York, Knoxville, and on the wires (mainly, I would suppose, for editors who had previously served the Pulitzer establishment). And afterward, there were letters to answer and phone calls to return. Also, I did have to await the preparation of all the prize publicity by Fred Knubel, who had succeeded Bob Harron and John Hastings as Columbia's director of public information. But other than that, and my last few classes, I seemed to have survived. Whatever my troubles, spread over more than a quarter century at Columbia, I was handsomely treated at the end.

To add to all else, the Gannett Foundation had engaged me to do a new book, *A Crisis for the American Press,* which was published two years later, and the Pulitzer board has been generous in citing my services to American journalism.

The 1976 Pulitzer Prizes, my last as administrator, were announced by

President McGill on Monday, May 3, shortly after 3 P.M. The Columbia Trustees, having disassociated themselves from the awards the previous year, had no part in the proceedings for the first time in sixty years. After that, I went home to relieve Dorothy's nurse who stayed with her in the last stages of her struggle against Alzheimer's disease.

There are a few more scenes in the process of separating myself from the Pulitzers and Columbia in 1976 that I remember and want to set down here just as they happened. They, too, are precious memories. And for that reason, I prefer to use once again the hasty record I scribbled in my diary at the time:

"May 11: When I went to President McGill's office this morning, he presented me with my Pulitzer Prize certificate and also with a formal, hand-illuminated resolution of the Trustees of the university thanking me for my services. I thanked everybody and left. . . . Then I took Rose Valenstein and Robin Holloway Kuzen [my secretaries] to lunch at Butler Hall and gave them each a bit of jewelry, my way of thanking them for all they'd done for me in the Pulitzer office. And tonight, Dorothy and I heard the D'Oyly Carte company at the Uris Theatre in 'The Pirates of Penzance,' a magnificent performance. All in all, quite a day."

"May 12: Commencement, our 49th, and I broke up my office and took my trophies home by cab, then asked Rose to ship my books and papers and went to a lunch given by Dean Abel for the school's guests. Had a lovely time with Abe Raskin of The Times, who won the Columbia Journalism Award; Judge Moe Potoker, Ed Barrett, Lou Cowan and others who have known me for many years. Next, I finished answering all my letters, kissed Rose and Robin good-bye and paid Mrs. Reams for the last time, wonderful Mrs. Reams who cared for Dorothy at home while I was at school.

"May 13: All morning, I packed our things at the apartment for storage in Aquebogue and put away others in camphor. All told, the apartment was prepared for an absence of 18 months but I didn't want to give it up, couldn't tell what might come next. All the while I loaded the car before taking off for Aquebogue I had the strangest feeling of going away—leaving Columbia at the end of the finest period in our lives, Dorothy and mine. And she, who made it all possible, knew nothing at the end—just followed me with an implicit trust that will always be fulfilled. . . . So I cooked at Aquebogue when we got there and fell into bed, exhausted.

"June 26: A nice swim in the Sound and a happy, happy day. It seems hard to realize that, in spite of Dorothy's mindless condition, we can still carry on and love each other but somehow we do—and we mean it. She cannot demonstrate by word or deed except for a cold little kiss now and then. But sometimes she takes my hand and suddenly kisses it and I know somehow, for a few moments, she is conscious of who she is and who I am. Then the curtain descends again.

"June 29: Dean Hileman phoned from Knoxville and I told him to take any apartment for me of which he approved for the coming academic year at the University of Tennessee. . . . Then more work on the Aquebogue house. I had a good swim, but again Dorothy seems strange. She said at the beach today that she would 'not be good,' but she was. I gave her an all-day sucker to make sure she didn't put stones in her mouth, a bad habit she's acquired recently.

"Tonight, I watched the movie '1776' and again was much affected by the final scene, the signing of the Declaration of Independence, just as I was at the play. Dorothy was asleep.

"June 30: Another muggy day of working and swimming—seemingly not at all out of the ordinary. And still it was—actually, a remarkable day in our lives, Dorothy's and mine, because it marked the last of our 26-year association with Columbia and the Pulitzers. Actually, counting our student experience, it severs a relationship that began in September, 1925, more than 50 years ago when I first saw her walking into the old newsroom in the Journalism building in a ratty old raccoon coat and floppy-tongued flat-heeled shoes. And I saw her smile and fell in love with her at once."

At the end of our time at Columbia, I was seventy and she was seventy-one in the forty-eighth year of our marriage.

23 ★ EXPANDING THE PULITZER PRIZES

The Pulitzer Prizes have served a worthy national purpose in this century. They have come to represent an ideal in journalism, literature, drama, and music in America. Many strive for them each year. To win one is considered a great honor.

But is there still room for improvement in the original purpose of the donor, to use his own words, "for the encouragement of public service, public morals, American literature and the advancement of education" among our people? Not too many years ago, a president of Columbia University and the third Joseph Pulitzer, the grandson of the donor, agreed that these cherished awards could be more venturesome. And I would concur in that opinion on the basis of my own twenty-two years as the Administrator of the prizes.

In public service, we have only one prize—a gold medal that is given to a newspaper for distinguished action in the public interest. For the advancement of public morals, there is no particular award except the implicit recognition in that field, which may be given to a book or a newspaper dealing with some aspect of that troublesome subject. For literature, there are five book prizes and one in drama, as contrasted with a dozen prizes for newspapers, and there is a separate prize for music. In education, Columbia has a well-established Graduate School of Journalism, which is in line with the donor's specification that a journalism school had to be in successful operation for three years before the prizes could be awarded.

At the very least, while approaching their hundredth anniversary, the whole Pulitzer experience, as well as the awards themselves, could well be made the subject of a combined professional and scholarly review based on all the accomplishments, current operations, and available resources of the Pulitzer establishment at Columbia. That decision, of course, would have to be made by the Pulitzer Prize Board under the terms of the Pulitzer will.

Should such a Committee of Review be appointed, for a fixed period of time and for a stated purpose, I would hope that strong consideration would be given to broadening the prizes to give greater emphasis specifically to a series of public awards, each to be recognized annually with a Medal of Honor. This, I believe, would be in keeping with the donor's central purpose to encourage "public service, public morals, American literature and the advancement of education."

The public service gold medal for a newspaper, which has been awarded for such initiatives as the Watergate and Teapot Dome exposés and the Vietnam War disclosures in the Pentagon Papers, ought to be the model for an elaboration of other Pulitzer awards in that field. Given sufficient funds, I see no reason why a new category of public awards should not be established to reward outstanding actions, not only by those currently eligible, but also for individuals and organizations in the United States that are worthy of recognition for their accomplishments in the public interest. I can envisage Medals of Honor that would be annually awarded for advances in the defense of civil liberties, the support of public education, the expansion of science and health, and, by all means, the strengthening of world peace.

I am well aware that the cry will be raised at once that the Pulitzers are out to rival the Nobel Prizes. Not so. The Pulitzer awards were intended from the outset to bestow recognition on American individuals and organizations and so they have remained, with few exceptions, notably in the fields of newspaper photography and combat correspondence. I see no reason for the Pulitzers to compete with the Nobel awards, which have done so well and are so highly respected in the international community.

As for the frequent suggestion that the electronic media should be recognized with Pulitzer Prizes as well, it is clear enough by this time that there are well-established separate prizes in these fields, and I see

The Pulitzer Board sits for its 1967 picture before the Statue of Liberty window.

On a trip to the Pacific Rim during the Vietnam era, I interviewed U.S. Ambassador Samuel Berger in Seoul, South Korea.

Honored with an L.H.D. *(honoris causa)* from Wilkes College in Pennsylvania, I make the commencement address.

no reason, once again, for the Pulitzers to compete with the Oscars, Emmies, and all the rest. What I would suggest, however, is that any American citizen and any American organization should be eligible to compete for the proposed new public awards with their Medals of Honor, should a Committee of Review and the Pulitzer Prize Board approve and work out specific guidelines, provided sufficient funding is made available. I know all this is a large order, but I deeply believe that it is necessary, not so much for the benefit of the prizes or of Columbia University, but for the strengthening of the democratic spirit within the United States as an example to the struggling new democracies that are emerging elsewhere in the world.

There is a more basic argument to be made for the broadening of the Pulitzer Prizes.

In these difficult times, an appalling amount of evidence already exists that large sections of the public have become disenchanted with the lagging emphasis on governmental progress, in whole or in part. And something must be done to encourage a more hopeful point of view in the development of the democratic function as we have tried to practice it in the United States.

Politics as usual, as most opinion polls have repeatedly demonstrated, cannot dissipate the concern that many Americans harbor toward demonstrable weaknesses in our government. The usual course of attacking the governmental process in order to improve it simply has not worked.

A more positive approach is needed, something that would be at the very basis of the creation of the Medals of Honor for public service if the Pulitzer organization believed it fitting and proper to do so.

Such awards would do more than merely bestow recognition on the winning individuals, agencies, or organizations. They would give encouragement to the fundamental purpose of improving the governmental process by respecting the efforts of those who work within the system.

This kind of action is long overdue in support of the public interest in this country. It accords with the spirit of the times. And it could be done with little effort if the will to act—instead of just wringing our hands—could once again dominate our public life as it has so often in the past.

In the depths of the Great Depression, Franklin Roosevelt rallied a whole great nation with his call to action: "The only thing we have to fear is fear itself." And so it is today, except that the paralysis of inaction, too, must be broken at some point. The example of those who strive for and win the proposed Pulitzer Medals of Honor could well give heart to others concerned with the improvement of the American body politic. But if the broadening of the prizes is to be successful, it will have to be undertaken wholeheartedly with the full support of the Pulitzer organization and Columbia. Any helter-skelter operation, done for the benefit of public relations rather than for public service, would be worse than useless and might well harm the very cause it seeks to support.

The last time this painstaking exercise in introspection was attempted occurred during the celebration of the fiftieth anniversary of the Pulitzer Prizes in 1966. It was then that Archibald MacLeish, the three-time winner of the Pulitzer Prize in poetry, asked a distinguished audience to pause,

Draw rein, draw breath,
Cast a cold eye
On life, on death . . .

and consider the consequences of Joseph Pulitzer's turn-of-the-century benefaction.

MacLeish, as the keynoter that night, saluted all the other Pulitzer laureates who were present, and the many who had preceded them, in these generous terms. "Whereas we, ladies and gentlemen—we who address you and a large proportion of you whom we address—*are* the consequences. We are Mr. Pulitzer's dream made flesh."

It was nobly done, worthy of a three-time Pulitzer Prize winner in poetry. For a fiftieth birthday, this was the proper tone, self-congratulatory in nature, and calculated to please everybody, offend nobody. It made all of us who heard MacLeish that night feel comfortable with him on the podium, with our achievements in behalf of the prizes, and even with the prizes themselves.

Am I a Philistine to have wondered then, and since, what would have happened if someone then had lifted a thin but cautioning finger and asked:

"Should we not examine what we have done with these awards, what we have failed to do, and where we go from here?"

I failed to do so then and have done nothing about it since; but now, having been separated from the Pulitzer Prizes since 1976, I wish to make amends. I am neither a poet, a keynoter at a grand anniversary, nor a disgruntled prize aspirant, having been honored on my departure. What I propose herewith is put forward in good faith and with the hope that a sufficient discussion will ensue over the points I have made, to cause a committee of my betters to "cast a cold eye" (as MacLeish suggested in his quotation from his own works) on the results of the Pulitzer benefaction.

The Pulitzer Prize Board, which controls the awards, consists of a group of public-spirited men and women whose efforts are based at Columbia University, as the donor intended. The Trustees of Columbia University have stepped aside. So have the dean and the faculty of Columbia's Journalism School, although the dean remains as an ex-officio member of the board, and the administrator of the awards, by custom, also is considered to be a member of the journalism faculty. (One of the major changes in the board came after my departure. It was then, finally, that the male journalists' domination of the board ended with the addition of qualified women and members of minorities who were not necessarily practicing journalists.)

In the beginning, the donor obviously had not intended for his fellow journalists alone to decide on the destinies of the prizes. It was he who proposed that the presidents of Harvard and Cornell should be board members, something that caused anguish to Columbia's president at the time, Nicholas Murray Butler (styled "Nicholas Miraculous" by his contemporary, President Theodore Roosevelt). For Nicholas Miraculous firmly vetoed the notion of having his opposite numbers at Harvard and Cornell peering over his shoulder. He may even have been conscious of a provision in the Pulitzer deed of gift that suggested the prizes should be moved to Harvard if Columbia's administration, for any reason, proved unsatisfactory.

However, the Pulitzer Prize Board has been able to adapt to changing times. Within the recent past, President Hanna H. Gray of the University of Chicago and Roger W. Wilkins, a senior fellow of the Joint Center for Political Studies, have served as prize-givers on the board. With the board's continually revolving membership, it follows that further changes are likely and that they are bound to be welcomed by the vast majority of those immediately concerned—the aspirants for Joseph Pulitzer's prizes, whose numbers annually increase.

In providing space, service, and facilities for the Pulitzer Prizes—from the beginning, more than seventy-five years ago—Columbia has tried to fulfill the wishes of the donor. Anyone who has stood before the great illuminated Statue of Liberty window in the World Room of Columbia's Journalism Building, where much of the judging has taken place, cannot fail to be moved by the symbolism of the process. The massive robed figure in itself, torch held aloft in its right hand, is emblematic of the intent of the awards.

This is a large operation that has to be seen and experienced to be fully understood. There is a vast and still expanding library of prizewinning exhibits as well as additional space and handling for the thousand or more literary and journalistic entries that are shipped in annually to be distributed before an army of judges, who examine them and make their recommendations each spring to the Pulitzer Prize Board.

The relatively small administrative staff and office cannot by any means define the extent of the total requirement in time and space, money and effort. And, more than once, I had to take advantage of the generosity of my erstwhile neighbors in the Journalism Building, the American Press Institute, which so quickly came to the rescue whenever I needed help or advice (often both).

Barring an unexpected rupture in their relationships, I see no reason why the Pulitzer Prizes cannot continue to be accommodated at Columbia. But that doesn't mean other publishers, universities, and public-spirited foundations cannot be represented on the prize-giving board.

This is neither a sentimental notion nor a delayed publicity pitch. I have always thought that the Pulitzer Prize Board ought to try to be representative of all the best in America, for as long as it alone decides the annual listing of laureates. I only wish, belatedly, that I could have worked out some method for reconciling the continued presence of the Trustees of Columbia University in their association with the Pulitzer board. For the Trustees, to give them their due, also were and remain broadly representative of an ever important aspect of American public opinion that is quite different from that of the Pulitzer board.

Now, the principal burden lies with the president of Columbia University as the sole member of the Pulitzer board who also is responsible to the Trustees of the university. It is a heavy load for one individual to bear, regardless of competence and public spiritedness.

Dick Baker, the first to succeed me as administrator of the prizes, once asked the third Joseph Pulitzer, while the three of us were together, "Why are the Pulitzer Prizes so chauvinistic? Why do they always have to be so all-American?"

Joseph Pulitzer, Jr., took the query good-naturedly. "Oh, that was old JP," he replied. "He always wanted to do something for the United States and the American people and the prizes were his way of doing it."

However, at another time, I well remember that the third Pulitzer, elaborating on his grandfather's bequest, also called it a "tradition of conscience," which I think is more to the point. For an elaboration of that tradition, for whatever reason, I always referred to the first Joseph Pulitzer's statement of principle:

"Always fight for progress and reform, never tolerate injustice or corruption, always fight demagogues of all parties, never belong to any party, always oppose privileged classes and public plunderers, never lack sympathy for the poor, always remain devoted to the public welfare, never be satisfied with merely printing the news, always be drastically independent, never be afraid to attack wrong either by predatory plutocracy or predatory poverty."

To my mind, that says it all. I accepted it as the tradition of conscience that governed my every act while I handled the day-to-day affairs of the Pulitzer Prize organization. It remains my life's ideal.

PART 5

A Different Life

24 ★ CHANGE AND CIRCUMSTANCE

All of us who lived far out on eastern Long Island realized that the Atlantic hurricane season was dangerous. It could begin almost any time in August. Storms could swoop down on the stoutest house or the best-built barn and rip them apart. And so, when I was preparing to leave for my new teaching assignment in Tennessee in 1976, I should have been alert to the possibility of a killer storm, but I wasn't prepared when it struck our old house.

On the night of August 9, I was packing for our trip to Knoxville and hadn't given the weather a thought. Nor had Dorothy. Now, all she could do, when not napping, was watch what I was doing.

Maybe I'd not have been caught short if I'd consulted friends or the fishermen on Peconic Bay. From the onset of August, they always were on the alert for a "line storm," the region's deceptively mild phrase that covered almost everything from a big wind to a full-fledged Atlantic hurricane. But I was too busy with my own affairs and hadn't consulted anyone.

The line the natives referred to out our way was merely the beginning of the autumnal equinox when the sun seems to cross the celestial equator from north to south, marking the onset of fall in the northern hemisphere, but in August that was weeks early for a change of seasons by the calendar.

What hurt all of us that year—the fishermen, the vacationers, and the in-and-out locals like myself—was that the line storms caught us completely by surprise. I was only midway through my packing chores and thinking about the drive to Tennessee when I heard a radio warning that Hurricane Belle would strike our little part of the world around 10 P.M.

Almost automatically, I stopped packing and began making the old house weather-tight, while the radio kept tracking the course of the killer storm. My routine had been the same for all my years in the old homestead in Aquebogue, so much so that Dorothy, jogged momentarily from her illness, noticed what I was doing and asked, "Hurricane coming?"

I told her as quietly as I could, trying not to alarm her unnecessarily, that I was taking precautions against the possibility of a storm, but that of course it might blow over, as it sometimes did. She nodded and paid no further attention either to me or the weather, and soon she dozed off in her chair.

I thought of the many times we both had worked together to make the old house secure at the outset of the hurricane season, then shook my head in irritation at my own sentimentality. It simply would not do. Bygones aside, there was work to do and I had to get on with it or invite disaster.

The routine was familiar enough. First, doors and windows had to be checked to be sure they were tightly closed and all screens locked into place. Next, the bathtub had to be filled with water from the basement pump. (We never did have town water, so we'd be helpless if the basement water pump conked out on us during a storm, as sometimes happened.) For good measure, I also filled every pot and pan we had with water for drinking.

I checked the batteries in our flashlights and radio, filled our kerosene hurricane lamps, put a large packet of tall white candles plus matches on the kitchen table with my candleholders, and made sure there was enough food in the refrigerator to last us several days.

By nightfall, I was done and put together a quick dinner for us, calculating at the same time that I wouldn't be able to leave for Knoxville for at least two or three days. A hard rain already was pelting our end of the island. And as I fed Dorothy and gulped down the food on my own plate, I heard the radio reporting that the storm now was bearing down directly on us. This was one time we were not going to be let off, the announcer said in a doomsday tone.

I wasn't worried about the old house. It had weathered many a hurricane from the time it was built in 1827, but I wasn't so sure about the line of tall elms between the house and the highway, which already were swaying dangerously. If any of them fell, depending on the strength and direction of the hurricane winds, the consequences could be drastic.

But I had no time to worry. Joe Hoppe, my neighbor to the west, made it through the storm to the old house in time to help me put Dorothy to bed downstairs. Also, Al Hubbard, an electrician who lived across the road, stuck his head in the front door a little later to make sure we were all right.

With such thoughtful neighbors, I felt secure enough around nine o'clock to go to bed myself on the downstairs lounge outside the bedroom, even if I couldn't sleep. At the time, neither the rising wind nor the lashing rain appeared to disturb Dorothy in the downstairs bedroom, and for that I was profoundly grateful.

All went as well as could be expected in a hurricane until 11:45 that night—I know the exact time because the electric clock stopped then—when one of our roadside elms went down with a resounding crash. At the same moment, our small electric bedside lamp beside Dorothy winked out, indicating that a power line had snapped. Within moments, I smelled smoke and realized the house was on fire. (Much later, I learned that a power surge caused by the broken line melted the basement fuses, and this touched off the flames.)

I tried to phone the Riverhead Fire Department three miles away but the line was dead. However, Joe Hoppe—always faithful, always dependable—had stayed up next door, seen the flames shooting from our basement, and sent in the alarm for us. At the height of the storm, he fought through wind and rain to get in our back door, helped me wrap Dorothy in a rain cape, and together we managed somehow to get her to his place where his wife, Fran, took care of her.

The Riverhead firemen did the rest. How they managed to control and douse the flames during the hurricane, I shall never know, but they're the ones who saved the old house for us. And Joe Hoppe, Al Hubbard, and their wives did the rest to get us back home at dawn. We were soaked, tired, and hungry as the storm eased off, but we were still together. And to me, that counted for more than all else.

Thanks to our insurance people and their adjusters, repairs were undertaken at once in the parts of the house that had suffered fire and smoke damage. The expense, too, was taken care of, except for a $250 deductible in my policy that I was glad to pay.

After that, toward the end of the month, it was high time for me to move out with Dorothy, and head south to Tennessee on still another risky adventure.

I did ask our doctor to examine her before our departure, but the examination didn't tell either of us much that we didn't already know about her condition. Physically, except for being about twenty-five pounds overweight and having a below normal red blood cell count, the doctor's report indicated, she was normal for someone her age. However, I was warned to make sure she continued her regular medication while we were in Knoxville and to arrange for another blood test within a month after our arrival. Other than that, our doctor could do nothing other than wish me luck.

Despite all my worries, the temporary move to Tennessee turned out reasonably well at first. To be sure, there were arguments with my Knoxville landlord, who had put us in a small first-floor furnished flat instead of the large third-floor apartment my Tennessee sponsors had contracted for, but this misunderstanding was eventually straightened out. And there also were discussions at the university about academic details—courses, hours, outside appearances, and the like—but that was normal enough.

As far as Dorothy herself was concerned, my arrangements turned out better than I'd dared hope for. A practical nurse, Nina Coatney, was wonderfully considerate, and Dorothy took to her immediately. Also, one of my first visitors was a former student at Columbia, Anna Paddon, now a professor at the College of Communications. She brought along the youngest of her three children, Joel, three years old, who at once captured Dorothy's attention.

I hadn't thought at first that I could take Dorothy to university receptions where she might be hemmed in by strangers, but Anna encouraged me to try it and everything seemed to go well. True, either Anna or I stuck with her, and some of the other faculty wives later helped with such chores. Even so, she seemed to adjust to new people and new conditions; even if she couldn't possibly have known what was being said around her, she still was able to smile charmingly and nod if someone addressed her, always a pleasant reaction. I liked to think that few who weren't aware of her condition could guess that she was anything less than the attractive wife of a visiting professor.

People at Tennessee were always considerate of me. Don Hileman, dean of the College of Communications, and his director of studies, Professor Dozier Cade (an old China hand), limited entry into my courses, an attractive mix of graduate and undergraduate subjects. As for the students, they won my heart from the outset—the decisive factor at Tennessee as far as I was concerned. There was, in addition, a bonus I hadn't expected—two Olympic-sized swimming pools, one indoors, the other outdoors, where I quickly signed up to do a half to three-quarters of a mile daily.

These are scenes from our first quarter at the university.

September 25: "After lunch this Saturday, Dorothy and I drove to the Great Smokies National Forest. It took an hour to get there so we didn't have too much time for inspection. But what we did see was lovely—great, jagged hillsides covered with beautiful, tall trees. There were not many cars on the road so we'll try again soon and give ourselves more time. . . . I think Dorothy was pleased."

October 12: "A luncheon with Dean Hileman and Tennessee editors and was glad to see a former Columbia student, John M. Jones, Jr., and his father, who invited me to see their paper, the Greeneville Sun. Also, there were other invitations from Tennessee editors including Tom Hill, of the Oak Ridger and Ralph Millett of the Knoxville News-Sentinel. . . . Had a pleasant interview in the News-Sentinel, done by Betsy Robertson, which was thoughtful."

October 16: "The 48th wedding anniversary for Dorothy and me and we had a little celebration, just for ourselves. I'm not sure she knew what it was all about, but I wanted to do just a little bit special that maybe might help her remember who she is. . . . Had her hair done early at the hairdresser's; then, after doing our shopping, I took her for our regular ride to the Great Smokies and she looked lovely in her bright yellow dress and slippers and her mink jacket with a little bunch of flowers pinned to the lapel. . . . I took pictures of her in the Great Smokies forest, then we had lunch in a little hideaway restaurant along the road. And when we came home there were more flowers, some from Mrs. Coatney, others from me. . . . Maybe she remembered, just maybe. . . ."

December 6: "This was the day I had my last classes for the year at Tennessee. Dean Hileman said he would get me a $10,000 Gannett grant for my new book about the press in equal parts during the first half of 1977. That's most agreeable to me and I'd like to do it.... So then I came home and started packing the car for the trip back to New York beginning tomorrow. Dorothy kept rubbing her right temple and saying her head hurt, which is worrisome.

"It developed, on examination by our doctor, that both of us were given a clean bill of health once we reached home. We had a pleasant Christmas at Aquebogue, saw some Broadway shows afterward, and also took in a New York Philharmonic concert with Leonard Bernstein as conductor, things we couldn't do in Knoxville. I think Dorothy enjoyed it all, but one never really knows...."

December 31: "We spent the evening with Sue and Dick Corwin at their home in Southold but didn't wait until midnight to go home. We have an 800-mile drive back to Knoxville beginning day after tomorrow and then ten more weeks of teaching at the University of Tennessee at the outset of 1977. As for 1976, it was a better year than I had any right to expect. Dorothy was still with me at year's end and our doctor said she remains in good physical health...."

The New Year began well in Tennessee. Mrs. Coatney decided as Dorothy's nurse that she wasn't getting enough exercise and began walking with her on nice days, which seemed to be good for her. My classes continued to be interesting, which made the last two quarters of the academic year pass quickly. Early on, I heard from the University of Kansas, where John Bremner had become a journalism professor, that I could have the new Gannett professorship there if I wanted it for 1977–78, at considerably more money than Tennessee can afford.

But once again, I had to tell him that everything depended on Dorothy's condition and I didn't want to do anything that would make life any more difficult for her than it has been. He understood and said he was sure Kansas would give us both time for a decision. I appreciated that.

When we returned from Knoxville after the end of the academic year, our doctor examined her and thought she had survived nicely even if she still was extremely vague mentally. There was, of course, nothing anybody could do about that. And yet, always being so hopeful that she had some inner feeling about her identity, I was encouraged to see her standing at the water's edge whenever I went swimming at Iron Pier Beach and waiting there until I returned. At home, too, I thought she seemed more aware of her surroundings than she had been for several years.

Perhaps I acted rashly, perhaps I was inconsiderate, but I became so supercharged with optimism that I accepted the contract offered me by the University of Kansas for 1977–78 and, at the same time, gave up the Morningside Drive apartment at Columbia and stored the furniture. I actually thought at the time that I could take another and even longer trip with Dorothy to the University of Kansas because she seemed so improved.

But midway through July that summer, her condition changed drastically and without warning. Twice, she stumbled and fell outside our old house near her rose garden, which caused our doctor to fear she might have suffered a series of small strokes. However, the X rays showed only the characteristics of Alzheimer's disease, although now somewhat exaggerated.

Despite that assurance, she fell again not long afterward, this time inside the house, and now there was no concealing the deterioration of her condition. Our doctor admitted, after more tests, that she had suffered a mild stroke, although he argued it had not been drastic enough for her to be hospitalized or confined to a nursing home unless it was a matter of my convenience.

It wasn't. I kept her with me, hoping against hope that we still would be able to travel together to the University of Kansas for the fall semester. It was not to be. The next time she fell in the house a few days later, she remained unconscious. And this time, our doctor had an ambulance from Southampton Hospital at our door within the hour.

Still unconscious, Dorothy was borne to the hospital ambulance on a stretcher. When she failed to improve overnight, she was transferred to the nearby Todd Nursing Home where twenty-four-hour care was more readily available. She died there in her sleep early on the morning of September 2, 1977. Two days later, after funeral services at the Old Steeple Congregational Church in Aquebogue, she was buried in the family plot across the road.

My last thoughts were of Dorothy—and of the young doctor who came into her room at the nursing home early on the morning after she died and asked me quietly, "What are you going to do now?" Although I cannot remember what my reply was, in particular, I know it had something to do with my Kansas teaching contract and my doubts that it would be either possible or even practical for me to attempt it now I was alone. The young doctor replied, "Kansas will be better for you than living alone out here now in the fall and winter. You should go."

After the funeral, I made an attempt to follow his advice.

25 ★ COMEBACK

When I drove my old Buick that fall into Lawrence, a quiet Kansas university town of about fifty thousand people, all was awash in the midst of a rainstorm. It was by no means the equivalent of an Atlantic hurricane, either in high wind or downpour, but it was tough weather and hard for me to take.

My car radio was blatting the discouraging news that at least twenty people already had died in Kansas City, Kansas, as a result of the storm. All things considered, it was scarcely an auspicious moment for me to arrive at the furnished house the university had rented for me from its owner, a professor absent on sabbatical leave with his family.

While I was walking around the place for the first time, wondering what was to become of me alone in these strange and unfamiliar surroundings, John Bremner came in and took charge of my destinies at once. I remembered him so well and so gratefully as the Roman Catholic priest from Australia who had been the number one student in the Columbia Journalism School Class of 1952, one of the best students in the school's history.

Now, however, this large-spirited and generous soul no longer was the Reverend Bremner but Professor Bremner, happily married and adjusted to an enormously useful life not only in the church of his faith but also in a great midwestern university.

It wasn't long before Professor Bremner discerned what was wrong with me and routed me out of the house, as soon as he had helped me unpack my car and my bags. He gave me no time for my sorrow but brought me instead to my new office on campus, introduced me to my gracious new boss, Dean Del Brinkman, and a half dozen members of the faculty who happened to be available. After that, as word spread that the visiting Gannett professor from New York had arrived, prospective students who wanted to register for my classes turned out in force for a firsthand view of the stranger.

From then until classes began, I had no time to continue to be distressed. If the students weren't hot on my trail at both my office and my new home, John and Mary Bremner, Del Brinkman, and others among my new faculty associates saw to it that I was seldom alone except at bedtime. Instead of continued mourning, my major problem at Kansas turned out to be that my students expected much more of me than I could possibly deliver. In good conscience, however, I had to try—and that was what saved me.

The kind of response that came from most of the students in my classes at Kansas was impressive. When I asked my class in investigative reporting for term paper proposals, more than 100 papers—1,500 to 2,000 words each—were handed in to be accepted, rejected, or returned with a request for further elaboration. This enthusiasm from all my classes resulted in a resurgence of my interest in working with ambitious young people.

I also was drafted as a speaker before professional meetings of various editorial groups that came to Lawrence for their conventions. For relaxation, there always was time for a vigorous swim of a half mile to a mile at the university pool, where I soon became a familiar figure. Also, for meetings and modest meals for faculty associates at my rented house, I could depend for help on my assistant, Jeanne Hierl, and her husband, Peter, as well as John and Mary Bremner. As my diary entries show, I had an interesting time.

September 24: "I spoke before a Kansas Editors' Day audience of about 250 at the Student Union at the induction of W. A. White, late editor of the Emporia Gazette, into the Kansas Editors' Hall of Fame. The student paper was nice enough to carry the text of my remarks and printed an out-of-proportion picture of me with a small head and large feet. That, I guess, is the way I come across to the kids. . . .

October 28: "I finished my second month of teaching at Kansas. My two big courses were lively, but I forgot to take lunch with me and I went hungry. It rained most of the day, but I took a long walk anyway to get the ache out of my muscles after jogging yesterday. I'm lucky it didn't kill me. I'd better stick to swimming."

November 18: "Clarke Thomas of the Pittsburgh Post-Gazette, the new president of the National Conference of Editorial Writers, was nice enough to handle both my large classes for me. It was very pleasant to hear him teaching my young people—and I thought he did very well. In the evening, I was invited to see a university performance of 'Camelot' with the vice chancellor, his wife and small daughters and some of their small friends. I thought of how I first saw the show with Richard Burton and Julie Andrews, and Dorothy went to sleep. . . ."

December 12: "This was my last full class day of the semester. Yesterday, a Sunday, I packed and put things away in the house, then went to a Vespers service with John and Mary Bremner and Evie Lazzarino in Hoch Auditorium. And today, I met my last two classes for the year. After I told them the story of Raphael Lemkin and the way he virtually forced the United Nations to adopt his treaty outlawing genocide—one man against the whole world!—the students stood and applauded me. I think I was more surprised than they were—and just a bit abashed, too. It was an amazing kind of classroom demonstration, I thought. And later, my assistant, Jeanne Hierl, came in crying and kissed me, which was more amazing still. After that, I turned in my grades and took off at 2:30 P.M. for New York in my old Buick. Somehow, I'd survived."

Everything on eastern Long Island that had belonged to me was untouched from the day I left for Kansas. And now, I'm sorry to say, the old house in Aquebogue seemed dishearteningly bare and empty. It was most discouraging, and I knew why. So did my old friends, who also saw to it that I was seldom alone during the holiday season and never was given a chance to get down.

There was shopping to do in New York City in the great Fifth Avenue stores because I had things to buy for all those who had been so kind to me—small remembrances, perhaps, but important to me. But in the process of shopping, after the quiet of Kansas, I was stunned by the extravagance of it all. It seemed as if the dollar had so little value that it was simply being thrown away by the most fortunate among us amid the joys of the holiday season.

Then, too, there were special events in which I was able to participate for the first time in many months. One of the most satisfying was the annual holiday party at the Council on Foreign Relations, where I had a chance to exchange greetings with Zyg Nagorski and Joe Johnston and others among the old Columbia and UN crowd. There, too, I saw Winston Lord again, only now he was very impressive as the council's newly elected president.

Another feature of my homecoming, without doubt, was Christmas dinner at Dick and Marge Baker's on Morningside Heights. His sister, Ruth, was there; so were a lot of others, who came for drinks. It was just as if I'd never been away; there were intense discussions of current affairs involving Columbia and the Pulitzers, small talk about faculty problems, and so on. Then, after dinner, Marge surprised me with some presents and Dick drove me to the garage on 125th Street where I'd always parked the old Buick, which I now picked up and drove to Aquebogue.

I thought at last I'd be able to stand the loneliness and silence inside the old house. But I couldn't.

The new year of 1978 came and went without much change in my outlook. New Year's Day itself turned out to be much more of a ceremonial effort—the usual routine of visits among old friends and telephone calls to others farther removed from the city. I was a little better at handling such things, or so I thought, until it came time for me to return to Kansas. Then, I had a terribly emotional downer while I was closing up the old house in Aquebogue. Anxiety over the future seemed for a brief time to paralyze me. And when, with an effort, I drove off west on Route 25 I did not dare look back.

It was just as if I was leaving for a foreign land, never to return. And this wasn't at all fair, because my time in Kansas actually had become a period of readjustment for me, and the people of the University of Kansas, particularly my students, had been enormously considerate of me. But this is how I felt, and in honesty I must admit it.

After a thirty-two-hour drive through freezing, even snowy weather for 1,332 miles from Aquebogue, I reached Lawrence on January 13 and found my rented quarters there to be warm, freshly cleaned, and comfortable. It made me ashamed that people had been so sensitive of my feelings, and I had thought so little of what already had been done for me.

The next night, John and Mary Bremner had me to dinner at their home and on the sixteenth, when I checked my mail at the J School, I found an urgent note to telephone Dean Hileman at Tennessee. It did not require any great feat of mental calculation to guess that I might now be asked to resume teaching in Knoxville at the end of my stint at Kansas. But certainly, it did seem to me, I owed it to my university superiors here in Lawrence to let them know about the Hileman message before proceeding to negotiate with him.

When I showed Dean Brinkman my note, I told him I would give priority to any new offer that Kansas might want to make.

He was just as forthcoming. He told me he would have no objection to anything I wanted to do to sound out the people in Tennessee for the next academic year. And at a guess, he added, the chances of my continuing at Kansas probably were less than 50-50. After that, when I called Dean Hileman, he made me a firm offer to return to Knoxville for the 1978–79 academic year, which I accepted subject only to a final talk with Dean Brinkman at Kansas. Once again, the Kansas dean had no objection, although he was nice enough to talk about inviting me back to Lawrence for 1979–80.

In my diary, I concluded, "So, it is done. I phoned Dean Hileman at the University of Tennessee that I'd be with him in Knoxville for 1978–79. He said he was delighted. And as for me, I am relieved. It was zero when I got up this morning [January 17]. . . . I'll be glad to be back in the South next fall. . . ."

I was doubly thankful, for a few days later Professor Bremner slipped and fell on the ice outside his home, broke his ankle, and was told he would be unable to function in his classes for from four to six weeks. It could just as easily have been me.

There are, after all, no rules that determine who shall survive unharmed and who shall not. Nor are there commandments to be observed that could accelerate one's chances of survival. From the time I had left Columbia as an emeritus professor, I could just as easily have dropped through the cracks in the academic system and been lost to sight. Not being a fatalist by any means, I could only mutter my thanks to some higher Power that I had been spared.

I have only the brightest memories of the latter part of my engagement at the University of Kansas. Beginning with my seventy-second birthday on February 17, when a wintry sun began to melt the season's accumulation of snow and ice in Lawrence, almost everything about me brightened with rapt promise for the future. That day, just before my big reporting class began, my best and most devoted student, Anita Miller, presented me with a bucketful of home-baked cookies and a large card of birthday wishes signed by everybody in the room. And afterward, another student, Julie Hutchinson, brought her own cake to my office.

That was only the beginning. I was well kissed in the hall. The faculty and supporting staff presented me with a houseplant. That evening, two girls and two boys from my big afternoon class took me to dinner, then escorted me to the Woodruff Theater on campus for an evening of Gershwin music sung and played by a team of eight talented youngsters. Finally, Jeanne and Peter Hierl had all of us to a late supper at their home where there was another birthday cake with candles that wouldn't blow out no matter how hard we tried.

I've never had a birthday that was celebrated with such vigor and goodwill by so many young people. And in the process, I was profoundly moved. No teacher, no matter how hardened to the academic routine and its sometimes graceless consequences, could have gone through such an experience as I did without being profoundly grateful to the host of admirable young people.

During our spring break in March, less than a month later, I had another heartening experience when I drove to Knoxville for the signing of my contract. (Actually, it turned out to be for three years, from 1978 through 1980–81.) I had decided it would be best to shift my teaching materials from Kansas to Tennessee so far as possible, which was another reason for the quick back-and-forth by car, and some of my former students at Tennessee decided to make an occasion out of my relatively brief appearance.

It turned out to be a lot of fun. There was a champagne buffet at the local Hyatt Regency Hotel, a reunion with some of my earlier Tennessee students who had done particularly well, and even a party and a spell of rock music afterward. Dean Hileman told me that students were already signing up for my fall classes for the 1978–79 academic year, which was heartening news as well.

By the time I returned to Kansas for the balance of my time there, the weather had changed dramatically. In early April, I wrote in my diary: "The spring-time blossoms in Kansas are fabulous. I have already seen the brilliant purple of the redbud trees, the fragrant white and purple of the magnolias, the dazzling gold of the forsythia. Now, the yellow daffodils and red tulips are just coming into bloom outside my door and the grass has been freshly mowed. It is a lovely spring, and very sudden, too."

I had one other surprise in Kansas that is worth noting. Toward the end of the academic year, Jeanne and Peter Hierl invited me to dinner where I met a lovely girl from Austria, Ingmar Lee, a native of the area called Hohenberg in lower Austria, and her husband, Professor J. K. Lee of the University of Kansas chemistry department, whose family were then among the trustees of the Chinese University of Hong Kong where I once taught.

That, too, was a diverting evening. I passed the time chattering away in German with Mrs. Lee about her home town in Austria, which then was observing its 650th anniversary, and later with Professor Lee who knew so many of my Chinese friends—Robert Ho, C. M. Li, Sally Aw, Jimmy Hahn, and others. In fact, I got on so well with the Lees that I was invited to have dinner with them the following Saturday night.

On the way out, Dr. Lee began the opening lines of his wife's well-loved song about old Vienna—"Wien, Wien, nur du allein"—and I happened to remember the next line, although my New York baritone was scarcely the equal of Dr. Lee's Chinese tenor, "Solstest die Stadt meine Träumen sein"(Vienna, Vienna, you alone / Are the city of my dreams). That made the evening for all concerned, and I thought at last that perhaps I could survive. When I met the Lees again, they had brought a Dr. Li of Nanking University to their home to meet me because he had been a classmate of one of my Columbia colleagues, Professor Frederick T. C. Yu.

So it developed at last, after all the heartache and all the mourning, that I managed to survive a most difficult year at the University of Kansas. And at the end, out of enthusiasm for a Chinese-Austrian couple, I had recovered enough of my zest for living to be able to sing a few lines of an old Viennese street song.

It was not that I had forgotten Dorothy. That would never happen. But somehow, in the altogether mysterious processes of humankind's ability to adjust to the most wrenching changes, I had been able to surmount my grief and go on with my life. And for this, I would be forever indebted to the University of Kansas, to my students and fellow teachers, and to all my other faculty colleagues who helped me through the worst time of my life.

26 ★ SECOND CHANCE

At the outset of the 1978–79 academic year at the University of Tennessee, my affairs seemed to be in reasonably good shape. My turnaround year at the University of Kansas had restored both my courage and my will to work. I rented a small house on the property of a Knoxville architect who was my neighbor. My three classes at the university had been oversubscribed. And I had managed somehow to survive the ordeal of "welcome home" parties.

My return to the Tennessee campus really was symbolic of homecoming. I felt comfortable there and had the distinct sense of belonging. To be sure, Knoxville wasn't New York City, and Gay Street (the main thoroughfare downtown) was a thousand miles from Broadway, in more than a literal sense. But the people around me, both on campus and in my new home, already had made me a part of their own lives—and to me that was more important than anything else.

My only real problem at first was partly my own doing. I was not up to the unseasonably hot weather that lasted through the late September and most of October after my return from Kansas. If I hadn't been able to hurry daily to the university's Olympic-sized outdoor pool beside the Student Aquatic Center, I don't believe I'd have made it through the year. Also, in my enthusiasm for swimming, I'm afraid I overlooked my age by thrashing through a mile every day instead of confining myself to lesser distances such as the half mile my doctors had suggested.

But then, my continual urge to make the most of a good thing far beyond plausible limits had always been one of my weaknesses, and I would have suffered for it but for the kindnesses of newfound friends.

My neighborly landlords, Bill and Catherine Ambrose, were among the first to try to divert my attention to less rigorous pastimes. What they did was interest me in local theater and concert events, some of the more interesting social affairs of the fall season, and, of course, Tennessee football games, which frequently attracted 85,000 zealots to the home stadium.

It also helped when I spent a few hours with the Ambroses of a late afternoon or evening, admiring their year-old baby, Elizabeth, and playing with their lively black-and-tan dog, Thumper. I had almost decided that this safe-and-sane routine outside my regular classwork was exactly what I needed, when I met JoAnn Fogarty on November 2, 1978. Then, I had serious second thoughts about life, love, the ultimate fate of humankind in general and of myself in particular.

Although JoAnn was still on the sunny side of fifty at the time we first met, this was an instance in which two mature people were almost immediately drawn to each other through a community of interest. JoAnn was sparkling and attractive. The impression she made on me was immediate and permanent, when I first saw her hacking away at a side of beef at a dinner party given by a colleague at the university, Professor Jack Haskins, and his wife, Tommie.

I couldn't have been expected to divine the future at that moment, but after awhile I did ask Tommie about the lady with the big carving knife and was told she was the recent widow of a Knoxville lawyer, Bob Johnston, and the daughter of Mr. and Mrs. John J. Fogarty of Knoxville.

If I had been considerably younger and much more the dashing romantic, I suppose I would have asked to see JoAnn home that first night. It was a mistake that I did not. For when she arrived home, as I later learned to my dismay, she found herself in the middle of an armed robbery. Showing presence of mind, she snatched up her elderly black poodle and ran outside with him in one direction, not noticing at first that the thieves had run off, too, in the opposite direction.

When the police arrived, they could do little more than ask a lot of questions she couldn't answer. And when I phoned to invite her to a concert the following evening, she was still badly shaken, but I didn't know why until I called for her to drive her to the concert.

It was then that I gave myself a sharp mental talking-to and resolved that I never again would permit any attractive woman, especially this one, to go home alone at night, whether or not I left her at her front door. Not that I could have fought off JoAnn's thieves single-handedly even if I had gone home with her the night we'd met (as I had to admit in all honesty). But at the very least, I might have been a bit more moral support to her than her elderly poodle. And, still being six feet tall and able to scowl menacingly if put to the test, perhaps (so I thought long afterward) the thieves might have been sufficiently startled to drop their booty as they escaped.

It was my good luck that JoAnn didn't seem concerned that I'd let her go home alone that first night. And even if the concert we attended the second night turned out to be less than artistically earthshaking, we did have a diverting night out together—so much so that I was encouraged to propose other such expeditions. To put it simply, I wanted to know her better and she seemed not to object.

As I learned thereafter, JoAnn's lawyer husband had died within the year, and she had two children by a previous marriage who now were teenagers away at school in Georgia. She was one of a large brood of Fogartys in Knoxville—the youngest of a family of three sisters and three brothers. All the others were married with children, and some had grandchildren as well. I had then been a widower for more than a year.

When we continued seeing each other during the holiday season, I soon became used to standing inspection among JoAnn's family and friends. And although I had long since survived nearly all my own family except for a few distant cousins whom I had not seen for years, JoAnn in due course also went through the same process of inspection by my former in-laws on eastern Long Island, my professional university colleagues, and old-timers from the news business who came to see me now and then.

On neither side were there any naysayers, to my knowledge. In fact, one of the nicest things that happened to me was a ceremonial holiday dinner that year at which I met JoAnn's mother, then in her eighties, who looked me over with sharp eyes, then kissed me and murmured, "Well, well, another John," a reference to her own late husband, John Fogarty.

I saw more of JoAnn's children, too. Never having had any of my own, I soon became interested in Pam, who then was close to her eighteenth birthday, and Eric, approaching sixteen but already bigger, broader, and stronger than I. It was a part of my luck that the children and I also got along well together, probably because I'd never learned to act the heavy father and now it was too late to try.

Early in the holiday season that year, JoAnn and I put together a dinner at her home for an intimate group including her mother, the mother and sister of her late husband, Professor and Mrs. Haskins and their two daughters, and JoAnn's two children.

This time, at JoAnn's insistence, I did the carving and afterward played rummy with her and Tommie Haskins, while the others sat in a family circle and chatted. It was, on the whole, a pleasant evening and I was grateful once again not to feel so dreadfully alone, even if JoAnn at one point warned me that, no matter what happened to us, she had two children to care for and educate. I understood the warning and appreciated it, but I refused to believe that two such strong, knowledgeable, and well-behaved young people could ever be a burden to anyone.

Over Christmas and New Year's, I flew home to Aquebogue to make sure that all was well at the old house, but I bogged down in near despair at being alone, amid all the memorabilia of what had been, except for the few years at the end, a very happy life. On sudden impulse, Christmas Day, I phoned JoAnn in Knoxville and asked her if she'd like to see New York for a few days before the end of the holiday break. She seemed delighted, which was a relief to me.

The next evening, I picked her up at LaGuardia Airport, drove her to a midtown hotel, then escorted her to the Rainbow Room in Rockefeller Center for a late supper. That was, I thought, a promising beginning, after which I did my best to give her the A treatment that born New Yorkers reserve for important people.

This included several fairish to good Broadway shows, a few decent meals at some well-recommended midtown restaurants, the red carpet tour at the United Nations where I still had friends, and another review of familiar sights from Washington Square to Morningside Heights. If she was a little breathless at the end, so was I. One day she was wearing a stunning white silk suit, had slippers with four-inch heels, and was carrying a small white mink stole—an attraction wherever we went.

Once we were in the Pulitzer Prize office, my former assistants, Rose Valenstein and Robin Holloway Kuzen, took over. What my own prize visitor then received was an intimate run-through of the best at Columbia University and also, I had reason to hope, a favorable comment or two on her professorial escort. All of us wound up at our favorite Columbia restaurant not far down Broadway.

Then came the risky part of the New York visit, for I wanted to drive JoAnn next day to Aquebogue for an inspection of the old homestead before I took her back to LaGuardia for her flight home. She seemed pleased when she accepted, but both of us were rather quiet during the ninety-mile ride to eastern Long Island that began next morning from her hotel. I never could be quite sure what JoAnn was thinking, but I do remember chillingly how nervous I was, afraid that merely being in my old home, with all its precious memories, might turn her off.

Still, when I swung the old Buick into my driveway and parked it beside the front door with its small metal shield, "A.D. 1827," I put on the boldest attitude possible and let her enter ahead of me. JoAnn said nothing, nor did I. After awhile, she relaxed, seemed to enjoy the light lunch I made, and admired my wonderful old Chickering grand piano in the front room as well as the antique furniture in the bedrooms upstairs and down.

But she didn't become her lively self again until we went to Southold for dinner with Dorothy's cousin Dick Corwin and his wife, Sue. When I drove JoAnn to LaGuardia for the flight back to Knoxville in time for New Year's Eve with the children, she seemed as relieved as I was that the visit had gone so well. I told her I'd see her in a few days, just before the scheduled resumption of classes at the university.

One rather painful decision loomed up unexpectedly for me in Knoxville with the beginning of the new year and the onset of the concluding two quarters of the 1978–79 academic year. Through a series of exchanges that I did not initiate, I received a written offer from the University of Florida to teach there for the next academic year, 1979–80, at a considerably larger stipend than Tennessee was paying me.

The Florida offer was tempting. And yet, I couldn't reasonably consider leaving the University of Tennessee without JoAnn. Nor did I have nerve enough just then to propose marriage in the immediate future, for fear that our most sensitive little autumnal affair would waste away and die.

Again, I ran into a lucky streak. The chancellor's office at Tennessee informed me a few days later, while I was brooding over my problem,

Top left: JoAnn on her first visit to Columbia as my fiancée—a lot of excitement for everyone. *Top right*: JoAnn inspects the old homestead at Aquebogue, with the woodshed in the background. *Bottom*: We took time out for dinner among all the festivities, and an obliging waiter snapped this picture of us.

that my professorial appointment at the College of Communications could be indefinitely prolonged if I wanted it. Having JoAnn very much on my mind, that suited me perfectly even though nothing was said about a pay increase. Nor did I bring up the superior Florida offer. Actually, since my emeritus status at Columbia was unaffected regardless of where I taught or what I earned, the monetary difference between Tennessee and Florida could not be the main consideration in my decision. JoAnn was.

There was one other hurdle that had to be taken before I was able to wind up this sticky problem. Usually visiting professors, especially emeriti, are not particularly popular with faculty who enjoy permanent status for the most part but who seldom are offered the special benefits and glamor that come with an appointment to an endowed chair. But at my college at the time, Dean Hileman had had a heart attack, Professor Cade was believed to be retiring, and another professor, Kelly Leiter, had been appointed acting dean pending Hileman's recovery.

Amid such uncertainties, any potential opposition to my reappointment among the J School faculty wouldn't have been practical. Accordingly, when I chose Tennessee, knowing that the Florida appointment might come at a later time, everybody seemed pleased.

To celebrate my reappointment, most of my faculty colleagues turned out for my first book promotion party away from Columbia. The event was the publication of *A Crisis for the American Press,* which I had completed under a Gannett Foundation grant awarded to me through the University of Tennessee.

Afterward, I was able to relax at a dinner with JoAnn and one of her childhood friends, Ann Weaver, who had helped make everybody comfortable at the party. Several students also were at our table, and at least one of them didn't know JoAnn and me very well because he kept calling her "Mrs. Hohenberg." When one of the other students finally corrected him, he was embarrassed and then asked JoAnn, "Well, *aren't* you Mrs. Hohenberg?" To which she responded lightly, "Not yet, but ask me some time around May or June."

The big date turned out to be March 9, 1979, during spring break.

We had a quiet wedding in Nashville on a bright, sunny afternoon full of promise. JoAnn and I drove there to be with friends, Professor and Mrs. Robert O. Wyatt, who had made the arrangements, and with Pamela and Eric, who had come from school. The brief civil ceremony was performed by Federal Judge Martha Craig Daughtry in her chambers, after which we celebrated at a champagne dinner provided by John Seigenthaler, then the publisher of the *Nashville Tennessean,* for which Professor Wyatt did literary criticism.

The next day was Pam's eighteenth birthday, which called for another celebration. For that, JoAnn and I drove to Atlanta with the children and dined at Hugo's in the Hyatt Regency Hotel. Pam had a cake with eighteen candles and champagne provided by Bill and Catherine Ambrose. Thereafter, we made JoAnn's condo in Knoxville our new home, I resumed teaching, Pam registered for her freshman year at Southern College in Collegedale, Tennessee, beginning that fall, and Eric was promised a car of his own in a noble effort on his new father's part to get his grades up at Georgia Cumberland Academy.

The second chance I had hoped for began with such a rush it took JoAnn and me a little while to catch our breath, settle down, and get on with our lives. Between my teaching and other commitments and JoAnn's affairs, we decided on a stop-go honeymoon—a celebration whenever the opportunity appeared. It couldn't have been done otherwise.

As a first stop, what we agreed on as a proper beginning for JoAnn, as a Fogarty born and bred, was the St. Patrick's Day parade in New York City on the weekend of March 17–18. It came off well—we stayed at the Waldorf, saw at least part of the parade outside Saks Fifth Avenue, had lunch at the Bull and Bear in the Waldorf, and enjoyed a matinee performance of a new musical on Broadway, then dined at the Rainbow Room in the evening.

Afterward, it was back to Knoxville once again for us both, more planning on further extensions of the honeymoon, and some urgent family matters. But in between, along with my classes and other academic affairs, the Socicty of Professional Journalists sent me my third Distinguished Service book award for *A Crisis for the American Press,* which brought me another flurry of correspondence including a congratulatory letter from President Boling of the University of Tennessee. Finally, both of us had to settle down. It would have been hard to imagine a better beginning for a late marriage, and one that would take us to far

Our wedding picture. JoAnn and I have been together ever since.

JoAnn and the children, Pam and Eric, the lively teenagers who became mine with our marriage.

places on earth. If this sounds like strenuous living for an emeritus professor with a bent for daily distance swimming, that is what it was.

Eventually, JoAnn learned to cope with the always exciting prospect of what would happen to us next. And as for Pamela and Eric, once they became reconciled to the notion that they had peripatetic parents, they grew up in a hurry. Pam, being older and wiser than her years, worked hard to acquire a first-rate education and clearly was headed for a college degree in business management and a business career. Eric, being younger and more venturesome, took something of a pounding (as did his mother and I) until he took over his own affairs in a surprisingly mature way.

JoAnn, as my wife and partner in this academic cavalcade, became the indispensable balancing force when we moved from one place to another both here and abroad and I undertook greater responsibilities than I ever would have dared assume by myself at my time in life. To be sure, love remained of tremendous importance to us. So was implicit trust in each other and also a reasonable assurance of economic stability. But I truly believe that the dominant reason for the satisfaction our union brought to us and to the children was the manner in which we were able to adjust to each other.

This was one late marriage that worked. And, as for all our devoted little family, that was good enough to last JoAnn and me for all the rest of our days together.

27 ★ THE MAKING OF A SOUTHERNER

During a long and active life, I seldom thought of a permanent attachment to the South until JoAnn and I were married in Tennessee. Up to that time, the most I'd ever dreamed of in that direction was to be washed ashore on an island within reach of the South Seas, preferably Maui, even Oahu in an emergency.

Like most born New Yorkers, I had always thought well of my heritage in the big city and had been content to spend most of my mature years there. To me, life had centered about Columbia University and the Pulitzers, after a quarter century of New York newspapering, and home meant the old 1827 saltbox on eastern Long Island when I could take leave of academe and Morningside Drive.

Growing up in the Pacific Northwest, too, had meant a lot to me. A smaller, greener, friendlier Seattle had always remained fresh in my memory. And every return journey west of the Rockies to places as widely separated as the Colorado ski resorts, Coeur d'Alene in Idaho, and San Francisco had been enormously appealing to me. I had even tolerated my few ventures north of the Arctic Circle although I'd never taken kindly to sneezes, coughs, and chilblains.

But now, having settled in Tennessee with every indication of permanence—a university professorship, a lovely new wife, and responsibility for her two handsome children, now my own—it seemed to me that I was on the verge of becoming a Southerner. Possibly even a Southern gentleman, if I behaved myself, which involved further changes in outlook and attitude. My hard-core New Yorker personality was beginning to change as the days passed, almost without my knowing it. Not that I ever would have become a drawling you-all type! That was beyond me. But Southern ways and Southern living were definitely different, and I had to make adjustments.

JoAnn was most accommodating, as were the members of her large and closely knit family in Tennessee—particularly her sisters, Margaret Beaty and Mary Cooper, and her brother, Bill Fogarty. And one of her cousins, Donna Beaty Brass, a portrait painter and the wife of Elder David Brass, did my portrait.

As for the University of Tennessee, where I spent so much of my working time as well as a daily swim of a half mile to a mile at its student Aquatic Center, everybody from Dean Hileman to the students in my overflowing classes did their best to make me feel at home. Right off, I was given to understand that this second engagement as a part of the Communications faculty would not be confined to just another academic year if I wanted to stay on. Which I did.

Still, it wasn't entirely easy for me to acquire an overnight understanding of the varieties of Southern speech. This wasn't because most Tennesseans have a distinctively Southern drawl. Had that been the problem, I wouldn't have lasted very long with my style of teaching—a continual back-and-forth with students, even in supervised writing courses. It seemed to me that most students and I communicated without particular trouble from the outset because we were working in a field of common interest. If anything, they may have had more difficulty with my sharp Pacific Northwest speech than I did with theirs.

But communications with JoAnn's family, in some cases, turned out to be more of a problem sometimes because I had to learn their way of handling personal problems and knowing, in a husbandly way, when to talk and when to remain silent. What JoAnn did instinctively, I believe (and the children seemed to follow her), was to break me in gently to differences in speech and customs. The Southernese that remained was JoAnn's occasional references to me as "Honey," when she was pleased with me, and the somewhat sharper "John" when she wasn't. (Thank goodness, I wasn't "Pa" to the children.)

Within a few weeks, as far as JoAnn's sisters and their families were concerned, the communications problems eased. But sometimes, if JoAnn,

Margaret Beaty, and Mary Cooper were talking together within my hearing, they might just as well have been using Choctaw for all the sense I could make of it. Finally, I followed the example of my sensible brother-in-law, Joe Beaty, and looked interested but remained silent.

It is not a myth that we Americans, each in our own sectional or bi-sectional manner, murder the English language at times with the same abandon as the Britisher who speaks loftily through his nose and expects to be understood. It is a small miracle that we understand each other, for good or ill, as well as we do. I shall never forget JoAnn's astonishment when we stopped at a Brooklyn garage once for gasoline, and the owner, a friend of mine, routinely asked her, because she was at the wheel of the car, "Check yer erl?" It was her introduction to Brooklynese, a special form of Northern speech.

Communications aside, what I learned to appreciate was that Tennessee, in whole or in part, by no stretch of my imagination could be made over into a semblance of upper Manhattan or eastern Long Island, my old neighborhoods. Even though I protested to JoAnn that this was not my frame of mind, ultimately I had to admit that this attitude was a handicap I'd given myself at the outset. I had imagined I could conduct my life in the South as if I were still in New York. It didn't work.

What I had to adjust to was that while Tennessee may not have been the storybook, made-for-the-movies South, where ladies wore flouncy dresses and peekaboo garden hats with floppy straw brims, it also wasn't the glittering movie version of limousine-driven New Yorkers with the women lounging casually in silks and ermine. As JoAnn put it to me, again using women as an example, most women in our part of Knoxville (except some of the elderly) were more inclined to wear pants than skirts on their daily rounds outside the home, no different than others elsewhere across the land. What she gently tried to remind me of was that Southern women in general were not a class set apart and did not want to be so considered.

I had to realize as well that there was little evidence of great wealth in Tennessee, either of the Rockefeller variety in New York or of the Kennedy variety in Boston. Taking JoAnn's solidly middle-class family as a standard in Tennessee's moderate society, it was a state that maintained reasonable stability at a time when many other parts of the country still were hoisting distress signals. Even for people who were well-off, the flaunting of wealth was considered bad form.

The moderate influence seemed to be dominant also in what I believed to be the cautious majority approach here to racial problems that could—and sometimes did—tear apart cities like New York, Los Angeles, and Chicago. Nor was there, so far as I was able to determine, anything more than a fringe response to rabble-rousers, more typical of the deep South, who had the notion of doing away with all people in the United States who were not made in their own unlovely image.

Although Tennesseans scarcely professed to have the solution to the nation's racial stresses, it was a relief to me to realize that few people in the state had been persuaded that racial warfare was the solution to differences between the white majority and racial minorities. But mere hope for something better wasn't the answer, either. In short, if Tennessee didn't have a formula for social progress for its 5 million inhabitants (almost 20 percent of them black with several hundred thousand Hispanics), neither did New York or California with their enormous influence and wealth. Racial problems, in effect, extend to virtually all parts of the nation and have to be considered nationally if any realistic effort toward progress can succeed. Whether I was a Tennessean or a New Yorker, that to me was the outlook and the one I had to content myself with for the time being.

In this frame of mind, I settled down with JoAnn and the children in Knoxville—a pleasant university city of fewer than 200,000 people. In many of its physical aspects, it reminded me of the much smaller Seattle of my youth, also a university town set in the middle of a dazzling scenic panorama on the Pacific coastal plain with the Cascades and Mount Rainier in the distance and icy-cold Puget Sound on its doorstep.

For Knoxville, academe meant the elaborate campus of the University of Tennessee in the nerve center of a well-planned urban landscape across the Cumberland plateau with a distant view of the Great Smokies and the Blue Ridge Mountains. And around both the home cities of my younger and later years, there was a luxurious surrounding of forestlands and picturesque waterways: for Seattle, the lakes, the Sound, and the Duwamish; for Knoxville, the Tennessee River. In the end, that comparison was what pleased me about Knoxville as we settled down and the children resumed their education away from home.

There came a time, two months after JoAnn and I were married, when I received my Tennessee driver's license, following an eye examination and a written test. I also fixed a Tennessee license plate on my old Buick. All this happened while JoAnn waited patiently nearby, even encouraged me, and silently clapped hands as I went through the various legal routines.

Then came the big moment, the legal transfer of my citizenship from New York to Tennessee, together with my registration as a Tennessee voter. In that too, there was a routine in which I signed documents canceling my New York registrations. To be doubly sure there was no mistaking my intent, I transferred my various deposits in New York banks to three banking institutions in Tennessee and recorded the net result in my diary as follows: "I think all that should unmake my New York citizenship and cause me to become a legally certified citizen of Tennessee."

As my first act as a Tennessee citizen, I drove with JoAnn to the graduation of our daughter, Pam, from her private secondary school, the Georgia Cumberland Academy in Calhoun, over the following weekend. It was all very pleasant, with the students thanking their parents and Pam pinning red roses on her mother and me. Having insisted on registering her at Southern College in Tennessee for the fall, I suppose I was insufferably smug during the graduation proceedings—but by that time, my new family had become used to my individual performances, and they put up with my attitude of comparing almost everything Southern with something I remembered from New York. By choice and qualification, I may have become a citizen of Tennessee, but it now remained for me to learn to act the part. And that, I must admit, took awhile.

It was particularly hard for me to get used to the twang of guitar-and-brass country-and-western music. But I learned to bear up through that indefinitely rather than submit to the numbing beat of heavy metal hard-rock bands and the screaming of professionals who were introducing the new sounds of music. When I had too much of that, I could always go to my old Chickering grand, which I had brought with me from New York, and soothe myself with whatever came to my mind and my ability to play through a fairly large routine of piano music.

What bothered me a lot more was the virtual death of the touring theater—the old road shows that sometimes brought the best of Broadway to the hinterland. But now, in the theater toward the end of the twentieth century, the Broadway shows were ever more expensive; few shows survived fierce competition with the movies and TV, and taking to the road was no bargain, either. To someone like myself, who had been used to going to what we liked to call the "living theater" regularly, it did matter that I had to settle for TV most evenings.

My attitude toward entertainment, I am sure, was unfair to JoAnn and the children because they couldn't very well miss first-rate theater or opera when they seldom had experienced either. But, wonder of wonders, they put up with my specialized, if grumpy, tastes.

There were compensations. On a winter's evening, we attended the performance of a Khachaturian concerto by the young violinist Eugene Fodor, a protégé of Jascha Heifetz. He played five other pieces too, backed up by a surprisingly fine Knoxville Symphony Orchestra. It was first-rate, and there were other evenings like it as my stay in the South lengthened and expanded.

Then, too, there were surprises in the form of talented student performances now and then, plus an occasional presentation of amateur theatricals such as a revival of the old Ben Hecht–Charles MacArthur comedy *The Front Page,* with Dick Smyser, editor of *The Oak Ridger,* in the cast. It may not have been stunning theater, but it was fun.

Sooner than I thought, I realized I was adjusting to my new life with much greater ease than I'd thought possible, with the exception of an occasional if minimal display of temper tantrums. After such lamentable lapses, however, JoAnn's patience and sweet reasonableness usually prevailed to such an extent that I became ashamed of my departures from grace and tried to make amends. It was an effort, I must admit; at an advanced age it was not a simple matter to wish myself into a different pattern of life and a better feeling for the uses of restraint.

My classes at the University of Tennessee helped a lot. They were lively, challenging, and crammed to capacity with enthusiastic young people who seemed to like their writing assignments and often kept me long after the end of class for one-on-one discussions of their work, their chances, and sometimes their future. To quote at random from my diary that year:

"My class in investigative reporting had 20 people plus a waiting list, another in international affairs had 19 plus a couple who were absent this particular day. A half-dozen had been students of mine at UT previously and it was good to see them again. I had two hours between classes and did my one-mile swim in the UT pool. . . ."

"My two classes today went beautifully. My 50 lap swim at the pool [about ¾ of a mile] was done in 35 minutes, pretty good for an old-timer. In the evening to Dean Hileman's and took two students with me, one French and the other German. Shirley Hileman had a fine pot roast dinner. I spoke good German and bad French to the students now and then. And Dean Hileman told me he was 99 per cent sure I'd be returning to UT for another year. . . ."

"My two classes were preoccupied with the returned and graded term papers, so I dropped my prepared lecture and made both a back-and-forth on anything within reason that anybody wanted to discuss. I thought it all went well even if I couldn't hand out high grades to the lot. Managed to swim my 50 laps at the pool and then, from 5 to 7 all my best ex-students at UT showed up with most of the faculty for my latest book party at the Faculty Club. Some of the editors of the newspapers in Knoxville and nearby communities, Oak Ridge and Greeneville, also attended. Kelly Leiter and Jim Crook [both professors at the Communications school] took care of the bill. . . ."

Far removed though I was from Columbia, I still had unfinished work to do there, and it pursued me quickly enough before I had even settled down as a Southerner. What had happened was that two of my previous books, both Pulitzer Prize anthologies including a number of my essays, seemed to have gone well enough so that a third volume had been suggested to me on the basis of more recent developments.

In response to queries from former associates at Columbia and the Pulitzer organization, I suggested doing a volume that would be based on the leading issues of the time—civil rights, the aftermath of Watergate and the Nixon resignation, the post–Vietnam War era and the difficulties of maintaining a free press, as disclosed in the Pentagon papers. The decision finally was left to President McGill, then in his final year before retirement, and he urged me to do the job. Columbia University Press was willing to publish it, I was ready to go to work, so JoAnn and I made our plans for a seesaw existence between Knoxville and New York to stay at the old house in Aquebogue weekends while I was burrowing through the Pulitzer records at Columbia or undertaking a lot of interviews in Washington, including in the White House, at a later date.

Between arrangements such as these, winding up the semester's classes, and the holiday parties over the Christmas break, both of us actually had more than we could handle. To quote from my diary for New Year's Day, 1980:

"This New Year and this new decade began for me with my first party at home for many, many years.

"With Judy and Bob Wyatt and Tommie and Jack Haskins, we had stayed up here at 5413 Riverbend Drive until long after midnight. There was singing, dancing, story-telling—a happy time for JoAnn and for me, the first New Year's Eve of our marriage. When we finally had the last bottle of champagne (and Eric tried it, too, at 16 years of age), the Haskinses went home, the Wyatts went to sleep in our room, we retired at 3 A.M. in Pam's room and Pam stayed the night with Karen, one of her friends.

"When I awoke, it was 10 A.M., a rather dark and disagreeable day. JoAnn and I had a leisurely breakfast with the Wyatts, then decided what we'd be doing soon enough in the New Year about the new book, which I am calling, with a total lack of originality, 'The Pulitzer Prize Story II.' After we said goodbye to the Wyatts, who drove back to Nashville (he is professor at Middle Tennessee State U), we spent the rest of the day quietly. There is a very strong realization on my part that I am well-started on a new life, that maybe there will be recompense somehow for all the tragedies of the 1970s.

"At least, I think I can face the future in good health with some assurance of a continued useful life, a loving wife and two admirable children. All this is more than I could have dared hope for two years ago when I did not know which way to turn and my wonderful Dorothy was so sick she didn't even know me.

"This is going to be a better New Year."

28 ★ THE USES OF TEACHING

I had barely settled into my teaching routine for the 1981–82 academic year at the University of Florida when I received insistent inquiries from the State Department and the University of Miami about my future plans. JoAnn was excited. And I was pleased after four years at the University of Tennessee, an Irish honeymoon with JoAnn in the summer of 1979, and an extension of that honeymoon through Western Europe in the summer of 1980. Both of us were ready for new adventures of consequence.

The State Department's inquiry was by far the most interesting. As relayed through the U.S. Information Agency, it was to inquire of my availability for another swing through the Far East, similar to the ten-nation speaking tour I'd conducted in 1964 under the department's American Specialist program. I was ready to go the next summer, provided I could have JoAnn with me, and I agreed right off to pay her way. To me, traveling and teaching had come together in a most agreeable manner.

What the University of Miami wanted to know was whether I'd be willing to teach there in the succeeding academic year, 1982–83. That sounded good to me, too. With JoAnn's encouragement, I kept that option open, reflecting that a year in Coral Gables would extend my stay in Florida and give me a better perspective on Latin American affairs in general and the always difficult American-Cuban relationships in particular.

Furthermore, continuing my teaching at Miami fitted in with everything else I was doing, which included a request from my publisher for a fifth edition of my textbook *The Professional Journalist*, which I was already working on. In addition, there had been some lecturing for me at such widely separated spots as the University of Alabama at Tuscaloosa and Harvard's Nieman Fellowship program.

Evidently, the rush of events had resolved my concern, on reaching emeritus status at Columbia, over how long I could continue such demanding professional activity as teaching, outside lecturing, and writing. Now, in my seventy-sixth year, it appeared that I would be moving around for as long as I wished and my health permitted. That suited both JoAnn and me perfectly.

She was enjoying Florida. And having already driven us almost seven thousand miles through Ireland, England, Scotland, Wales, and Western Europe in our two-part motorized honeymoon, she was ready for the next installment, our projected Asian venture.

We had been reunited at Florida with Ralph Lowenstein, an old friend from Columbia, who was now the dean of the College of Journalism and Communications at Gainesville. With his wife, Bronia, he made sure we were well settled in a comfortable house nearby, with a grand piano, an organ, some impressive antiques, good furniture, and extra rooms for Pam and Eric when they came visiting. Our own homes in Knoxville and eastern Long Island remained available for Pam and Eric, too, in breaks from their educational routines.

I had a full academic load that year at Florida—and then some. In the fall semester, there were twenty-four students in a graduate course in Mass Media and Society and a smaller workaday group in a course in community journalism, which I'd inherited from an indisposed faculty colleague. Curiously, no matter how intensively I worked with the graduate students in what amounted to social studies, it was the practical effort to put out a weekly community newspaper that seems to have made a lasting impression at the university.

More than ten years after my pleasant experiences at Gainesville, I received an impressively thick and up-to-date copy of the weekly we'd originated in the community course, which I called *The InvestiGator* after the tag used for Florida's sports teams. I don't know who inherited the paper, courtesy of Dean Lowenstein, but in my year I gave a lot of the credit to the *Florida Times-Union* in Jacksonville and its managing editor at the time, Fred Hartmann.

This kind of introduction to the day-by-day, hour-by-hour responsibilities of the working journalist has always seemed to me to be the first business of any journalism school, along with necessary background in specialties ranging from editorial and critical commentaries to national and foreign correspondence. This did not mean I was slighting the legal and ethical problems of the journalist or the profession's often overly conservative approach to social and political affairs. To me, it was a matter of putting first things first, a view I often advanced before faculty seminars and university accreditation teams.

I had another successful semester in two courses for the spring of 1982. The smaller was like my Columbia seminar in foreign correspondence for graduate students, another practical course. The second class, centered on journalistic ethics, suddenly turned practical when it developed that a Pulitzer prizewinner from the *Washington Post,* Janet Cooke, had faked her story about two eight-year-old drug addicts. The twenty-five members of the ethics course were thereby given a taste of reality along with the dozen in the foreign seminar who were immersed in the practical business of dealing with the Cold War and Castro's Cuba among other subject.

During my year at Gainesville, in a break with my teaching routine, I was able to take JoAnn with me for a brief reunion with old friends at the University of Kansas. She was impressed in particular with my former student and distinguished colleague, Professor John Bremner, The introduction came at a magnificent dinner prepared by another Kansan, Alex Lazzarino, an Italian feast over which he had labored for the better part of a day. Before we returned to Gainesville, I met Jerry Sass of the Gannett Foundation and thanked him for Gannett's sponsorship of my year at Kansas as well as my current stay at Florida. JoAnn loved it all.

Back at Florida, with the publication of *The Pulitzer Prize Story II,* I was lucky enough to get TV time to talk about the book, which had been given a string of favorable reviews. And even though I was far removed from an international news center, the University of Florida made it possible for me to complete a report for the German Marshall Fund that analyzed the foreign news content of eighteen American newspapers and selected electronic media. At the Lowensteins' home one night, I met a team for the Association for Education in Journalism and tried once again to make a case for more practical work in J-schools.

Left: They had me play the piano for their wedding. Mr. and Mrs. Eric Kenney, the former Tracey Nichols, and Eric's sister, Pamela Jo Kenney, who was a bridesmaid. *Below left*: My first professional piano engagement, at Eric's wedding. *Below right*: Farewell to the old homestead. The picture was taken shortly before JoAnn and I moved out and settled permanently in Knoxville.

I also appreciated an invitation to appear before an editorial conference of daily newspapers to name the newspaper commentators whose work I believed to be the most influential in the country. My choices: Ralph McGill of the *Atlanta Constitution* for his courage in facing up to the nation's racial issues; James Reston of the *New York Times* as the most influential journalist in Washington, D.C.; Marquis Childs of the *St. Louis Post-Dispatch* as the most graceful stylist of the lot; John S. Knight of the Knight newspapers as the leader of protests against the Vietnam War; Erwin Canham of the *Christian Science Monitor* as the most respected editorialist in the nation; and Vermont Royster as the most influential writer on financial affairs in his *Wall Street Journal* commentaries. (My apologies for omitting women from the list, but this was somewhat in advance of the ascendancy of women in journalism.)

I was grateful, as well, to Dean Lowenstein for releasing me from teaching in the spring of 1982 to serve with four colleagues on the Pulitzer international jury. It also gave JoAnn a chance to see an opera, a few shows, and to shop for clothes. And I can't forget the Florida places that were fun: the nation's number one tourist attraction, Disney World; swimming at Ormond Beach, Cedar Key, Flagler Beach, and for my daily routine the city and university pools at Gainesville.

After we visited the University of Miami and settled our schedule for 1982–83 with Dave Gordon, the head of the Communications Department, it was time for farewells to the University of Florida—our open house and dinner for all comers included faculty, staff, and students. We closed our house, packed for the Asian trip that had been arranged meanwhile, and took off, first for Knoxville, then for the lovely old house in Aquebogue and a visit with all our friends there before our departure. One night neither of us will ever forget came at Douglas Moore's old home where his son-in-law and daughter, Brad and Mary Kelleher, introduced us to the Broadway composer John Kander, the star of the evening, with a collection of songs he sang to his own piano accompaniment.

My Asian mission, simply put, was to discuss a proposed New World Information Order (NWIO), an anti-American, anti-Western propaganda ploy that was being pushed at the time by a number of radical-minded Third World delegates before the United Nations Educational, Scientific, and Cultural Organization (UNESCO). To those of us in the news business who knew something about both UNESCO and NWIO, the pitch was nothing more than a poorly concealed effort to censor the work of American and other Western correspondents stationed in Third World countries (mainly in the Far East and sub-Sahara Africa). The objective seemed to be to present to the world a more favorable image of the larger and more important developing nations, India being the most prominent.

The targets of NWIO, without doubt, were mainly the Western news agencies, networks, newsmagazines, and syndicates—particularly those that served the United States. What the American and other Western UNESCO delegates offered as a substitute to the Third World offensive was a UN-sponsored program for the training of better-informed Third World journalists and more support for their news organizations in the form of the latest in communications equipment—computers, cellular telephones, and other advanced electronic data processing.

However, in several countries that had been taken over by dictators or military governments, the UNESCO issue already had been determined. They had, for the most part, installed their own version of conditions under which they would permit foreign correspondents to operate, to the end that only "positive" information—that is, only favorable news of the country being covered—would be cleared for worldwide transmission. To be sure, there was no way any such censorship could stop a correspondent from leaving the country and filing his dispatches elsewhere. The trouble was that such a correspondent would not again be admitted into that particular nation as a part of the working press.

All this was explained to me in detail by John Hughes, Than Lwin, and others in the U.S. Information Agency when discussing the objectives of my trip and the manner in which I was expected to carry out the State Department's policies. Actually, it was to be my third mission for the State Department, and there had been others, more limited in scope, that I had worked on in and out of the Pentagon for the Air Force Secretary's office.

(At the time, USIA was called the International Communications Agency for reasons known only to the government experts in nomenclature. Actually, the name was an embarrassment to the State Department because the initials, ICA, were continually being confused with CIA, whose methods were quite the opposite. So in the end, it became apparent that USIA was the more useful designation consisting, as did ICA, of the U.S. Information Service (USIS) and the Voice of America (VOA) with a few other agencies included whenever necessary.)

On the basis of previous experience, I could plainly see that neither I nor anybody else in my position would be able, in a single swing around the Far East, to persuade so powerful a bloc of Third World governments not to press their censorship proposal before UNESCO. In that organization, the developing countries formed a majority, had Soviet support and could do much as they wished. Regardless of what the United States desired, that seemed to indicate UNESCO's eventual acceptance of the censorship program for foreign correspondents.

Why, then, the long and in many ways difficult speaking mission for me and perhaps others like me elsewhere? Without raising the question with my USIA people, it occurred to me that my arguments against action by UNESCO as an American government agent, however temporary, was being designed to prepare Third World governments along my route for an unfavorable reaction if U.S. objections were ignored (which was, as President Ronald Reagan's public statements already had indicated, a probable American boycott or even withdrawal from UNESCO).

The subject wasn't mentioned in our discussion that day. About the closest we came was the repeated assurance I was given that neither my wife nor I had anything to fear on the trip, once it was undertaken. No government, however hostile, so I was told, would want to harass an American citizen on an official mission for his government or go so far as to hold him or his wife hostage.

What it all amounted to, I guessed, was that I was to be sent across South, Southeast, and East Asia as a kind of human lightning rod. As I was to learn along the way, the Reagan administration already was giving serious consideration to a proposed American withdrawal from UNESCO. So this trip, quite unlike any previous swing I had made along the same general route, could have serious repercussions. And it also had no connection whatever with my previous Pentagon service in the Eisenhower administration.

Just before our departure, Than Lwin, who was to be my control officer, wanted to wish JoAnn and me well when he handed us our schedule. JoAnn was very impressive that chilly day in Washington in a new black suit and a long mink coat, an outfit she hadn't been able to wear in the sunny South. And I did my best to look the part of the privileged husband. We also had a useful talk with John Hughes, a Pulitzer prizewinner when he worked for the *Christian Science Monitor,* who was soon to become Assistant Secretary of State for Public Affairs. At any rate, I became satisfied that this was to be a necessary mission on which future American policy toward UNESCO would be based in a realistic way. It seemed to me that I would be able to report, at the end of the trip, whether I believed it possible that any of the governments along my route would be likely to drop their attempt to censor American and other Western foreign correspondents. And none, in any case, would be able to say that they were unaware of the American distaste for UNESCO in general and the NWIO program in particular.

The only question JoAnn had after we left Hughes and Lwin was the usual query about any venture to the Far East: "What about China?" My answer was the same as I'd always given to suggestions that I might be willing to teach for a year at the university in Beijing: "I don't see much use in going unless the Chinese change their policies toward the United States." What actually happened later was that I did agree to teach at a more Westernized Chinese university, the one in Hong Kong, where I was to be interviewed that summer between stops at the Philippines and Japan.

JoAnn now had reason to be excited when we began making our final preparations for the Asian trip at the old homestead in Aquebogue. It had dawned on her, outside the political speculation I'd finally decided I'd better discuss with her, that this might be one of the factors on which President Reagan would base his decision to cause the United States to quit UNESCO.

She put it to me wonderingly. "Is that it? They hate us in UNESCO?"

"We'll soon find out," I said.

She brightened. "Anyway, we're actually going all around the world, aren't we?"

"Quite so," I said, trying to sound blasé.

She thought about that in silence for awhile, then, asked somewhat wistfully, "What do we do for an encore?"

The Asian trip that summer was tough enough without thinking of encores. The Pakistanis at successive stops in Karachi, Lahore, and Islamabad were polite but critical although they did turn out mass audiences for me.

In India, the major objective of the mission, I had the surprise advantage of working with a lot of devoted professional journalists, some had been friends of mine at the UN, like Krishnamachari Balaraman, and others had been in my Columbia classes. Regardless of the government's opposition, the journalists on the whole supported me at something close to a hundred meetings, interviews, and professional conferences—a break I hadn't expected in making my rounds at New Delhi, Bombay, Calcutta, Poona, Madras, and Bangalore.

Nepal, Sri Lanka, and Thailand were easier because the struggle within UNESCO didn't mean as much to their governments. And in the Philippines, where I had so many friends and colleagues (beginning with the foreign minister, Carlos Romulo), I had the best time of all. There was a brief stopover in Hong Kong to complete arrangements for my service at the Chinese University there at a later time. But, fortunately for my peace of mind, JoAnn's Irish was up when it was suggested to me once again there and elsewhere that I should spend a year later in the 1980s teaching at the university in Beijing. (Had I accepted, I would have been trapped in the uproar over the brutal Chinese repression in Tiananmen Square.)

At the final stops of my mission in Japan, there never was any question about the position of the Japanese government and Japan's large and powerful organizations of print and electronic journalists. I had so many former students from Columbia who turned out for my meetings that I never had to worry about disruptions like the ones that occurred at sessions in Pakistan, which their government people blamed on Russian "interference."

When JoAnn and I returned to our home in Knoxville by way of Hawaii and its marvelous beaches, we needed a rest. But afterward, in doing my report on the position within UNESCO on the Third World's bid for censorship control of foreign correspondents, I had to give a split verdict on the support the United States might expect within UNESCO against the Third World's sensitivity to criticism. It seemed to me that India and Pakistan—despite the independent position taken by most of their journalists and university people at my meetings—would be unlikely to change their lines. Moreover, I believed they would take with them smaller countries within their orbit, which left us with Filipino sympathies and probable Japanese support.

If this position was confirmed by our embassies elsewhere in the Third World, I wrote the best we could do would be to try to postpone a vote on the NWIO or perhaps quit UNESCO altogether. Eventually, in 1985, President Reagan chose the latter course, which seemed to me to be regrettable but necessary for as long as the Cold War affected our foreign policies.

I was grateful throughout for Than Lwin's support and his thoughtful arrangements. And I congratulated John Hughes on his appointment as Assistant Secretary of State for Public Affairs. The Asian mission turned out well for us all. As I concluded in my diary, "I have lived much longer than I expected and enjoyed it more than I anticipated."

From the outset everything came up roses for us at Miami. Before we had a chance to settle into the academic routine at the university and get used to our new home on San Amaro Drive in Coral Gables, another old friend—Larry Jinks, the managing editor of the *Miami Herald*—had us to lunch there. It was old home week because I renewed friendships with John McMullan, the executive editor; Don Carter, who handled the editorial page; and Bill Montalbano and George Beebe, whom I'd known at Columbia.

Then came the class arrangements, which Dave Gordon had made for me in my absence with the consent of his superior, Dean Arthur Brown of the Faculty of Arts and Sciences. There were two seminars, one on news interpretation for a dozen students and another on foreign affairs for nine others. And the big class, for around forty, was, as might be expected, in newswriting. And so the academic year began with a rush, in summer heat that leveled off mercifully into a late fall and winter of comfortably warm weather that made year-round outdoor swimming possible for me. The attraction of the changing seasons in south Florida also helped draw Pam and Eric back to us in Coral Gables at every break from their own university routines and caused old friends from the frozen North to drop in for much appreciated visits.

For JoAnn, that meant more fun in the South with one of her constant companions from eastern Long Island, Liv Sawyer, a registered nurse who reveled in the winter sunlight as much as we did. And it also gave me a chance to look up Kathleen Gilmore, Herbert Bayard Swope's secretary, who now was handling the affairs of a retired British diplomat, recently knighted for his services, on Jupiter Island off the Florida coast.

While we were at Coral Gables, we also were able to maintain contact with most of JoAnn's big family. Her brothers, Bill and Fred Fogarty, and their wives all liked Florida winters, so much so that Fred and Betty located permanently in Fort Myers. And Bill and Peggy had us to dinner while they were vacationing in Miami Beach and later visited us in Coral Gables. Of course, we always saw a lot of Joe and Margaret Beaty and Mary Cooper whenever we were in Knoxville.

Old friends and new ones were a part of our lives. We hadn't been at Miami for a month when Professor Bob Wyatt and Judy invited us to stay with them for a weekend in Nashville while I lectured on the Middle East at the Jewish Temple there. And whenever we needed help at Coral Gables, our friends in Gainesville, Fay O'Neal and Richard Lester, were generous with their support. They came to Thanksgiving dinner with us at Coral Gables to make it a party of six with Sue and Dave Gordon.

Toward Christmas that year, there was sadness, too. Trudy Murmann, whom we'd known at Columbia, told us that J. Montgomery Curtis, the founder and director of the American Press Institute at Columbia, was in a hospital near us being treated for pneumonia. I was able to visit him several times there before his death and reflect that he had done more for American newspapers through the API than most of its editors and publishers.

Otherwise, social activity at Coral Gables reached such a peak during the year-end holidays that sometimes I had to get away in the early morning to take my daily swim of three-quarters to a full mile at the Venetian Pool, my refuge from academe. When the children came home and brought their friends, that was an added treat. And there also was a lot of back-and-forth entertaining with Sylvan Meyer, editor of *Miami* magazine, and his wife, Ann, Larry and Claire Jinks from the *Miami Herald*, the Gordons, and others at the university.

JoAnn, competent and unflappable as always, did the honors and the meals and even a little singing to my piano playing for all who came and went from Christmas through New Year's at our Coral Gables home. And there was, never to be forgotten, a wreath of red roses for Dorothy's grave in Aquebogue in the old cemetery across the road from the white steeple church. All that, too, remained a precious part of my life.

The new year of 1982 began with bids from Syracuse, Louisiana State, and Miami for another teaching engagement for 1983–84. Professor Cleve Mathews at Syracuse even indicated broadly that I might be offered a two-year contract at the Newhouse School if all turned out as well as he anticipated when I came there in late January. That stimulated JoAnn's interest and mine because we had been talking idly about a cross-country auto tour and wondered how we'd be able to swing it. A two-year contract, if it materialized, meant we'd be able to travel once again in the summer of 1984 and return to academe for the 1984–85 year at Syracuse.

That, and a projected travel book about the United States, which I'd been thinking of for a long time, explains why I arranged for a brief absence from the University of Miami to fly to Syracuse in late January. There, Professor Mathews and his wife gave me a tour of the Newhouse School, introduced me to some of the students, and then took me to Henry Schulte, an old friend I'd known at Columbia from the time he and his wife, Irene, were classmates there. Hank was another reason why I was attracted to Syracuse, all of which made a lunch with Dr. John Prucha, the Syracuse vice-chancellor of academic affairs, all the more pleasurable.

When I left, the two-year contract seemed a distinct possibility, dependent primarily on the completion of negotiations between Dean Ed Stephens and me at spring break. I wrote in my diary for my seventy-seventh birthday on February 17:

"To most people my age, this is a time for sitting in the sun and dreaming, doing nothing, letting the mind slip gently downhill into the final void. But not I! For reasons neither my doctors nor I fully understand, the aging process seems to have been delayed in me so that my life has become a series of drastic moves, much traveling, enormous changes since leaving Columbia at age 70. These past seven years, I've shifted around so much in so many different places—more than ever before. And although JoAnn smiles and gracefully plans our lives and the lives of

Liv Sawyer, who kept the home fires burning in the old homestead at Aquebogue.

The University of Tennessee's Communications Building, where I worked longer than at any place except the old Pulitzer Building at Columbia.

the children and our homes with the greatest efficiency, it must be hard on her. Yet, she never complains, only looks forward to new scenes, new experiences, new people. . . ."

The weeks before spring break at Miami passed quickly. I still had my two seminars, one on public affairs at the local and state level this time and a foreign seminar that emphasized Latin American relations, plus the usual newswriting course. I also had to finish correcting the galley proofs of the fifth edition of *The Professional Journalist* and return them to the publisher, do some TV appearances for the new Pulitzer book, and fulfill the usual outside speaking engagements.

Before JoAnn and I quite realized it, we were off for New York City and the icy North once again, for my second year of jury duty for the Pulitzer international award at Columbia. Prior to that three-day stint, we made arrangements with Liv Sawyer to open the Aquebogue house for us so that JoAnn could stay there while I went to Syracuse after the Pulitzer judging, and Liv, as usual, did far more than was necessary. With her maid, Bessie, she cleaned the place, made up fresh curtains and a new shower curtain, provided us with new linens and all manner of other useful things, and saw to it finally that both the furnace and water pump were in good working order. She was still at the ironing board when we walked in after Paul Gaydos, who had always brought us to and from New York's airports in his car, let us off in our driveway and helped us stow our bags upstairs.

Next morning, as I left for Syracuse, all I had to worry about was the completion of my arrangements with Dean Stephens. It all turned out well, and he announced my appointment as the Newhouse Distinguished Professor of Journalism. Salary, expenses, classes, and the rest of our contractual arrangements had been settled with little argument on either side. And in addition, I received suggestions on where to look for a place to live, all of which pleased JoAnn when I reported the details to her on our way back to Coral Gables to wind up our Florida living and teaching experiences.

The climax, however, came after the end of my classes, when JoAnn and I drove to Southern College at Collegedale, Tennessee, to witness Pam's graduation with a degree in business education. In academic cap and gown, Pam made both of us proud parents that day, a feeling that was intensified when she worked at Knoxville City Hall as one of the mayor's assistants, appeared a few times on television, and later became a member of the staff of the Democratic National Committee in Washington, D.C. Directly after graduation, however, Pam came to Aquebogue with us before facing the world, and Eric joined us, too, for the beginning of one of the best summers our little family had ever experienced. All of us had earned it.

29 ★ MOVING ON

JoAnn and I ran into trouble as soon as we arrived in Syracuse after a delightful summer at the old homestead on eastern Long Island. We had rented an unfurnished apartment in a high-rise called Jefferson Towers, which was near the campus, and we had counted on rented furniture to be there in time to make us comfortable. It didn't, which caused us to spend our first night at Syracuse sleeping on a hard mattress on the floor.

But next day, while I was at the university making arrangements for my classes, JoAnn resolved the furniture problem temporarily. Then she set about renting an upright piano for me and finding a usable cargo of antique furniture here and there, which she refinished during the two years we were at Syracuse. Indeed, she made such progress with her self-imposed furniture assignment and her salesmanship that we were able to rent a larger apartment at Jefferson Towers for our second academic year, so I could do more of my academic work at home (at the Newhouse School, I had to share an office with a colleague). I stress these mundane housekeeping details because nobody who moves about the country and the world at large as much as we have always done could take all the necessities of comfortable living for granted.

Well-meaning faculty people did their best to help us get settled, especially Hank Schulte and his wife and the Mathewses. But as JoAnn frequently reminded me, permanent faculty, no matter how friendly, could not be expected to form a management team to resolve all the problems facing newcomers who wouldn't be around for more than a year or two.

"You're on your own," she often told me when the going seemed unnecessarily rough, at Syracuse or elsewhere. "You do your work and

I'll handle the housing and everything else." Which is the way our setup at Syracuse eventually was resolved.

My thirty-fourth year of teaching began early in September of 1983 at the Newhouse School with twenty graduate students in a newswriting class, including a Britisher, two Canadians, a Malaysian, and a Japanese. I had fifteen more in a news-reporting class, including a Nigerian, and at a later time there were other subjects over the two-year period—ethics, national and foreign correspondence, and a few special ties in critical writing.

Throughout, I seldom had fewer than forty student papers a week to read, edit, and criticize, plus the usual assortment of academic and professional obligations outside classes that I had come to expect. And early on, I found my way to the Syracuse gym and a crowded swimming pool where I worked out several times a week with three-quarter-mile swims. Between that, the piano at home and JoAnn's watchful supervision, I believe I was able to do what was expected of me from my seventy-eighth to my eightieth year.

We formed new friendships early, among them Bill Rivers, with whom I shared the office at the Newhouse School, and Harry Marley and his wife, Lillian, who insisted right off on taking us to dinner at a first-rate restaurant, the Poseidon. It was Marley, too, who introduced me to Donald Newhouse and encouraged me to bring more first-rate newspaper professionals to the school. And as time went on, the Newhouses became interested in a proposal for a conference at the school for professionals—something on the order of a discussion of the relationships between the presidency and the press. Although former President Gerald Ford and others were willing to participate, nothing ever came of it.

In retrospect, what maintained JoAnn's interest and mine at Syracuse as much as anything else was our love of travel and our continual fascination with the exploration of our new surroundings. Whereas the winters in central and western New York often made us sigh for the sunny warmth of Hawaii, south Florida, and Gainesville, the pleasures of spring and early autumn in our new surroundings also were rewarding.

Many a time during my two years at the Newhouse School, when I was overly tired of the academic load, JoAnn had the perfect remedy—a leisurely auto trip around the beautiful Finger Lakes region nearby or a brief venture across the border to Canada. When we didn't take the long weekend ride to the old homestead in Aquebogue, which was risky in inclement weather, we usually settled for a drive of about 400 miles to Niagara Falls and back. Or, as an alternative, we'd take the colorful auto route along the St. Lawrence Seaway.

The work at Syracuse was hard, the classes for the two years were demanding, but the total effort, as JoAnn concluded, was good for us both. And swimming at Syracuse's Webster pool, crowded though it usually was, helped keep me in good shape physically.

Almost everything we wanted to do at Syracuse in the winter depended to a great extent on the weather. For with a heavy rain or a snowfall of ten inches or more overnight, even my classes sometimes had to be curtailed or abandoned altogether in favor of make-up work at a later date.

I well remember how my will and my strength were tested the first time I struggled through wind and heavy snow during a bad storm to meet one of my classes and found only three hardy souls who had been able to make it out of a total of twenty. Under the circumstances, I could not penalize the rest who had either not dared brave the elements or failed to get through. After that experience, I fell back on the usual faculty routine when class work was interrupted by an emergency—make-up lectures or comparable student-teacher sessions at a more favorable time. The system, I thought, worked fairly well at Syracuse. Cornell, so I learned adopted similar measures.

However, I was also told that students who were eager for a particular aspect of instruction or who thought well of a special course or a teacher sometimes reached classes through the worst kind of weather. I never really believed it until I slugged through heavy snow to meet a class of twenty-three at the Newhouse School, in the belief that I owed it to the handful of students who were likely to show up. That time, to my surprise, all but one out of a class of twenty-three were waiting for me in a chilly classroom when I arrived, and the delinquent telephoned me later to apologize.

Such situations as these weren't easy to handle during my time at Syracuse, but neither the students nor I appeared to have suffered unduly. Everybody else in up-state New York was in the same fix. One winter's day when a deep freeze congealed Niagara Falls, I well remember that most of us at the Newhouse School, both students and faculty, were able to function, although I, for one, wouldn't ever want to face such a record cold spell again.

While I was at Syracuse, I was given leave to judge the Pulitzer international prize at Columbia for a third year, and I joined my four colleagues for the better part of three days of almost uninterrupted reading of exhibits from all parts of the country. As usual, JoAnn helped out in the Pulitzer office with secretarial chores, as she had done in the past and joined me for the few social functions at the midday break.

My luck as a juror seemed to vary with the composition of the juries as a whole. It seemed to me that when we took more time for discussion of our choices on the third and last day of the judging, we were able to reach sounder conclusions. It was on this basis that my first jury (in 1982) voted unanimously for John Darnton of the *New York Times,* a choice the Pulitzer Board accepted. However, when my second jury (in 1983) split its verdict because there seemed to be no other possibility for agreement, the Pulitzer board had to make its own decision. The third time (in 1984), we voted 3–2 after considerable discussion for a *Wall Street Journal* correspondent in the Middle East, Karen Elliott House, a selection the Pulitzer Board also endorsed.

Curiously, my attitude as administrator had been quite the opposite from my frame of mind as a juror. When I needed a jury verdict, I was impatient and did everything I could think of to force jurors to finish their report, which may have pleased the Pulitzer board but most certainly annoyed the judges.

It was on this note that my formal association with the Pulitzer Prizes ended after a quarter of a century, although I continued to participate in Columbia University affairs whenever possible. Most faculty, staff, and alumni who had known me over the years seemed to take it for granted that I would remain a part of the university for all the rest of my days. One former student, then well along in years himself, greeted me during my last Pulitzer service with an intense scrutiny and a command, "Look old, John!"

There would be time enough for that in years yet to come, but the prospect of aging, somehow, seldom entered my mind. During the Pulitzer judging that year, what JoAnn and I did with our time off in late afternoons and evenings was to take advantage of the pleasures New York City offered that we would find nowhere else—the shows and the shops, the sights and sounds, the visits to special places where we were known and welcomed. In particular, that early spring, I spent as much time as I could at the United Nations for interviews, impressions, and documents to take back to Syracuse with me for some of my classes.

Once we returned, the rest of the academic year passed quickly. And with the completion of arrangements for a second year at Syracuse, we prepared for our cross-continent journey. We left eastern Long Island on May 13 in our durable 1974 Cadillac and returned on June 24, having traveled almost 9,000 miles, crossed twenty states, seen such natural marvels as Yellowstone National Park, the Grand Canyon, and Yosemite Falls, experienced freezing cold and snow in the High Sierras and 116 degree heat in the Arizona desert.

At the halfway point, we were taken in by Colonel and Mrs. Syd Fisher who sheltered us, entertained us, cleaned and fed us first at their home in Scottsdale, Arizona, and later at their Los Angeles apartment. Refreshed and reinvigorated, we continued on our way and wound up back at the old homestead in Aquebogue with more than enough information in my notebooks for the writing I had wanted to do for so many years on the American experience in the twentieth century.

What we had seen on our six-week journey considering that we had traveled at the height of the Reagan boom years, when he was about to be reelected by a record majority, was a country of tremendous wealth and power, unmatched by any other I had seen in a lifetime's *weltanschauung*. In the light of what happened to the economy when the recession deepened during the Bush years, our cross-country expedition became a glittering memory—one that I would try at a later date to preserve in book form.

There were other works I had contracted for while I was at Syracuse, which also required thought, research, and planning. One of the most necessary, it seemed to me, was the projected examination of the Presidency and the political circus in Washington that I had suggested in my earliest days at the Newhouse School. The more I considered the subject, beginning with the slumping public opinion affecting both major parties and the presidents they had elected, the more it attracted me.

Eventually, I submitted a general proposal of that nature to the Gannett Foundation and received assurance of sympathetic consideration for a grant when I was ready to begin work. That, however, seemed unlikely until I was able to wrench myself away from teaching, which I tried to do after my second year at Syracuse.

JoAnn meanwhile had come across several novels I'd written as a young man during the Great Depression when I was working six days a week for New York newspapers. One of the novels—based on what I'd known of young Americans in Paris while Hemingway was there writing books all of us both applauded and envied—eventually appeared in paperback form, primarily because JoAnn was enthusiastic about it. When she offered it to a publisher and he asked how soon she could get it to him, she suggested, "Do you think this afternoon would do?"

I also produced a new textbook, through arrangements with another publisher, in this fallow period when I was trying to decide where to go next and what I should be doing. The most difficult problem was to determine the fate of the old homestead in Aquebogue once I determined to end my teaching career despite several offers for the 1985–86 academic year. JoAnn and I had agreed, after Syracuse, that we wanted to stay in one place, maintain one home instead of three, and concentrate my work and our resources. Just where we would alight hadn't been decided at the time, mainly because we weren't sure how much of our respective properties we wanted to sell and when would be the best time to do it. I suspect, too, that JoAnn may have wondered whether I could stand the strain of moving from Aquebogue with the Chickering grand and a lifetime's collection of books, pictures, and antiques, and leaving so many old friends behind me.

These were important considerations, true enough, but they did not seem insuperable to me. My closest friend, Dick Corwin, Dorothy's oldest surviving relative, always was with us no matter where we were; otherwise, I had no other kinfolk except for Norma Slivonik, Dorothy's niece, who also lived in Aquebogue. As for old friends, I was sure we'd not lose touch with each other.

For as long as I could take my daily distance swims, I did not worry about my health no matter where we settled. My only serious illness, a blood condition, had been cleared up long ago by Dr. Richard L. Geltman, a New York hematologist, who had told me on my latest visit while I was at Syracuse that all symptoms of anemia had disappeared. That judgment was concurred in through separate examinations later in Knoxville by Dr. Alan L. Grossman, a hematologist, and Dr. Michael Douglas Leahy, JoAnn's family physician. In discussing the importance of my daily distance swims, Dr. Grossman suggested to me that my physical activity had a great deal to do with both my good health and my longevity. "Think I'd better do some swims myself," he said with a big grin.

That was why, when the time came, I was prepared to sell the old homestead in Aquebogue and stay in Knoxville. JoAnn hesitated, however, and it was plain enough to me that she feared I was doing it only to please her. At any rate, when we talked it over, we couldn't come to any agreement about when to offer the place for sale while we were in Syracuse. And then, upon returning to eastern Long Island after our long trip that summer, everything seemed so lovely to us both that we couldn't summon up the resolution to proceed immediately.

Liv Sawyer and Bessie once again had done wonders with the old house in our absence, and our neighbors Al Hubbard and Joe Hoppe had made certain that it was well protected from intruders. Also, Marshall Jackson, who had always helped me with the gardening, showed up promptly after our arrival to assist with the hard work of keeping the grounds and the five acres beyond in good shape.

Straightaway, I forgot all about selling the place. Instead, I was out in the rose garden, trimming and spraying and planting new bushes to replace the ones that had died during the winter. I built a new trellis for the enormous growth of wisteria that shaded the back porch and that spread out as far as the woodshed and toolhouse beyond. The massive old elms beside the road, in front of the house, had long since vanished in Atlantic hurricanes, but the maples I'd planted to replace them now were so large that they, too, needed pruning.

While I was preoccupied out of doors, JoAnn once again was rummaging through the basement, a favorite hunting place in old houses, and had come up with more antique pieces that she had previously overlooked, a Tiffany lamp and some other eighteenth-century leftovers. In the house itself, there was also work to do—antique rockers, tables, and a wooden sewing box that Dorothy's mother had painted white or black, as the mood seized her—desecrations that JoAnn vowed to restore to their original condition. And that summer, taking up where she'd left off with her refinishing project at Jefferson Towers, she tackled the paint-encrusted antiques in Aquebogue.

Of course, Dick Corwin approved. He was even able to place dates on some of the antiques and give us a bit of the history for some of the art in the house, including portraits and a painting of the place itself that had been done by an artist who came by in a horse and buggy. That, at least, had been Grandmother Shirley's account of the origin of such decorative pieces, something Dick liked to talk about at our frequent dinners together.

Almost every day when the weather was fine, I returned to Iron Pier, the rocky beach on Long Island Sound just two miles north of us, where the swimming seemed perfect in the summertime. In the pre-automobile era, there once had been an Iron Pier jutting from the beach to accommodate steamers that plied the Sound, but that structure had collapsed years before and disappeared.

Most of the old crowd at Iron Pier also had gone. Bishop MacLean no longer floated on his back while smoking a cigar just beyond the surf. And the resident lawyers weren't around any more to argue over cases won and lost. But in the only beach cottage that was open in July, I found Peggy Carstensen and her husband, Krag, who now presided over the little circle of sunbathers and swimmers at the water's edge—the new generation that had taken over. As a native Long Islander I'd known from her childhood, Peggy was not one to greet me with a remark like "Look old, John!" She was quite matter-of-fact about the aging process, pointing to our mutual friend, Ebenezer Young, who still was working hard not far away at ninety-one and showing no sign of weakness. "You'll go on for quite awhile," she assured me, and sent me off to swim in saltwater—one of the pleasures of Long Island summers.

Not long afterward, while visiting with Mildred Hubbard, the widow of my friend and lawyer, Seth Hubbard, I renewed acquaintance with a retired businessman, Moncrief Jefferson, whose passion was the repairing of old clocks. He, too, made no great point about his age, arguing that there were too many of us around now for him to try to make himself out to be a modern Methuselah. When JoAnn heard about him, she wasted no time getting our own ancient clock to him for repairs, something he was able to do with such skill that it still keeps time fairly accurately and strikes the hour with impressive regularity as long as it is wound daily.

In return, Moncrief came to our house for dinner with his friends Mildred Hubbard and Lizette Hand and assured us its stout construction would preserve it for many years yet to come. Such enthusiasm as his caused us to delay for still another year our decision to sell out and go south where the winters were milder.

With the death of JoAnn's mother, Grace Fogarty, and the relocation of both our children in Atlanta, there was no particular urgency about the move to Knoxville. Pam was happy in the sales department of Bell South, and Eric was casting about for a suitable business opportunity in the Atlanta area. Whenever they could that summer, both were with us, as always, and sometimes they brought their friends. So it gave us much more satisfaction to take them to New York City for a show and dinner at Sardi's than try to visit them in Atlanta during the summer heat. Then, too, it seemed to us that Pam may have had an attraction for New York City when she brought two friends with her for a vacation and asked us to take them to the United Nations, something I thoroughly enjoyed.

The upshot was that we stayed put with homes in Aquebogue and Knoxville, going back and forth as usual when it seemed necessary to us on the various undertakings for books that I'd accepted. In a very real sense, what I was doing, in effect, was to taper off a long career as a journalist, teacher, and sometime prize-giver, and to settle down to the life I had always desired, that of a writer.

At the beginning of 1987, there was an interruption in our plans. It was back to class again, this time at the University of Tennessee where there was an emergency. I was asked to teach the spring semester for my former associates Kelly Leiter and Jim Crook, and I was glad to do so. We had come to Knoxville for the winter and temporarily closed the Aquebogue house as usual, so there was no great problem in my making the effort to accommodate my colleagues. The three classes I handled were all applications of practical journalism instruction—public affairs, newswriting, and ethics—so my preparations were minimal and my lectures covered familiar ground.

My diary tells the story of my return to class in Tennessee:

"January 8—What should have been a routine event was turned into a circus through no fault of my own or the dean's office. Notices had been sent to the newspapers and to the local NBC-TV affiliate so several reporters and photographers came around for interviews and pictures and some very pleasant professional talk. Then later, I also had a number of students who wanted interviews, too, but these were about the courses—and did I ask for a lot of written work? I tried to be pleasant about it, but left no doubt that writing, in my opinion, remained a basic part of the news business. Then, there was a two-hour class in the afternoon that was large enough and active enough to keep me going. I think I'll make it for the semester."

I did, with a lot of help as always from Kelly, Jim, and others in that Tennessee communications faculty. Outside class, one of the particular nonacademic university attractions for me was the year-round swimming routine that I'd always enjoyed at the university's outdoor and indoor Olympic-sized pools. And as Jim Crook obligingly assured me, the privilege would continue to be mine as a faculty member from then on, whether I taught or not. It was one of my biggest extra inducements to Southern living, for winters in Aquebogue had become increasingly trying and the only available pool on Long Island within a reasonable distance of our home was a YMCA forty miles west of us.

I am well aware that it sounds incongruous to stress exercise—the kind at least of which I am capable—as a reason for making decisions that bear on academic accomplishment. But this was my position and I had to face up to it honestly, which is why I set it down here as the deciding factor in still another drastic move for me late in life. There was more than enough work for me to do whether I taught or not—a Gannett Foundation grant for still another book, a political commentary that I had hoped to do for some time, and the autobiography—this book—that I'd promised JoAnn and the children I would write.

Once the semester ended at Tennessee just as nicely as it had begun, I told my students I'd be available to help them if they needed me, thanked my faculty colleagues, and took off for our quarters in Knoxville. I knew now what I had to do. Depending on time and circumstances and the nature of the offers we might expect, the old homestead on Long Island would have to be sold and we'd buy another, with ample grounds, in Knoxville.

I knew, of course, that it might take a certain amount of time to arrange for a sale at the valuation placed on the house, but I expected that eventually we'd find a buyer for it and the acreage that went with it.

During the next five years, while I wrote my books and contributed to various newspapers and magazines when asked to do so, the big change was completed. With the sale of the old homestead, we bought a new place in a quiet residential area of Knoxville, and JoAnn supervised the move from Aquebogue—the Chickering grand with the rest of the furniture, all my books and other academic possessions, and the antiques she was in the process of refinishing.

In Knoxville, we were housed on one floor with three bedrooms, a large living room dominated by the Chickering, and a dining alcove beyond the kitchen. My study, the walls lined with my books except for pictures and trophies of our travels, faced a large glassed-in wall that looked out on a broad, sloping lawn lined with trees and, in the distance on a clear day, the jagged heights of the Great Smokies.

Necessarily, the typewriter on my desk faced a solid wall without such distractions. It was there that I spent my mornings and at least a part of my afternoons, a routine that usually was broken only by the two hours it took me to drive to the university for a long swim and return. More often than not, JoAnn left me to my own devices; she was always in demand, for all manner of work from acting as a census supervisor to running a mortgage company. And even though she spent as little time as possible in the kitchen, she always was capable of putting on lunches or dinners for as many people as showed up, including me.

It has always been fun being with JoAnn. I have watched her in a kelly-green suit, being swung from her heels by two husky lads to kiss the Blarney Stone in Ireland, or charming a Parisian cab driver without knowing a word of French, or chasing a beggar boy in Katmandu, or bargaining with a shopkeeper in Hong Kong, and being the grand lady at the Metropolitan Opera in New York City. She can change personalities in a few moments, depending on the time, the place, and the mood. I have seen her throwing snowballs at me in June in Yellowstone Park, agonizing over the conditions of life in Calcutta, paying her respects to Shakespeare at Stratford-on-Avon, or making dinner in Knoxville for two hungry Somali graduate students at the University of Tennessee who were worried about their families at home.

But I am sure one of her happiest evenings was December 12, 1992, when she saw our son, Eric, married to the lovely girl he'd been going with for years, Tracey Nichols, at a church wedding in Atlanta. It was sedate and formal, the bride in a sweeping white gown and veil, the groom in white tie and tails, sister Pam in blue velvet among the bridesmaids and—by request of the couple about to be married—I was at the piano playing the wedding march. After years as an amateur, I finally performed at my first professional engagement, and I don't believe I hit a clinker. But after the minister had completed the ceremonial, I couldn't help varying the monotony of Mendelssohn and Wagner by breaking into "I Get a Kick Out of You."

JoAnn, in a spangled red dress with red slippers to match, danced with her son at the reception, where a lively combo took over from me, and he in turn did a furious jitterbug routine with his Aunt Margaret, while Tracey was changing from her bridal costume. Eric, I reflected, was lucky, and so was I. Both of us had been able to marry the girls we most wanted.

What's next, then? For those who ask me to foretell the future, I like to respond with the story of Tom Fogarty, JoAnn's uncle, who hit a cow one day on the tracks of the Southern Railway between Knoxville and Harriman while he was at the controls in the cab of his locomotive. At the subsequent trial, the opposing lawyer demanded, "Tom Fogarty, how far can you actually see?" It was an intimation that Uncle Tom hadn't seen the cow on the tracks in time to stop the engine.

Uncle Tom's Irish was up. He responded, "I can see the moon. How far can you see?"

In this waning century and perhaps into the next, we move on.

INDEX

NOTE: * denotes Pulitzer Prize winner and † symbolizes past or present board members.

Abel, Elie, 139, 214
Acheson, Dean,* 68, 97, 123
Ackerman, Carl W., 52, 62, 71, 72, 82, 83, 107, 110, 112, 113, 114, 117, 157, 167
Advisory Board on the Pulitzer Prizes (since 1974, the Pulitzer Prize Board): judging and reporting the prizes, 173-77; powers of, 201. *See also* Columbia University: Trustees; Hohenberg, John; Kirk, Grayson; McGill, William J.
Air Force, Department of the, and JH, 114-16, 131-32
Akron (Ohio) *Beacon Journal,** 192-93
Albee, Edward,* 170
Ambrose, Bill and Catherine, 243-44
American Assembly, 113, 154
American Press Institute, 62, 271
Anderson, Jack,* 199, 200
Anderson, Maxwell,* 176
Anderson, Paul Y.,* 204-6
Arafat, Yasir, 92
Arnett, Peter,* 189
Associated Press, 127-29, 187, 189, 211-12
Association for Education in Journalism, 263

Atlanta Constitution, ix, 12, 265
Austin, Sen. Warren R., 96

Baker, Richard T., 110-11, 144
Baker, Russell,* 183
Barrett, Edward, 167, 214
Bartlett, Charles L.,* 166
Baruch, Bernard M., ix, 69, 166
Beaty, Margaret and Joe, 254, 255
Beech, Keyes,* 211
Berlin blockade and airlift, 77, 78, 79
Bernadotte, Count Folke, 96
Bernstein, Leonard, 176
Best, Robert H., 24
Bingham, Barry,† 172
Black, Justice Hugo L., 197-98
Bradlee, Benjamin C.,† 206
Brass, Donna Beaty, 254
Brass, Elder David, 254
Bremner, John, 232, 235-37, 238-42, 263
Brinkman, Del, 239
Broder, David,* 208
Bromfield, Louis,* 27
Browne, Malcolm,* 187
Bunche, Ralph, 95, 96
Burns, James MacGregor,* 178, 180
Bush, George, 92, 178, 280

Butler, Nicholas Murray, 222
Byrnes, James F., 66

Cade, Dozier, 249
Canham, Erwin,† 265
Carmody, Nancy, 182
Carter, Hodding,*† 162
Carter, Jimmy, 11
Castro, Fidel, 127–28
Cather, Willa,* 175
Catledge, Turner,† 161
Chattanooga (Tenn.) *Times,* 166
*Chicago Daily News,** 169–70, 211
Chicago Tribune, 43, 170
Childs, Marquis,* 265
China, 269
Chinese University of Hong Kong, 146, 269
Christian Science Monitor, 136, 265
Churchill, Winston, 50, 66–67
Clapper, Raymond, 46
Clark, Donald L., 71–72, 80, 81
Clinton, Bill, 92–93
Cold War: beginnings, 64–65; at the UN, 65–69; Truman's warning on, 69–70. *See also* Berlin blockade and airlift; Marshall Plan; Truman Doctrine
Columbia University: JH teaches at, 107–8; Trustees of, and Pulitzer Prizes, 110, 164, 180, 200–201, 213–14; Vietnam war riots at, 130–39; founding of J-school at, 150–52. *See also* Butler, Nicholas Murray; Cordier, Andrew W.; Eisenhower, Dwight D.; Kirk, Grayson; McGill, William J.
Conniff, Frank,* 166–67
Cooper, Mary, 254–55
Cordier, Andrew W., 95, 99, 138
Corwin, Richmond and Sue, 247, 283
Council on Foreign Relations, 91, 113, 133, 145, 238
Crook, James, 284

Cuban crisis, 127–29
Cuero (Texas) *Record,* 165
Cunliffe, John, 16, 19, 152
Curtis, J. Montgomery, 62, 271

Darnton, John,* 279
Dashiell, Sam, 27
Douglas, James H., Jr., 115
Dryfoos, Orville, 134

East-West Center, Hawaii, 146
Eden, Anthony, 119, 120, 123
Egypt, 91
Eisenhower, Dwight D.: at Columbia, 108, 109; sent to lead NATO, 109; wins White House, 109–10; and U.S. intervention in Indochina, 131–32; advises against land wars in Asia, 186
Ellsberg, Daniel, 197
Esper, George, 210–11
Evatt, Herbert V., 95

Fall, Albert B., 204–6
Faulkner, William,* ix, 152, 162
Felt, Adm. Harry D., 188
Ferguson, J. D.,† 178
Filo, John Paul,* 193
Fisher, Col. and Mrs. Syd, 116, 154, 280
FitzGerald, Frances,* 184
Fitzpatrick, D. R.,* 163
Florida, University of, xiii, 247, 261–64
Florida Times-Union, 264
Flynn, Edward P., 52
Fodor, M. W., 24
Fogarty, Bill and Peggy, 254, 271
Fogarty, Fred and Betty, 271
Fogarty, Grace, 245, 284
Fogarty, John Joseph, 245
Fogarty, Tom, 287
Ford, Gerald R., 277
Ford Foundation, 91, 133, 146

Gandhi, Indira, 95, 103–4
Gannett Foundation, 148, 213, 249, 263, 281
German Marshall Fund, 263
Gershwin, George, 18, 176
Ghali, Boutros Boutros, 94
Giles, Bob, 193
Gorbachev, Mikhail S., 91
Gordon, Dave, 265, 270
Graham, Katharine, 206
Greeneville (TN) *Sun,* 231
Gromyko, Andrei A., 66–67, 96

Halberstam, David,* 187, 188–89
Hammarskjold, Dag, 95, 123, 129
Hammerstein, Oscar II,* ix, 176
Harding, Warren G., 8–11, 204–6
Harms Inc., 14–15
Harron, Robert, 108–9, 182
Haskins, Jack and Tommie, 244, 260
Hastings, John, 213
Hearst, W. R., Jr., 42, 180; team* wins Pulitzer Prize, 166–67
Hearst, W. R., Sr., 40–44
Hemingway, Ernest,* 27–28, 162
Hendrix, Hal,* 128
Hersh, Seymour,* 190
Hierl, Jeanne and Peter, 236–37, 240
Higgins, Marguerite,* 190
Hileman, Don, 215, 239, 249, 250–51
Hills, Lee,*† 213
Hofstadter, Richard,* 183–84
Hohenberg, Bernhard (uncle), 19, 20, 24, 34, 36, 37
Hohenberg, Dorothy Lannuier: and JH at Columbia, 19, 20–21, 22; correspondence, 28; marriage, 29; in depression years, 37–39; during World War II, 152, 161; return to Columbia, 90, 91; in university life, 109, 155–56; illness of, 230–31, 232; return to Aquebogue, 227–29, 230; death of, 233

Hohenberg, Jettchen S. (mother), 3, 4, 13
Hohenberg, JoAnn Fogarty, xii, 244–45; JH's courtship, 245–47; wedding of, 249–50; with JH on teaching engagements, 265–79 passim; permanent home in Knoxville, 286; returns to New York with JH, 274, 279; marriage of son of, 287
Hohenberg, John: birth and early life, 3–6; covers President Harding's arrival in Seattle in 1923, 8–11; first job at *Seattle Star,* 12–13; sells first article to *New York Times,* 14–15; works nights at *New York Graphic* and attends Columbia, 15, 18–22; graduates from Columbia with Dorothy, 22; wins Pulitzer Traveling Scholarship in Europe (1927–28), 23–29; marries Dorothy on return, 29; works at *New York Evening Post,* 30–32; during depression, 33–34, 35–37; hired by Hearst's *New York Evening Journal* (later *Journal-American*), 38–39, 40–43; and World War II, 44–58; return to New York after war, 61–69; teaches first class at Columbia (1948), 71–74; covers Palestine and birth of Israel at UN, 74–76, 78; offered and accepts Columbia professorship, 82, 107–8; month-long tour of Israel, 83–89; appointed administrator of Pulitzer Prizes, 109–12; and Vietnam War riots on campus, 130–39; visits to Southeast Asia during Vietnam War, 130–60 passim; and Pentagon Papers case, 176, 194, 195–202; and Watergate scandal, 176, 202–4, 207, 209; his last Pulitzer board session, 210–12; move to University of Tennessee, 231–32; Dorothy's last illness and death, 233; at University of Kansas, 238–43; return to

292 ★ INDEX

Hohenberg, John—*continued*
Tennessee, 243–47, 255–59, 284–85; courtship and marriage to JoAnn Fogarty, 244, 249–250; at University of Florida, 261–64; at University of Miami, 265; at Syracuse University, 272, 276–79; as Pulitzer journalism juror, 274, 279; USIA tour in Asia, 266–70
—books by, 144, 146–49
Hohenberg, Louis (father): gold seeker in Alaska, 3; in Seattle, 5, 7, 12; settles in New York City, 13; opens children's shop, 17
Hohenberg, Simon (uncle), 26
Holocaust, 26
Horton, Philip, 145
House, Karen Elliott,* 279
Hubbard, Mildred and Seth, 283
Hughes, John,* 136, 266–70
Hussein, king of Jordan, 93

Intervention and isolation, Americans on before and during World War II, 43–45
Iran at the UN, 66–67
Iraq and the Gulf War, 92, 104
Israel: Palestine case at UN, 74–76; state of, 75–76, 78–79; admitted to UN, 80; JH's visit to, 83–89; Israeli-Arab wars, 90–91; Egyptian peace, 91; position in Gulf War, 92; PLO/Israel peace effort, 92, 93
—territories occupied by: Golan Heights, West Bank, Gaza Strip all won in 1967 war, 90–91; negotiations with PLO over, 92, 93; assessment of chances for peace, 94

Jefferson, Moncrief, 283
Jessup, Philip C., 113
Jewish Agency for Palestine, 75
Jinks, Larry, 270
Johnson, Lyndon B., 134

Johnston, Joe, 238
Jones, John M., Jr., 231

Kander, John, 265
Kansas, University of, 232, 235–47, 263
Kaufman, George S.,* 176
Kelleher, Brad and Mary, 265
Kennan, George F.,* 183
Kennedy, John F.,* ix, 127–29, 177–78, 188
Kenney, Eric, 249, 250, 287
Kenney, Pamela, 274, 275
Khrushchev, Nikita S., 128, 129, 130
Kirk, Grayson,† 110–11, 113, 114, 141, 142, 144, 162, 163, 164, 166, 167, 173, 181, 182. *See also* Columbia University
Knight, John S.,* 187, 207, 265
Knight Foundation, 147
Knoxville, 255–57, 284
Knubel, Fred, 213
Kohlmeier, Louis M.,* 207
Korean War, 65, 96
Krock, Arthur,*† 110, 161, 165

Lash, Joseph,* 183
Laurence, William L., 60
Lee, J. K., 241
Leech, Margaret,* 183
Leiter, Kelly, 249, 284
Lewis, Anthony,* 165
Lewis, R. W. B.,* 183
Liberty window, 21, 112, 113
Lie, Trygve, 68–69, 94–109 passim, 123–24
Lindsay, John V., 155
Lippmann, Walter,* 37
Literary Digest, 42, 44
Los Angeles Times,* 200
Lowenstein, Ralph L., xii, 262, 265
Lwin, Than, 266–70

MacArthur, Gen. Douglas, 50, 51, 65, 99
McCord, James W., 208
Macfadden, Bernarr, 15–16, 17–18
McGill, Ralph,*† ix, 182, 265
McGill, William J.,† 138, 182, 200, 201, 213, 214, 259. *See also* Columbia University
MacLean, Bishop Charles W., 143
MacLeish, Archibald,* 221
McNamara, Robert S., 197
Marja, Fern, 75–76
Marley, Harry, 277
Marshall, George, 77, 79
Marshall Plan, 77–78
Massolo, Arthur, 75–76
Mathews, Cleve, 272
Maxwell, Don,† 170
Meeman Distinguished Professorship, 212
Meir, Golda, 95
Mencken, H. L., 151
Meyer, Sylvan, 271
Miami, University of, 261, 265
*Miami Herald,** 270
Miami News, 128
Michener, James,* 175–76
Miller, Arthur,* 176
Milwaukee Journal, 178
Mitchell, John N., 195, 206
Mitchell, Margaret,* 175
Moore, Douglas,* 265
Morison, Samuel Eliot,* 183
Moyers, Bill, 134
Murrow, Edward R., 44, 45, 165

Nagorski, Zyg, 238
Nashville Tennessean, 250
Nehru, Jawaharlal, 103
Newhouse, Donald, 277
Newhouse Distinguished Professorship, 276–77
Newsweek, 167

New World Information Order, 265–66, 267–70
New York Graphic, 15, 18, 19, 22
*New York Times**: public service prize for Pentagon Papers case, 194–202
*New York World,** 12, 20, 21, 37–38
Nieman Fellowships, 157
Nixon, Richard M., 131, 137–38, 176, 195–202 passim, 208–9
Nobel Prizes, 217

Ochs, Adolph S., 150
O'Neal, Faye, 271
O'Neill, Eugene,* 152, 176

Paddon, Anna, 230
Palestine Liberation Organization, 91, 92
Pearl Harbor, 50, 131–32
Pearson, Drew, 179
Pearson, Lester B. (Mike), 95, 96, 99, 123
Pentagon Papers, 176, 194, 195–202
Persian Gulf War, 92
Philippines Herald, 98–99
Polk, James R.,* 207
*Providence Journal-Bulletin,** 207
Pulitzer, Joseph: *World* newspapers sold to Scripps-Howard, 37–38; on plan for prizes and journalism school, 110, 150–51, 201; his principles quoted, 224
Pulitzer, Joseph, Jr.: succeeds to *St. Louis Post-Dispatch* and Pulitzer board leadership, 110–12; activities as board chairman, 126, 161, 162, 163, 167, 169, 174, 177, 180, 199, 201, 216
Pulitzer, Joseph II, 110–12, 161–63
Pulitzer Prizes. *See* names of individuals and newspapers with asterisks

Quarles, Donald A., 166

Rabin, Yitzhak, 92
Raskin, Abe, 214
Reagan, Ronald, 102, 280
Reston, James,*† 265
Rockefeller, John D., Jr., 68
Rodgers, Richard, 176
Romulo, Carlos P.,* 95, 98–99, 123, 269
Roosevelt, Eleanor, 95, 102, 103
Roosevelt, Franklin D., 33, 41–42, 43–44, 50, 51, 58–59, 60
Royster, Vermont C.,*† 265
Rusk, Dean, 133, 134

*St. Louis Post-Dispatch,** 37, 191, 204–6, 265
Salisbury, Harrison,* 135–36
Sass, Jerry, 263
Sawyer, Liv, 271, 282
Schanberg, Syd,* 210–12
Schiff, Dorothy, 52
Schlesinger, Arthur M., Jr.,* 183
Schulte, Henry, 272
Seattle Post-Intelligencer, 43
Seattle Star, 9, 10, 11
Seattle Times, 5, 8
Seigenthaler, John, 250
Sheehan, Neil,* 194, 199, 200–201
Sherman, Gene,* 200
Sherwood, Robert E.,* 176
Shirley, Mary Adelaide, 34, 35–36
Shor, Toots, 168
Smith, J. Kingsbury,* 166–67
Smith, Merriman,* 129
Smyser, Dick, 258
Society of Professional Journalists/Sigma Delta Chi, 148, 250
Solzhenitsyn, Aleksandr, 154
Sovern, Michael I., xi
Soviet Union: in World War II, 54, 59, 65; in Cold War, 66; at the UN, 66–67; explodes A-bomb, 69; threat to Greece and Turkey and to Western Europe, 77; Berlin blockade, 78–79; role of Khrushchev and others, 128–30
State Department American Specialist program, 145, 261
Steinbeck, John,* 175
Stephens, Ed, 272
Sullivan, Ed, 17, 19
Sulzberger, Arthur Ochs, 188
Swanberg, W. A.,* 181–83
Swope, Herbert Bayard,* 12, 112, 114
Syracuse University, 272, 276–79

Talbott, Harold, 166
Teapot Dome scandal, 204–6
Tennessee, University of, 212, 231–33, 239, 243–47, 258–59, 284–85
Thomas, Clark, 237
Time Inc., 188, 202
Towery, Roland K.,* 165
Truman, Harry S., 60, 61–62, 64, 65, 69, 75–79
Truman Doctrine, 77
Tuchman, Barbara,* 184

UNESCO, 102, 265–70
United Nations: founding of, 94–95; JH assigned to, 61–62; and Iranian crisis, 65–66; Rockefeller's gift of headquarters site of, 68; temporary operations of, 68–69; Truman dedicates headquarters site of, 69–70; creation of Israel by, 78–79; and Mideast wars, 90–92; and Arab-Israeli peace accord, 93; summary of, after fifty years, 94–104
United Press International, 129, 200
USIA, 261–66, 267–70

Valenstein, Rose, and Robin Holloway Kuzen, xii, 214, 246
Valley Daily News (Tarentum, Pa.), 193
Vietnam War, 132–33, 135, 136, 137–38, 139, 192–93
Vishinsky, Andrei, 69, 123

Wagner, Robert F., 112
Wall Street crash, 32–34
*Wall Street Journal,** 207, 265, 279
Washington, University of, 5–6, 13
*Washington Post,** 195–202, 203–9
Washington Star-News, 207
Washington Times-Herald, 43
Watergate scandal, 176, 201–4, 207–9
Watson, Thomas J., 109
Weizmann, Chaim, 79
Westmoreland, Gen. W. C., 133
Wharton, Edith, 175, 183
White, Jack,* 207
White, William Allen, 148, 150, 236
White, William S.,* 183
Whitman, Walt, 140, 141
Wiggins, J. Russell, 122

Wilkins, Roger W., 222
Williams, Talcott, 156
Williams, Tennessee,* 162, 176
Willkie, Wendell, 44, 64
Winchell, Walter, 17
Wingspread conference in Wisconsin, 135
Woodward, Bob, and Carl Bernstein, 203–4, 207–9
World War II, 23, 49–60 passim
Wyatt, Robert O. and Judy, 249–50, 260, 271

Yu, Frederick T. C., 241

Ziegler, Ron, 206